Managing Crises Overseas

Managing Crises Overseas

Scott Ast

CRC Press
Taylor & Francis Group
Boca Raton London New York

CRC Press is an imprint of the
Taylor & Francis Group, an **informa** business

CRC Press
Taylor & Francis Group
6000 Broken Sound Parkway NW, Suite 300
Boca Raton, FL 33487-2742

© 2017 by Taylor & Francis Group, LLC
CRC Press is an imprint of Taylor & Francis Group, an Informa business

No claim to original U.S. Government works

Printed on acid-free paper
Version Date: 20160719

International Standard Book Number-13: 978-1-4822-4579-0 (Hardback)

Visit the Taylor & Francis Web site at
http://www.taylorandfrancis.com

and the CRC Press Web site at
http://www.crcpress.com

Printed and bound in the United States of America by
Edwards Brothers Malloy on sustainably sourced paper

CONTENTS

FOREWORD

Security management and crisis management are strongly linked with each other and always will be. There are several areas of security functions that might quickly escalate into crisis situations, and several areas for crisis managers will require security input and assistance. The two functions, to say the least, cannot work well without each other.

The liaison and relationships with those who operate in security and crisis management circles within organizations are very important and groups must cross train and drill as a unit. They must share ideas and concerns. There should not be anyone fighting for turf or territory, and the easiest way to avoid this is for the two groups to meet and decide who handles what and when. There are crisis management certified planners (CMCPs) and board-certified protection professionals (CPPs). One should not debate which group of professionals might be better at dealing with emergencies, crises, and all things considered.

Effective crisis management requires the support of senior management. This statement is important enough to say again: Effective crisis management requires the support of senior management—not just in the conceptual sense, but also in the nuts and bolts and practical sense. Senior management is so important that I would not recommend that any organization commit to a crisis management program unless and until senior management puts some "skin in the game," as the saying goes—skin in the form of money for supplies, training, materials, the time for employees to meet and discuss, create, and formulate plans, and to drill. Drilling is very important and it takes time and effort. Employees will have to be away from their jobs. Members of the crisis management team (CMT) will be required to spend time and effort in becoming familiar with aspects of the plan and their responsibilities in the performance of the plan.

Any mention of senior management is not intended to be a lecture to people in these positions. What it is intended to do is to alert security and crisis professionals to the fact that, for any crisis plan to be worth managing and developing, it has to be worth the complete support and involvement of senior management. If senior management, the chief executive officer, vice presidents, or others within the organization will not back up the crisis management team and crisis management planning, all of these efforts might be just wasted time.

Another pitfall to consider in the area of crisis management is to have the buy-in, support, and participation in the planning of crisis management by the affected functional organizational areas. For example, the Human Resources and Legal Departments must be involved in the development of training and planning for a crisis involving a workplace violence incident. Information technology professionals, including the chief information officer, would be involved in crisis planning for an incident involving the organization's computer system, and so on.

The pitfall or area to avoid is something that happens all too often. You might not know that in some corporations, plant, facility, project, or country managers, especially those who are removed from headquarters and operating around the country (or around the world), often operate as though they are kings or queens. Sometimes, they operate with impunity as they oversee what can only be called fiefdoms. That's correct: They operate as little kings and queens, right down to the little crowns with brightly colored jewels. And, unless their little corporate entity or republic is not operating at a profit or this particular person is not in good favor with headquarters (in which case they don't last too long in their postings), they will most generally be allowed to get their way.

All of this is not to say that anything improper is going on in such situations. It is just a matter of stating that you might run headfirst into such bramble bushes only to realize that you have to now deal with someone who is not willing to see anything differently than what he or she is used to or how things have operated in the past.

Another important thing for security and crisis practitioners to realize is that country, project, or facility managers generally have enough political power, seniority, or senior management influence to cause one professional hardship if you get on their bad sides. So, the recommendation would be to make sure you make every attempt to work effectively with these personnel and their managers. In-country managers can be of two varieties: those who want to work with security and crisis management professionals and those who do not.

As previously referred to, senior management support is critical to any crisis management program, especially those that involve projects and facilities located away from headquarters. The further away from the Mother Ship, the more senior the management person might have to be to wield some influence.

Citing an example, an in-country project manager, who had spent several years in the region and in country, began to drag his heels and stall when crisis and security management professionals began to inquire about the status of his project crisis management plan. The country was free of strife, and although the region had been somewhat unstable, there hadn't been any terrorism to be found. The country manager fancied himself an expert on the country where he had lived and worked for five years.

Now, the intrepid security/crisis manager who was visiting from afar was not one to go looking for arguments and, yet, over dinner, postulated that opposition forces within that country's military might present problems for the ruling government in the future. The manager from afar was there with a colleague to try to convince the country manager of the necessity of completing and, in this case, actually beginning to formulate a crisis management plan for employees and assets. The two travelers spent the rest of the dinner being lectured on why what had been said was ridiculous. And yet the travelers didn't come up with this theory in a vacuum. They had read about this in credible reports coming from the region. Had the travelers' senior manager approached senior management then with their concerns, a lot of forthcoming trouble, lecturing, and cost could have been avoided.

Flash forward 18 months: with no crisis management plan in hand because nothing had been done by the country manager or subordinates, the country, the government, and the military were in turmoil. Protests had turned violent and the country was breaking apart. Before all was said and done, emergency charter flights had to be arranged (at considerable cost and effort, more so than would have been required had even limited advance preparations been made). Employees were placed at risk simply because no forethought had gone into emergency evacuations. It is at times like these that professionals should always resist the urge to say, "I told you so."

No particular region in the world is completely free from what one might call emergencies, crises, or disasters—or the possibilities of such. What is safe by one standard—say, a quiet, stable, and dependable political system—might be plagued by annual brush fires or seismic activity involving the surrounding countryside. Flooding in one country might occur just as frequently as violent protests and demonstrations.

What often seems so obvious to those looking in from afar, those close to the issue can be blindingly unable to see. Conversely, those who are looking at an issue from thousands of miles away may have little or no knowledge of the true situation on the ground. Living and working in foreign locales, especially for professionals who have done so for quite some time, provide certain insights that cannot be ascertained without living and working in country. Living in a country or region gives cultural and political insights and offers the opportunity to feel more comfortable, especially as language skills and social sensitivities improve.

Working, growing up, or being educated in foreign countries can give valuable insights, to be sure. It can, however, lead to *astigmatism*—creating a blind spot for what might be truly taking place. It might be summed up as leadership culture/organizational culture prompting an attitude of local bias. That is, the boots on the ground obviously know better about what is happening in the country they live and work in than someone at headquarters 2000 miles away. If a company or organization has worked in a particular region or country for an extended period of time, such as years or even decades, an institutional memory might form. If an organization was based in Iran during the late 1970s and witnessed the US Embassy in Tehran being seized, such a company might invest heavily in planning and resources for emergency evacuations of its employees and dependents, if dependents were ever allowed to live alongside their significant others working in Iran or the Middle East. If another group had a gut-wrenching experience of a company executive being kidnapped or murdered in a foreign location, it would most likely take planning to mitigate such occurrences more seriously. In other words, most crisis programs in most organizations are developed *after* something bad has happened. This is all too frequent to be happenstance. And, it is not uncommon for many professionals in security, safety, or crisis management to lament that the only way their suggestions and observations are ever to be put into place would be in the aftermath of a disastrous incident.

AUTHOR

Scott Ast has 28 years of international crisis and security management and consulting experience in both the private and public sectors. His responsibilities have included crisis management program development and management, risk assessments, vulnerability assessments, disaster and emergency management, awareness training, and liaison with state, local, federal, and international agencies.

Mr. Ast's background has included implementation of extensive crisis and emergency management assessments and programs at remote, austere, and hostile reconstruction sites throughout Iraq and Afghanistan, as well as around the world. His efforts led to the protection of some of the first private contractors deployed in these areas. He has expertise in crisis management across a wide variety of critical infrastructure, including water- and wastewater-treatment facilities, oil and chemical infrastructure, oil and chemical operations, and traditional and nuclear power generation facilities.

Mr. Ast is a board-certified protection professional (CPP), certified fraud examiner (CFE), and certified crime prevention through environmental design (CPTED) planner. He has assisted the Department of Homeland Security, the Environmental Protection Agency, the White House Office of National Drug Control Policy, the US Department of Agriculture, and the RAND Corporation in developing national policy. He has chaired the production of guidelines for the protection of people and assets used as a model by these federal agencies. Mr. Ast has been recognized by the Federal Bureau of Investigation as a subject matter expert and has received letters of commendation from this agency and the US Secret Service. He has presented at international security and crisis management conferences. He is a published author in the American Society for Industrial Security's *Security Management* magazine and of the textbook, *Managing Security Overseas* (Auerbach Publications, 2009). Mr. Ast earned a BA in political science and a masters of public administration from the University of Missouri-Kansas City.

1

Introduction to Crisis Management

Do not pray for an easy life, pray for the strength to endure a difficult one.

Bruce Lee

This book explores examples of serious crises in international settings that require security professionals to make quick decisions—and to always be correct!

The aim is to explain concepts, goals, strategies, and procedures relating to corporate crisis and security management, operating in some of the most extreme and most dangerous countries and regions in the world. What it takes to manage crises with confidence and effectiveness from anywhere, taking place anywhere, facing anything is frequently learned by fits and starts, by trial and error, and by extreme circumstances. The intention of this book is to give readers an explanation of the proper types of instructions, manuals, standard operating procedures, planning, implementation, and drills—the never ending and never to be underestimated process of drills and exercises and to cover some of the pitfalls and problems associated with crisis planning and management.

When life safety is involved, having proper planning and effective management systems in place before a crisis occurs can make the difference between life and death. Systems must be constructed in such a way that if a crisis event occurs half a world away, in different time zones, on different days, while corporate headquarters are closed for the night, the plans can be implemented and run with precision and effectiveness.

Crisis management, in the opinion of many professionals, goes hand in hand with security management. Although corporations might have certified crisis management managers in place, whose sole responsibility is planning for and directing corporate personnel before and in the event of crises, this function, more often than not, falls upon security professionals.

Security professionals must hone their skills in the area of crisis management because often the worst case scenarios concerning security breaches, such as trespassers; breached security perimeters; or a kidnapped individual quickly morph into corporate crises. Suppose an arson fire in an Asian capital engulfs a high-rise building housing your corporate personnel. You are operating in a region where firefighting equipment and personnel are less than effective. The firefighters, if there are any, are poorly trained, inadequately staffed, and marginally equipped. The fire system in the building, if it works, is often improperly connected or programmed. Fire exits and stairwells have been known to be padlocked and barricaded to prevent unauthorized persons from entering the building. Fire exit pathways may have become obstructed by file cabinets, copiers, appliances, and even walls.

As a security professional, did you know this? Were you aware of the threat to your personnel? Have you met with building management, first responders, and political entities to do the most that you can to protect your principals? Have you "been there, done that?"

Crisis preplanning and coordination encompasses a broad spectrum of corporate functions and areas of expertise. Human resource professionals, including benefits managers, relocation specialists, housing specialists, corporate payroll, and many others; corporate counsel; building services; corporate security; safety, engineering, and operations departments; senior management; insurance managers; and many others must meet, plan, and train together in advance and go through the *what if?* scenario.

Meetings must take place, with roundtable discussions designed to look at the emergency and disaster histories of the corporation's operations in given countries and regions. What types of crises have taken place before? What actions were taken? What were the outcomes? The lessons learned? By meeting and discussing the previously experienced forms of crisis and discovering what had been done, correctly or incorrectly, much time and effort can be saved and improved upon. There is, of course, a great deal of historical knowledge within corporations and organizations of all sizes that have international background and experience. This institutional and operational knowledge can be of great value for a number of reasons.

One corporation with expats posted at a far flung project had personnel on the ground when political and ethnic violence spiraled out of control. Communications were lost with the expats and their dependents, who, surprisingly, had not been preevacuated when conditions were tense but not so serious. As the violence spread, the expats, fearing for their safety, gathered essential items, fueled their vehicles, and headed to the highways, and, they hoped, to safety.

As the caravan of vehicles headed toward the coast, the expats came upon their first rebel roadblock, not five miles from their main camp. As one might imagine, no pleasantries were exchanged, but the rebels demanded valuables, and, thankfully, even surprisingly, not the vehicles in which the expats were riding. Shaken, but not deterred, the expats continued on their lonely journey (the highways were empty) toward the coast. Undaunted, and with only useless mobile phones, owing to the nation's phone systems being down, and without satellite phones (these had never arrived) or GPS (not requested from HQ) they traveled along hoping for the best. Fifty miles farther down the road, the second set of roadblocks appeared. This time, those manning the roadblocks were not so easy on the travelers. All were forcefully pulled out of their vehicles and asked where they thought they were heading.

The expats were ordered to line up and as one armed militia member strode along the groups of men and women, he paused at each female expat standing in line. He leaned in and made a big show of smelling each woman and then turned to comment to his laughing compatriots. While the entire luggage was being tossed from the backs of the Land Rovers and SUVs, the man in charge demanded that all expats approach him, raise the sleeves of their shirts or blouses, and empty their pockets. He and two of his men took all of the watches, rings and bracelets, billfolds, and money they could find. The expats had sensibly hidden all of their passports under their seats, and the guerrillas never asked for these. The expats were allowed to get back into their now much roomier vehicles and continue on their way. Fifteen miles from the coast, the group encountered one last roadblock, this time manned by government military forces, who asked for money while holding automatic weapons. On being told the harrowing tale by the travelers, they allowed them to pass unmolested.

3

As a result of the experience, this particular institution now has a knowledge base, institutional knowledge, an ingrained understanding of why it is not always the best decision to grab your go-bag and hit the roads not knowing what is out their waiting for you. In the scenario described, the expats were lucky to have made it to the coast alive. As a footnote, by the time they reached the coast, the violence had abated and the group was able to travel back to the main camp after a few days of resting and recovering at the beach. The next time hostilities threaten expats in a remote location, the first inclination won't be to evacuate first and think later. Perhaps hunkering down and standing fast might be the more prudent option.

Security professionals are used to dealing with the "what would we do if?" for scenarios that have been dreamed up or considered from past experiences. Security must ensure that it has the contacts with law enforcement, or if not, the knowledge and resources required to make these liaisons and connections to plan for and ensure the corporation's people and assets are protected.

Of course, life safety trumps all. It is the number one concern, in security or crisis matters. As is illustrated in the following case study covering Fukushima, Chernobyl, and Three Mile Island, the capacity for humanity's ability to create and build powerful machines and achieve engineering feats, such as nuclear reactors, is often surpassed only by its inability to realize the potential risks and dangers of such creations. Secondarily, and important in its own right, is the protection of the corporation's assets. Assets are the tangibles—the nuts and bolts, the brick and mortar, the trucks and turnstiles. Assets are intangible as well—corporate reputation, for example. The way an organization handles a crisis situation will affect not only those who work for the organization who are placed in harm's way, but also the future of all employees who continue to work there, along with many who may or may not choose to work there in the future.

Life safety is not just ensuring things work when they need to. It is also a requirement if corporations want to remain free of liability and a massively damaged reputation. In most instances of kidnapping, for example, whether or not the corporation is successful in the effort to rescue and return the victim, it will most likely be sued by the victim and/or the victim's family, alleging the organization didn't do enough to protect the employee.

Crises are often a result of the caprices and whims of Mother Nature. It might be an earthquake and tsunami in the Far East or in Japan, or the resultant release of radiation in the aftermath of a tsunami. It might be

CASE STUDY   FUKUSHIMA, CHERNOBYL, AND THREE MILE ISLAND

FUKUSHIMA

Located about 180 miles north of Tokyo is the prefecture of Fukushima. At 2:46 p.m. local time on April 11, 2011, northeastern Japan was shaken by an earthquake of magnitude 9 that churned a massive tsunami. Thanks to Tokyo's early warning earthquake monitoring system, residents received a one-minute warning before the quake. A wall of water 50 feet high rolled into Fukushima Daiichi's 865-acre nuclear power generating facilities housing six reactors. The wave overwhelmed and destroyed the cooling and power to three of the reactors. Over the next three days, the nuclear cores of these reactors, unable to be properly cooled and maintained, melted. A fourth reactor would later be listed as damaged beyond repair. It took two weeks to cool the three reactors properly. Two years after the tsunami, about 300 tons of irradiated water was still leaking each day from Fukushima (Hsu, 2013).

The aftermath of investigations conducted by the Nuclear Accident Independent Investigation Committee concluded that "...the situation continued to deteriorate because the crisis management system of the Kantei (Office of the Prime Minister of Japan), the regulators and other responsible agencies did not function correctly." Specifically, the report found that the nuclear site operator Tokyo Electric Power Company (TEPCO) was to coordinate efforts from the point of the emergency with the Japanese Nuclear and Industrial Safety Agency (NISA) under the Ministry of Economy, Trade and Industry (METI).

The Kantei chose to bypass the regulatory chain of command of NISA and began to work directly with TEPCO. TEPCO management was not prepared for an emergency of this size; nevertheless, the Kantei and TEPCO formed a team to respond to the emergency. The prime minister himself, Naoto Kan, visited the nuclear power plant. By doing so, the process and protocols in place were subverted, and TEPCO was allowed to deflect and not take responsibility for actions in the aftermath of the quake. What ensued was a massive state of chaos related to when to evacuate local residents from the

5

area surrounding the facility. Shelter in place orders were initially issued, keeping residents in the area rather than evacuating. Many residents didn't even know of the accident when evacuation orders were issued and some residents were evacuated to high-radiation rather than safe areas owing to the lack of coordination, communication, and direction.

The investigating commission found that the Kantei delayed in advising the locals about the accident and how great the extent of the damage was. The regulating agencies procrastinated and dragged their feet in forcing improvements in emergency and disaster plans.

CHERNOBYL

The city of Chernobyl is located in the Ukraine, near the borders with Russia and Belarus. Chernobyl became part of Russia when Poland was dissolved in 1793 and part of the Ukraine in 1921. Construction of reactors began in 1977 and by 1983 four graphite reactors had been completed, with two more to be built.

On April 25, 1986, a planned maintenance shutdown was taking place. The unit 4 reactor was to be shut down for routine maintenance that day. The shutdown was discussed as an ideal time to test whether or not a slower turning turbine could generate sufficient power for the water cooling pumps until the backup diesel generator kicked in. Even though the reactor was still a genuine nuclear reactor, which required cooling to ensure the core did not melt, safeguards such as auto shutdown capabilities were disabled. When the extremely hot fuel rods were exposed to water intended to cool the power source, steam overbuilt to the point of explosions. Two employees were killed during these explosions and an estimated 1300 tons of graphite glowed as radiation released approximately 400 times more radiation than the atomic weapon dropped on Hiroshima. Over the next 3 months, an additional 28 people would die from radiation poisoning as a result of fighting the fire and attempting to contain the radiation. The fatalities included firemen, plant staff, and an unfortunate person who had been conducting business at the plant at the time of the accident. Soviet authorities didn't begin evacuating persons surrounding the facility for two days. The Soviet Union announced the accident on April 28, after nuclear facility workers in

Sweden noticed radioactivity on their uniforms. The radiation originated from Chernobyl.

THREE MILE ISLAND

By laughing at me, the audience really laughs at themselves, and realizing they have done this gives them sort of a spiritual second wind for going back into the battles of life.

Emmett Kelly

People in and around Harrisburg, Pennsylvania, would require some comic relief when on the day famous clown Emmett Kelly passed away—March 28, 1979—a series of mechanical malfunctions and human errors at the Three Mile Island nuclear generating plant resulted in an accident that profoundly affected them and the nuclear utility industry. On this day, a series of mishaps involving faulty equipment and human error resulted in a partial melting down (some reports indicated 90% of the core) of one of the reactors. Radiation was released into the outside environment that, according to the owners of the facility—Jersey Central Power & Light Company, Pennsylvania Electric Company, and Metropolitan Edison Company—was equivalent to about two million nearby residents receiving a chest x-ray. For years to come, the Three Mile Island accident led the nuclear power industry and the nation to question the safety and wisdom of building more reactors in the United States.

In thinking about the incidents at Three Mile Island and Chernobyl and the aftermath of the earthquake and tsunami involving the Japanese nuclear facility in Fukushima, some may say that hindsight is 20–20, to use a common cliché. However, shouldn't the very smart and well-educated people who were busy designing and building such immense technological achievements, with such great potential for inadvertent damage and destruction if these were to fail, have planned more carefully for unforeseen circumstances?

What can be said without hesitation is that even in the presence of a power as awesome as the atom (in the words of J. Robert Oppenheimer, "I am become death, the destroyer of worlds."), at Three Mile Island, Chernobyl, and Fukushima nuclear power stations, emergency preparedness and crisis management were not considered paramount to everything else. In other words, in dealing with something as potentially hazardous as nuclear power generation, one would think that the FIRST consideration BEFORE building such an operation would be the creation of emergency plans, crisis management, and thinking about the what-ifs in case the worst should happen. Instead, these facilities were engineered first and foremost for functional performance—harness the heat, heat the steam, turn the turbines, generate the electricity. This was indeed accomplished. But the facilities and planners lacked preparation for contingencies were the system to go amiss. As J. Robert Oppenheimer said, "No man should escape our universities without knowing how little he knows."

Why is it that people focused on crisis management believe that a leading consideration for the groups building, fueling, and operating the nuclear facilities is to protect those who work at and live around the plants? The obvious legal considerations should be taken into account, but in the case of Fukushima the commission investigating the incident for six months found that "The TEPCO Fukushima Nuclear Power Plant accident was the result of collusion between the government, the regulators and TEPCO, and the lack of governance by said parties." (The National Diet of Japan, 2012, p. 16.) In the area of crisis management, the commission found "...that the situation continued to deteriorate because the crisis management system of the...regulators and other responsible agencies did not function correctly." The Chernobyl accident took place in the Ukraine. Although the facility was built by the former Soviet Union, it wasn't the Soviets who neglected to evacuate those who lived around the reactors. The Soviets, were not, as many might believe, indulging in any particular Cold War skullduggery for not releasing information relating to the extent of the accident. As we now know, many people heroically fought to contain the accident, and paid with their lives.

At Three Mile Island, reports have shed light on a theory that Metropolitan Edison was aware of the extent of the damage to the reactor, that radiation was already being released into the community, and that by not sounding any alarms sooner, the US government's Nuclear Regulatory Commission was propping up this wholly illogical explanation. Chernobyl is located far from Moscow, just as Three Mile Island is quite a distance from Washington, DC. If the two reactors were closer to the respective capitals, would the response have been different? In each of these cases, a combination of mistakes made by technicians and engineers, the lack of emergency and crisis management plans and training, disconnected departments and working groups, and management not pushing for planning and cooperation led to debacles.

> Don't you know about the praying mantis that waved its arms angrily in front of an approaching carriage, unaware that they were incapable of stopping it? Such was the high opinion it had of its talents.
>
> Zhuangzi
> *The Complete Works of Chuang Tzu*

The designers, builders, and operators of Three Mile Island, Chernobyl, and Fukushima didn't intend to release radiation or threaten the lives of those who lived nearby or of employees who worked in proximity to the reactors. But they were blinded by their fascination with their projects and a belief in the infallibility of their designs and handiworks. Had they not been so, they might have perhaps tasked subordinates with drawing up emergency plans and formulating crisis management plans. We know that in the cases of Three Mile Island and Fukushima, relationships between regulators and operators were unethical at the least and criminal at worst, or government regulators took for granted and gave too much credit to operators for possessing the knowledge to adequately manage a crisis involving their facilities. Perhaps when the radiation was leaking and it became clear just how dangerous the situations at Three Mile Island, Chernobyl, and Fukushima were the operators gave the highest priority to evacuating nearby residents and employees, rather than considering the bottom dollar and how much they could stand to lose from prying eyes or penalties, fines, and lawsuits.

It is the role of crisis and emergency managers, hopefully working with the engineers, designers, and builders of corporate infrastructure and assets, to ensure that people, buildings, and properties are protected. If crisis managers are not considered a vital part of corporations and organizations, crisis management often becomes a *check off* or *check the box* item at best. More often than not, crisis management is a cut-and-paste job—taking a crisis plan from a previous project and putting it at the tail end of this new endeavor. Often, crisis management, emergency procedures, and security concerns are requirements those involved with government contracting must meet. Without these actions, a bid will not be considered. Adequate crisis management, with plans in place for protecting expats around the world, may become a means of attracting or retaining valuable employees who know the corporation is concerned for their well-being. Crisis management must become for corporations and organizations a vital function of their corporate governance. If crisis management planning and response continue to be afterthoughts, we will continue to experience gaps and monumental failures in how we deal with crisis.

forest fires in Colorado, flooding in Europe, the bird or swine flu epidemic, or extensive and continuing dangerous pollution in a large Chinese city. The manner and variety of disasters the world can produce appears to be inexhaustible (Figure 1.1).

Whether you have been tasked to be the responsible person to manage and plan and train for a crisis in Iraq and Afghanistan, or will be called

Figure 1.1 In 2012, Mother Nature wreaked havoc with some of the largest fires Colorado had ever experienced. In these areas, businesses and homes without disaster planning would not have fared well. (Courtesy of Master Sgt. Christopher DeWitt, US Air Force, http://www.nasa.gov/content/goddard/nasa-fire-towers -in-space-watch-for-wildfires-on-the-rise/#.Vq95Hk10zoo.)

on to evacuate expats from Egypt and Israel when one or both countries erupts with violent protest, or is the victim of missiles rained upon indiscriminate targets. Your duties might include training and procedures for employees avoiding surveillance in Africa and South America, or planning for health concerns in Algeria. In whatever would be considered a crisis—that which has happened and that which is likely to happen—it will be expected that you should have planned responses or conducted exercises to deal with the event and manage it on the ground.

What can be learned and should be understood about crisis is that people can survive if they know what to do, if they have prepared mentally and tactically to respond to circumstances. As with anything in life, practice makes perfect. And, practice in crisis management means the sometimes dreaded *D* word—drills and more drills.

Crisis can sometimes be mitigated and contained, as for example, in a crisis involving a corporate tragedy involving bad press in the aftermath of a product recall, or a death of an employee in an accident. But crises involving natural disasters must be dealt with, and dealt with effectively.

This book seeks to illustrate the crises affecting corporations, whether specific to personnel working in the United States or people and assets in far-flung locations, with consideration from a crisis management and security perspective. Readers may or may not have had experience with crisis preplanning and drilling, or with actual crisis situations. The objective of this book is to add some background and suggestions for dealing with potential and eventual outcomes.

In terms of crisis planning, this book does not intend to illustrate or elevate the tired old practice of creating a crisis plan, only to place said plan upon a shelf, never to be seen or heard of again. Many an organization has a spaceholder for a crisis plan, a thick brightly colored binder containing all the thoughts and recommendations of the team that was assembled after the CEO or board member read or heard about a disaster or crisis halfway around the world. Or, a nervous insurance company account representative may have fired off a memo to his or her senior management and the executive floor rumbled to life and demanded its clients come up with a Plan (Figure 1.2).

The Plan is then developed and distributed with much fanfare. The recipients marvel at its weight and girth and seek a suitable location to display this worldly tome, and there it sits. The team congratulates itself, goes out for a meal, and the members go about their normal jobs as HR managers, logisticians, and engineers. As for the Plan, immediately after it is placed prominently upon the bookshelves or desks of many cubicles

11

Figure 1.2 The 1964 Alaska tsunami exhibited to the rugged individuals living in the state to prepare for nature's possibilities. (Courtesy of NOAA/NGDC, US Department of the Interior, http://www.ngdc.noaa.gov/hazardimages/picture/show/160.)

and offices from Ann Arbor to Afghanistan, it begins to become dated. Frank from accounting has now moved to distribution. Sally from HR has moved to finance, and Joe from safety has become a statistical engineer. Employees have moved or had to change phone numbers; people have retired or been asked to leave. Some have passed away. The relevancy of crisis management plans is dependent on keeping current with every piece of information contained within the documents.

REFERENCES

Hsu, Jeremy. Radioactive water leaks from Fukushima: What we know, August 13, 2013. www.livescience.com/38844.fukushima-radioactive-water-leaks.html.
The National Diet of Japan. "The Official Report of The Fukushima Nuclear Accident Independent Investigation Commission," 2012.

2

Crisis Conditions and Reality

It is better to offer no excuse than a bad one.

George Washington

Crisis. The word means different things to many different people. For example, in 2008, the United States suffered a financial crisis that is still affecting the economies of the United States and the world to a certain extent. Many scholars attribute this financial crisis to the *housing bubble* and the *bursting* that followed, when what many labeled the *subprime mortgage crisis* slowly enveloped US and world markets. The financial crisis of 2008 was a huge event of an intangible nature to many, unless one lost a job as a result of the downturn in housing starts, credit swaps and defaults, or if a house was lost to foreclosure. One tangible effect of the housing bubble bursting and the subsequent financial crisis was that many corporations spent less on security and crisis management apparatus and systems, and on hiring security and crisis management professionals. This caused a personal financial crisis for persons in these professions.

> The wise man does not expose himself needlessly to danger, since there are few things for which he cares sufficiently; but he is willing, in great crises, to give even his life—knowing that under certain conditions it is not worthwhile to live.

Aristotle
Greek philosopher

There are personal crises, and one might have a crisis of conscience. There are crises of confidence, and sometimes people or organizations

13

say they are in crisis mode. Things might reach crisis or epidemic proportions. You might have heard the saying, "A lack of preparation on your part does not constitute a crisis on mine."

Some of us recall epidemic or pandemic preparations of a few years ago. What began as media-inspired interest over a few years reached its apex in 2009 when a worldwide panic prompted many US corporations with a national and especially an international presence that had never sat down for any discussions concerning crisis management to develop pandemic plans. In May 2009, Afghanistan quarantined the only pig located in the entire nation. Fear of H1N1, or the swine flu, prompted nations such as China to construct biometric monitoring stations in international airports and even quarantine passengers as they disembarked if they had higher than normal body temperatures. The flu concerns persisted for much of 2009 and by 2010 had largely quieted from the panic mode of the previous year (*Globe and Mail*, 2010).

Crises often begin with emergencies, that is, an emergency situation might turn into a crisis based on its duration or severity. In almost every situation a fire is an emergency. A fire in a home is an emergency, requiring residents to extinguish the fire or to evacuate the building if the fire is out of control. If the home becomes completely engulfed, and a family or homeowner is injured or loses everything in the fire, a true crisis now exists from the aftermath of an emergency. The crisis is made worse if the homeowner does not have a sufficient amount or the correct type of insurance to cover the loss of the home. Now the home is gone and there is no means to rebuild it. As illustrated in the following case study, conditions or situations that might have become more or less commonplace to some populations, such as a history of risk of rockets and missiles being occasionally lobbed at civilian populations, might face employees of organizations who have suddenly found themselves working on a valuable project in such a region.

A medical emergency at a plant site might be the type of incident considered for immediate actions to save or protect lives. Often procedures are drafted for dealing with such emergencies in what are called emergency action plans (EAPs). EAPs consist of the steps to take in the event of the types of emergent occurrences to which your particular location or industry may be vulnerable. An EAP for a medical emergency might include the steps to take by the front gate security officers, the receptionist, the emergency response team (ERT), and so on. EAPs can be *table topped*, as one form of exercise, and these plans may be drilled. Participants can become very familiar with the steps to take in such emergencies.

CASE STUDY   ROCKETS AT DAYBREAK

A semi-large project involved the placement of expats outside of a major metropolitan area in a hospitable location. Hostilities between the host government and rebels outside of the country and just across a nearby border had been ongoing for years and were recently coming to a head at an unfortunate time for the project. This particular project required frequent inspections of work around an approximately 700-acre project area. Rebel groups had been threatening to bombard government facilities, actually indiscriminately given the lack of targeting and aiming ability for the rockets at any given time. In addition, the rebels claimed to have at their disposal chemical weapons that could be fitted to their rockets. Finally, the rebels fired off some rockets in other locations around the country, causing little damage and no injuries, but raising the desired level of terror among the population. The news media and the government began to warn the citizens of the range of the rebel missiles and the threat of poisonous gases being contained within.

Back home, the corporation had been monitoring conditions and began to query its employees about the situation on the ground. The headquarters (HQ) disaster management team (yes, there was one in place!) inquired what precautions were being taken at the jobsite. The expats replied that the in-country managers of the project were installing bomb shelters around the jobsite and were issuing gas masks: comforting in one sense, disconcerting in another. The shelters were constructed such as to prevent injuries or death due to the effects of shrapnel from exploding missiles and for limited but not extended shelter from any gases present on the projectiles. None of the shelters were capable of withstanding a direct impact of a missile.

HQ became concerned that the project might be taking things a bit too cavalierly, with the shelters being built, yet little done with an actual written and practiced plan, which might in some sense be expected because such missile attacks had taken place in the country some years before, and the populace had become well trained and steadfast in its defiance of the missiles. A plan was set forth to develop hard and fast methods and procedures geared toward keeping the employees safe and protected.

The first item of concern was communications. The expat employees hadn't bothered to pick up the recommended satellite

15

phone (satphone), which had been considered because the in-country communications were often unreliable or were shut down because of security precautions in times of national emergency. The idea was that if landline and cellular telephone service was unavailable, at least the satphone might work. It wasn't clear if such a theory would prove out during an emergency, as even though many people no doubt possessed satphones, in this particular region they are suspect by the host government, and, at any rate, in case of an actual emergency, would the satellite networks be kept up and running, or would there be too much phone traffic, and so forth? If communication networks are unreliable—landline, mobile, Internet, satphone—what shall the project do, and what measures should HQ be responsible for ensuring?

In this situation, obviously with missiles or other sorts of attacks possible at any time, and with very short notice, HQ and the expats on the ground for the project needed to devise a plan that could be enacted quickly AND even without the ability to contact HQ. The plan would have to be clearly developed and put forth. It would have to be quick and nimble and something else would need to take place. The leader of the expats involved in the project would have to be given and accept the authority and responsibility to act immediately and without permission from or even the ability to notify HQ of the actions that must be quickly initiated.

It would first be imperative to ensure that the intelligence, the real and true information concerning what might be happening, would be guaranteed and verified. If rebel groups were forming to stage another attack, if negotiations were going badly and were in danger of being terminated completely, the project team and HQ would require timely and accurate information. If rebels were making plans for a large demonstration, peaceful at first but one that had a high likelihood of becoming violent, fomenting nationwide troubles, the project employees and HQ would need these data as soon as possible. To gather such vital and useful information HQ sent someone in the country to make contact with US Consulate personnel to discuss the ongoing security situation and to place a face with the State Department men and women who would provide an early warning when necessary. HQ also contracted with a private travel intelligence organization to get some additional perspective from their in-country and regional security experts.

Next, HQ decided on placing a measuring stick in the ground in-country. It was decided, through meetings with their crisis management team, that if rockets were to start up again and land anywhere within 20 miles north of the project, the expats would immediately drive 40 miles south to the closest major city—well out of range of any of the rebel missiles. The expats would contact HQ whenever they were able to do so, either before they left for the southern sanctuary or once they arrived. There would be daily conference calls to discuss the situation and to check the expat's satphone reliability—the expats would be calling in on the satphone each day.

The expat and crisis management team calls on Sunday through Friday were fairly uneventful. There was discussion of the preparations the expats had put into place should the situation again become dangerous. During the evening hours of Friday, the situation on the ground became quite precarious for the expats. The rebels had become hostile again and began to lob rockets toward populated areas. The expats gathered their *go bags* and boarded the project buses that had been loaned to them by the project management. They attempted to contact HQ, to no avail. The satphone could not be located; it had been misplaced by a member of the expat team. By the early morning hours of Saturday, all the expats had reached the corporate apartments in the southern town. The exhausted expats tumbled into their beds and were quickly consumed by sleep. When they awoke the next morning, they were met with cable news broadcasts of direct hits upon the area from which they had departed the previous evening. What the newscasters could not know, but what project management passed on to the expats, who then relayed the information to HQ, was that two missiles had made direct impacts on their jobsite. In fact, one missile struck and completely destroyed an empty bomb shelter, which would have been theirs had they remained and not evacuated.

EAPs are often confused with crisis management plans (CMPs) or a crisis response plan (CRP). These plans are not the same thing. Emergencies may lead to crises, of course, and crises may catapult ahead during an emergency that is of catastrophic proportions. A tsunami, for example, is a crisis at the moment it touches land. In the past, governments in tsunami-prone regions did not believe it necessary to develop crisis plans for giant ocean waves hitting their coasts, but history has taught them that it is prudent they have these now.

A crisis, then, may develop immediately on the heels of an emergency, but in many cases, the emergency takes place first. A plane strikes a skyscraper, and many personnel feel an accident has occurred. Building and floor emergency procedures and responses are initiated. The fire and destruction is immense. A second plane strikes the adjacent tower, and now a crisis has ensued. However, emergency procedures remain in effect and many personnel are successfully evacuating the buildings using the emergency stairwells.

Corporations and organizations, if the truth were to be told, often feel immune to crisis, even emergencies, as evident by the number of companies and organizations that rely on *911* for whatever might arise. Managements of high-rise office buildings, even chemical plants, often rely on law enforcement and first responders for their crisis plans. This is not a desirable proposition in crisis situations in which law enforcement agencies may be quickly overwhelmed in the case of widespread emergencies and disasters. Consider, for example, emergency services in the aftermath of Hurricane Katrina. One might assume that big city police departments, sheriffs' offices, and fire departments of a city the size of New Orleans are well equipped and trained to handle multiple emergencies and step up in time of crisis with no lack of resources (Figure 2.1). As Commander Timothy Bayard of the New Orleans Police Department vice and narcotics unit advised a panel of US senators:

> We did not coordinate with any state, local or federal agencies. We were not prepared logistically...we relocated evacuees to two locations where there was no food, water or portable restrooms.... We did not utilize buses that would have allowed us to transport mass quantities of evacuees expeditiously have allowed us to transport communications system. (p. 54)
>
> Jenni Bergal (2007)
> *City Adrift: New Orleans Before and After Katrina*

The same holds true for all first responders. In many towns and cities, volunteers make up the fire and rescue squads, without whom these locales would have no first responders. In many jurisdictions, first responders double as fire and police. The lesson one might draw is the following: plan for the worst, but hope for the best. Plan for no one from the police department showing up very soon, and hope that they do. Or,

Figure 2.1 Residents of New Orleans couldn't have imagined taking refuge in the Superdome awaiting rescue from regional and federal authorities. (Courtesy of FEMA, https://www.fema.gov/media-library/assets/images/47153, September 4, 2005.)

don't plan on medical care arriving quickly when your city has just been flattened by a tornado, or the coast was battered by a hurricane. Don't plan on the fire department; as has been mentioned, multiple agencies will be set about in search and rescue operations.

The work of police departments, such as that during the Katrina event in New Orleans, will be hampered by the collapse of a city's infrastructure, flooded or blocked roads, power down or sparse, and officers dealing with their own personal losses and devastation. As illustrated in *City Adrift: New Orleans Before and After Katrina* (Bergal, 2007), police unit cohesiveness and effectiveness can be tried as much as the patience of its citizens.

> The situation worsened with the erratic police performance in the days after the storm. Though many officers performed heroically during Katrina, the department sustained new blows to its esteem after dozens deserted their posts. Some were investigated by the Louisiana attorney general's office in connection with the theft of vehicles from a downtown dealership. (p. 107)

If police departments can react like this during times of disaster, how can private corporations and organizations rely on them?

19

Hospitals didn't fare much better during Katrina, even with planning that had been mandated by the state of Louisiana.

> New Orleans hospitals thought they were prepared for any disaster. For years they had gone through plenty of hurricane planning sessions and emergency drills…in 2001, when Tropical Storm Allison caught that city (Houston) off guard, causing nine area hospitals to close because of flooding. Many lost primary and backup power, leaving them without lights, air conditioning or even ventilation after their basements were submerged. Since then, many have moved their equipment to higher ground. While the hospitals in New Orleans knew about such potential problems, most either didn't have the money or the will to make such changes. (p. 79)
>
> Jenni Bergal (2007)
> *City Adrift: New Orleans Before and After Katrina*

The problem with relying on first responders for your emergency and crisis response is a lack of numbers and of timing. As emergencies and crises dictate, a large number of police and fire personnel may be called on for more pressing issues than checking on or responding to the situation where your facility or personnel are located. In the case of damages limited to your facility or the area surrounding your facility or personnel, you may be able to count on an emergency services response.

So, don't plan on police, fire, paramedics, utility repair trucks, trucking companies, vendors—anyone—being able to arrive in a timely manner. Your organization will do right planning that, at some point, first responders will arrive during or after a crisis has occurred. And, if local services are not completely tied up, you may still see responders at some point. However, you should construct your plan with the knowledge that resources might be too slow in responding or that these services may be unavailable to do so. Does this mean you should have the capability to sustain your business in the absence of vital services and assistance usually taken for granted? Yes, this is exactly what that means.

In discussions of crisis among security and crisis professionals, the topics often turn to what constitutes *domestic* versus *international* crises. Domestic crises, or those that happen within the US, Canadian, or Mexican borders if you are so based, can be seen as circumstances for which there is some limited amount of control or capacity to respond to such events. For example, the United States has a robust, well-funded, highly technical capability to monitor hurricanes in the Atlantic or the Gulf of Mexico and to predict whether or not these storms will make landfall, and where.

20

Based on experiences throughout history, various regions are notably more likely to be hit by hurricanes. Planning for hurricanes, including preparations for the onset and the aftermath of hurricanes, should therefore take place in these areas. Likewise, facilities and personnel located in San Francisco or other earthquake-prone regions and areas should prepare for such events happening again.

Other examples of incidents to plan for include power outages in regions and cities where heat- and storm-related power surges and blackouts might occur. In states and areas that are prone to forest fires, planning should include the capability to address evacuations of fire zones, if required. If one operates in zones known to be frequented by criminal gangs or with high crime rates, planning should take into account protection for people and assets based on these risks.

Planning for crises taking place outside of North America must take into account all of the aforementioned types of crises, plus a few that are not so familiar in our locales. Coups, mass strikes, moving checkpoints, and violent protests often take place in many foreign countries. One crucial aspect of crisis planning and management that planning for crises in foreign locations must take into account is that these locations are far enough away from many corporate, North American-based headquarters that time zones, great distance, laws, customs, and capabilities stand in the way of effective crisis management.

One thing is certain when planning for crisis response and management: nothing will ever go exactly as planned. You cannot plan for every outcome, but you can plan for those within the realm of possibility. Here's a common dilemma: you have expats thousands of miles away and they are located in a hot spot. Rockets launched from terrorist cells have been peppering the area surrounding their jobsite and personnel camp. HQ calls the project manager and begins to assess what they are seeing and hearing on the ground. Suddenly, communications are lost. HQ receives an e-mail from the project manager saying a cell tower must have been taken down and to expect Internet to be next.

HQ is now forced to rely on the wits and decisions of the project manager. They are cut off, no longer able to pass along intelligence and information that might help him or her make critical, possibly life or death decisions. HQ must now totally rely on the project manager for the safety and security of the expats under his or her control. Do you have a robust, flexible plan in place? Does the plan include triggers so that if action A occurs, action B is taken by the expats on the ground? If you don't have a plan in place, or if communications are down, can you rely on the project manager to act in the best interests of the personnel in place? Will he or she make the correct decisions to protect the full-time employees, the contractors, and local nationals?

When one is considering just the nonnatural types of disasters, the list can become extensive considering all the different types of businesses and organizations. There can be cases of crime involving either personnel or a corporation itself, such as an employee being assaulted or murdered at a facility or while traveling. Kidnappings can occur anywhere in the world. The company's executive might be targeted for threats or extortion or attacks. Organizations can suffer a loss of information through economic or competitive espionage. Networks are susceptible to denial of service attacks or hackers taking or destroying data or releasing or stealing confidential customer financial information. Union or union organizing activities or strikes might place companies in a crisis situation, along with attempts to take over a corporation through stock or other business transactions. Corporate actions or other occurrences might cause customers to organize against purchasing the company's goods or services. Employees might be injured or killed in vehicular, airplane, or other accidents, or a competitor might have infringed on a patent. Food products in a grocery store may be tampered with, causing a panic across the nation or the world. Oil spills or chemical releases may take place. Lists of what can happen should be compared with what has happened in the past to a particular corporation. And, the corporation should take into account what is likely to happen. Comets impacting with Earth, given their nature, might be a difficult disaster to plan for, let alone survive. Pick your battles, choose the crises likeliest to happen, and plan accordingly.

The reality of crisis management is that actual crises are different from the presuppositions. Seems logical? For anyone who has experienced a crisis, either on the ground in the midst of such an event, or at HQ trying to manage the response and mitigate disastrous occurrences, this truth has become self-evident. One can write about crisis, make presentations concerning crisis, lecture on crisis, or conduct crisis exercises and training, but unless and until one experiences a crisis down and dirty, in the trenches, the true complexities and evolving nature of crisis may not be completely appreciated. In crisis situations, personal limits of endurance and levels of tolerating stress are tested to the fullest.

See the Appendix section "Emergency Funds Contact List" for a suggested contact list for corporate individuals who have control of emergency funds for crisis response.

REFERENCES

Bergal, Jenni. *City Adrift: New Orleans Before and After Katrina*, Center for Public Integrity. Baton Rouge: Louisiana State University Press, 2007.
Globe and Mail. H1N1 is over, but the next pandemic awaits, August 9, 2010.

3

Four Stages of a Crisis

When written in Chinese, the word *crisis* is composed of two characters. One represents danger and the other represents opportunity.

John F. Kennedy

If you believe the first stage of a crisis is PANIC, then you probably haven't done enough planning in preparation. Panic is a human condition, resulting, in my view, from stimuli over which the recipient feels he or she has no control and few options for a response. Successful crisis managers rely on continuous planning and tweaking of emergency action and crisis management plans to avoid panic and mitigate loss of life or property.

For many organizations or people stationed overseas the first stage of crisis often might very well be panic. It immobilizes their brains and bodies, numbing their senses and making them susceptible to mistakes, injury, death, and destruction. Panic can be avoided and dealt with in positive ways, making use of the adrenaline resulting from such an onset to keep the mind clear and focused.

For the purposes of this discussion, consider there are four stages of a crisis in the same manner that the International Fire Service Training Association (IFSTA) explains as the four stages of a fire: incipient, growth, fully developed, and decay.

During the first stage of a fire, termed the incipient stage, the reaction takes place between the essentials: oxygen; heat; and something to burn, the fuel. In a crisis of a political nature, for example, one might consider the sudden change of a government, by coup or a rigged election, to be the incipient stage. Of course, in the case of political, ethnic, religious, or economic tensions, the *fuel* may have been collecting for some time. Demonstrations might be a reaction to higher fuel prices, the cut off of utilities, or suppression or oppression of opposition groups. Preaching to the masses in a bombastic, hateful, and rhetorical manner might intensify the incipient stage of the crisis. And, if government police or military armed forces move in to respond to protestors with violence, oxygen may be added to the mix. Such situations may be somewhat predictable given the nature of an indigenous police or military force. For example, if the government security forces are of an aggressive nature, one could predict a hostile and violent confrontation. It would be prudent to warn employees to remain at their homes, avoid certain areas, or limit travel as appropriate. Planning should begin at this incipient stage and consider the preparation of *tripwires*.

This incipient stage may be prognosticated well in advance of the actual circumstances. For example, an opposition group beating the drums of localized or nationwide transportation service strikes might lead management to deduce that there may be issues involving public or private transportation means and venues. In some countries, roadblocks are a favorite form of disruption of automobile traffic, while blockades of public transportation, including subways and trains, might be set up. Corporations or organizations are able to use the time during this incipient phase to begin looking at their crisis management plans, or quickly developing these if none exist.

Sympathy strikes or masses of workers calling in sick have been known to drastically curtail and halt public transportation with little effort. Alternative means of transportation may be arranged or recommended by in-country management. Or, offices may be closed if public/private transportation blockage will adversely affect the ability of the office to conduct business.

The incipient stage of a crisis might consist of news reports or press coverage of opposition groups making threats of civil disobedience or warning of violent confrontation or acts. In ongoing crises, such as what one might call the ongoing acts of terrorism directed against Western interests and countries perpetrated by Al Qaeda and other supporters or groups, no such warnings or incipient indicators might be observed or witnessed.

The growth stage of a crisis might be clearly obvious to onlookers, such as flames now tickling a ceiling, the fire clearly having made the leap from the incipient to the next stage. In the growth stage of a political crisis, one might see the swelling of a protest—ever so subtly, almost imperceptibly, to a point where a mass of people is ready to move on the forces arrayed against them. Then, as mentioned previously, the addition of military or police forces, violently descending upon protestors, sets about a night or days of sporadic violence and destruction. During the growth stage law enforcement and military may be gearing up for potential use of mass force. Harsher tactics to deal with protestors might ensue. Civil services and utilities may suffer from breakdowns, closures, or shutdowns. Organizations may consider the evacuation of nonessential personnel and of flying dependents out of the country, if it may be done safely. It is time for all employees and contractors to have a serious discussion of whether it makes more sense to stay or to leave. It is time to ask, is my life/their lives worth more than the completion or continuation of this project, than this office ceasing to operate for a short time, even longer, in this endeavor? Chairs, desks, vehicles, and even buildings can be replaced. People cannot.

Whether in times of strife or turmoil or not, it makes a great deal of sense always to keep your passport and important personal documents with you whenever leaving the hotel, the office, the jobsite, or buildings. You might be stopped and asked to produce such documents by police, government agencies, or the military. But, in addition, if you have to leave a region or a country hurriedly for whatever reason, it's best not to have to return to your hotel to retrieve these items. Plus, these are safer with you than at any hotel.

A fully developed scenario, what one might consider the third stage of this crowd–protestor–police/military example, might be the death of protestors and police, destruction and firebombing of structures or vehicles, and running violence as protestors and police forces move in battles from area to area, cascading like pinballs with an ominous outcome. During fully developed stages, incredibly violent protest events or actions taken by the protestors, the police, and/or the military ensue. One frequently sees vehicle roadblocks and checkpoints set up in various locations. The roadblocks are sometimes set up by the police or the military, or by protestors or self-appointed loyalists to a regime. The roadblocks might be constructed to keep neighborhoods safe. No matter who is manning these checkpoints, they are ideal locations for criminal behavior including violence by all involved. Avoid checkpoints at all costs. In surrounding areas, gunfire and explosions can be heard. It is extremely unsafe to be on the streets or even to venture outdoors during such incidents. The time for evacuation has come and gone. This now becomes the most critical stage of a crisis event, requiring the greatest amount of courage and forethought.

Decay is the final aspect of a crisis event, if one is considering the four stages of a fire as an example. Although decay might lead the team on the ground or those back in headquarters to believe the crisis is not only diminishing but also subsiding, this might be the furthest thing from the truth. An event or series of incidents can and often does rise back to a fully engulfed stage with little warning or provocation. If telephone and Internet services are restored, the decay phase might present an opportunity to reestablish contact with headquarters and loved ones, to let everyone know what might be needed and that everyone is OK, or not so.

Tripwires or preplanned procedures in reaction to key events should be put into place. For example, in some countries or regions, history and events often repeat themselves. And, in planning for crises, security and crisis professionals can anticipate similar occurrences and reactions to events. Opposition political opponents under an autocratic regime might gather large supporting rallies. What starts as a peaceful public demonstration or celebration attracts police or military, which begins violent crackdowns on peaceful crowds. These rallies attract opposition groups hired by the party in power to cause trouble and wreak havoc. The military and police have been known to become violent with little or no provocation.

Some examples of tripwires might include the following: Students begin protests in the city central square. Protests are peaceful and the government and police forces are merely standing by; there have been no violent actions by these forces. Headquarters advises corporate and contract personnel on the ground that they are monitoring the situation and are ready to *stand up* crisis support should the project request this or should the situation warrant. In country personnel are reminded to review the crisis management plans and to be ready should the situation worsen.

Personnel on the ground in country would do things like review their crisis plan and procedures. They should strongly consider looking over travel and project schedules. They might hold a tabletop exercise or at least hold a meeting to go over the plan, reemphasizing key responsibilities and functions. Personnel might begin to check their *go bags*, satphones, and other equipment.

By way of progression, the next preset tripwire might be akin to the following: Peaceful protests have given way to fighting and violence in the streets. The tide perhaps looks like it is turning toward the government showing itself as being more in control, more heavy handed. Riot police have been called in and have used tear gas and water cannons. As of yet, the military has not shown up to quell more demonstrations and protest. A decision could be made in advance that the next tripwire would consist of a circumstance such as the military showing up and essentially taking over the police action against the protestors. Shots are fired and demonstrators are killed. Right away, in-country personnel need to be looking at the actions to be taken if they need to curtail their movements to and from the office, jobsite, or project. There should be a review of the next tripwire to be considered, that of violence by protestors or forces loyal to the ruling regime and if this would necessitate sheltering in place or standing fast. If deemed to be safe, based on consultation from multiple professional safety and security sources, company management would think about nonessential personnel being flown or otherwise transported out of the country.

Crisis should not sneak up on an organization if it has its antennae up and its feelers at the ready. Crisis planning and management must not take over an inordinate amount of valuable time and resources of an organization. It must, however, be considered and dealt with, not grudgingly, but with the understanding that the work that is being done might save someone's life down the road.

Understanding the stages of a crisis does not lead one to discover the solutions for each level, but it does help one to realize where they might be with respect to the level of risk. During the initial stages companies that haven't done any planning might still have time to allocate resources and personnel and assemble a group to deal with what might come next. If it is the right group of people, and if they have the appropriate resources, this task will be much easier. To keep in mind the fire analogy, just because a fire has no flame, it does not mean the smoldering embers might not again ignite. Stay on guard during what might seem to be a cessation in violence or intensity that might just be a lull before more fuel such as anger, government actions, or other factors reignite a blaze of retaliation, violent protest, or retributions.

The bottom line here, what every organization wants to avoid, is the initial Phase One, Level One, First Step, Numero Uno thing to do when plans are not in place—PANIC! By understanding the phases of a crisis one can more effectively categorize and plan for responses as each level of crisis manifests itself.

See the Appendix section "Improvised Explosive Device (IED) and Bomb Threat Plan" for suggestions relating to planning for the mitigation of threats from suspicious packages and parcels and improvised explosive devices.

4

Assessing Risk

The Edge.... There is no honest way to explain it because the only people who really know where it is are the ones who have gone over.

Hunter S. Thompson (1966)
Hell's Angels: The Strange and Terrible Saga
of the Outlaw Motorcycle Gangs

Think of assessing risk as peeling an onion. The brownish skin is on the outside, and the part you want to get to is under this layer. The tough skin needs to be peeled away, and as you do so, you are presented with a substance that burns your eyes and makes it difficult to see. Yet, if you are going to reach the fruit, you must persevere and keep peeling and cutting away.

One of the first processes in determining what is required to mitigate and deal with risk is to assess what potential hazards are facing your corporation or organization. Assessing risk can be difficult, and assessing all aspects of such risk might be even more strenuous. One tried and true method for assessing the risk of crises taking place is tackling crisis as if one were conducting a security or risk assessment in the area of physical security, that is, working inward from the outlying areas. In looking for where risks concerning physical security are, many practitioners work from the outside, the perimeter, and move closer and closer toward the interior, identifying and testing the layers or sections of security. Risk assessment for crisis management can start as simply as looking over a map of the outlying area and determining what of any significance has taken place, or might take place, and what is taking place now.

For such assessments, many organizations use multiple means of intelligence gathering and formulating ideas and opinions. One such method of ascertaining useful and timely information is to join organizations such as the US Department of State's Overseas Security Advisory Council (OSAC). The Council was formed in 1985 to encourage information sharing and cooperation between the private sector in the United States and the Department of State. Today, OSAC comprises more than 4700 US private sector companies and educational, faith-based, and nongovernmental organizations. Some of the more beneficial aspects of becoming a member of this group are the training opportunities and many contacts available.

As an example, the State Department in 2000 opened up a two-day class for non-State Department personnel entitled the "Security Overseas Seminar." Initially designed "...to meet the security awareness needs of US Government personnel and families going overseas..." it now provides much more (US Department of State, n.d.). The topics open to the private sector include safety, health, and environmental hazards; explosives: identification and safety measures; fire safety; evacuation planning; and crisis management, to name just a few. The information is presented by experts who have lived and worked overseas for many years and provide real-world examples and training.

Risk is important to understand and hard to quantify. One might consider risk as a blend of the tangible and intangible. Tangibles of risk might be placed into categories such as loss of life, loss of property, or the inability to rebuild or restart a business. Intangibles might be considered loss of reputation due to a plane crash found to be caused by improperly maintained aircraft, or the inability to attract or retain employees as a result of expats being kidnapped and murdered while working on a foreign assignment.

Risk can be calculated by many variables and scenarios. Insurance companies utilize actuarial life tables to determine a person's likelihood of dying at a certain time based on age, national origin, occupation, to name just a few areas, in addition to complex charts and algorithms. When calculating risk one can often overlook the obvious. Such is the case with hurricanes. The fact is, after hurricanes do people along the coastlines evacuate and choose to never return? On the contrary, cities and communities are rebuilt in the face of hurricanes that come around every year around the same time and in the same relative regions. As of 2010, approximately 70% of Americans lived around 100 miles from coastlines that frequently experience the ravages of hurricanes (Ripley, 2008, p. 37). Why do such people tempt fate? Why do they play with their lives? Is it

CASE STUDY   AVAST YE SWABS!

A regional sales representative for a multinational corporation was in a faraway location negotiating the purchase of a large shipment of bulk materials. The shipment was, in fact, on board a large ship. This particular salesperson was known to be a bit of a swashbuckler himself. He would dart off to a remote locale or exotic country with little regard for letting anyone back at HQ know of his plans or whereabouts. And, his first-line manager did nothing to control his actions because the sales rep always exceeded his targets. He was happy, his manager was happy, and the corporation was happy. The tanker was approximately two days out of harbor, so the salesperson drove himself (also in violation of corporate policies and procedures) to the port city and began to check out the local nightlife and social activities. What cannot be known by the author, but what is suspected, is that at some point during the daring and intrepid salesperson's soirees he must have divulged his purpose for being in the port city. He was about to score a very big deal of locating some very precious raw materials, purchase these for cash, and turn these into massive profits for his corporation.

The ship neared the coastline, and from out of the mist appeared two small rapidly approaching watercraft. Within minutes, the two boats emptied their heavily armed and determined crews of modern-day pirates. They violently seized and bound the crew. They telephoned the hotel where the intrepid sales jockey was sleeping off a hangover and asked the front desk to be connected to his room. Groggily answering the call, the salesperson slowly began to comprehend the predicament he was in. The pirates demanded one million dollars in US currency be delivered to the boat, that no military or police be contacted, or the crew would be murdered and the tanker would be blown up.

Our intrepid sales guru began to sweat bullets. The alcohol from the previous night oozed from his pores and he began to shake a little. Seizing a cigarette, he gulped loudly three times and then eased into his best negotiating spiel. Why not, he offered, accept $10,000 cash, right now, which he would personally bring to the ship, and let bygones be bygones? The pirate commander pondered this for a moment. He knew he would never see a million dollars in his

33

hopefully long existence. He needed a new engine for his boat and his wife was soon to deliver their third child. He would keep the lion's share and disperse the rest among his pirate crew. Not bad for three hours of work. He agreed to the $10,000 cash.

The intrepid salesman had now added hostage and pirate negotiator to his impressive resume—two new skills he would be sure to share quickly with anyone willing to listen along his many bar and restaurant stops over the coming years. He raced to the hotel lobby, grabbed the first cab he saw, and sped to the bank. With a $10,000 cash advance in hand, he and the cab driver headed to the port. Fifteen minutes later and with a hastily rented john boat and captain, he set sail toward the anchored tanker. The handover of money was pleasant enough; the pirates had even brewed tea and provided biscuits, and they were handed and then counted the money. Seeing the booty was all there, they quickly bade our intrepid salesman goodbye and sailed off, slapping each other on the back as they did so.

Answer the following:

What do we know about the salesman?

A. He is very lucky to have survived this adventure.
B. He most likely will someday be kidnapped, or worse.
C. He most likely never let his employer know what had taken place until it was all over.
D. His employer most likely did not have protocols in place for such incidents.
E. All of the above.

The correct answer is E.

part of the "it can't happen here," or, more importantly, in some areas, "it can't happen here again" syndrome? As the case study for this chapter illustrates, risk comes in varying sizes, shapes, and dimensions. Is it possible that the corporation involved in this case study might have been forewarned of the potential for piracy in the ports and areas in which they were operating, and therefore could have been forearmed?

Again, time after time, we have seen images of rescuers who are placed in harm's way rescuing people from areas that were previously under mandatory evacuation orders. First responders have cleared many areas, going door to door, using bullhorns and the media to order persons to evacuate. Many people still refuse to move, and contrary to what some believe, studies indicate it is not just poor people who refuse to leave because they don't have the means or resources to do so. In fact, a Harvard School of Public Health survey indicated the number one reason for people who chose to ignore evacuation orders during Katrina was the ill-placed confidence that their homes were constructed well enough to stand up to the power of the hurricane (Ripley, 2008, p. 39).

In considering a region, country, state, or province, ask, What has happened in the past? Volcanoes? If so, plan for (or plan AGAINST) those. Tornadoes? Yes, take these into consideration. Train derailments near your plant? Yes, take these into consideration. You cannot ignore what HAS happened and focus only on what MIGHT take place. If a nuclear reactor is built next to your employee camp, obviously one should consider purchasing protective suits, vehicles, a helipad, or perhaps moving your operations. Planning for what has occurred and focusing on means to mitigate the effects of these natural or man-made disasters will successfully prepare your operations for what might take place (Figure 4.1).

While a history of natural disasters can be as easy to determine as searching the Internet or *National Geographic*, political and man-made crisis

Figure 4.1 Even many years after Mount Saint Helens erupted in 1980, it is considered to be a highly dangerous location. (Courtesy of Federal Emergency Management Agency (FEMA), *NOAA News*, https://www.fema.gov/media-library/assets/images/37848, March 18, 1980.)

can be more difficult to assess. As previously mentioned, there are US government sources for information on dangerous groups and movements. There are private intelligence sources that can provide the same as well as analysis of the security and safety risks for regions. Man-made issues are often extremely difficult to assess correctly or even plan for. In the digital and 24-hour news age, however, protests and demonstrations are covered in detail from almost any region on Earth.

So, how does one plan for such events? Protests and demonstrations, military crackdowns, coups, and countercoups happen in many countries and in several of them, with relative frequency. But there are circumstances in which such events come out of nowhere and sweep the country or region like a wildfire. Without warning, corporations and organizations could be susceptible to sudden occurrences of violence and mayhem. Facilities and employee camps can be surrounded or damaged. Shipments and transport can be damaged or stolen, and many sources of problems can arise. Organizations can prepare for these eventualities.

Crisis and security personnel should visit the operations areas of project work and determine the topography and logistical concerns, such as whether there are adequate roads, airports, rail terminals, or seaports. Crisis managers might rely on a security consultant to visit the far-flung projects for such determinations. By knowing which means of emergency egress are possible, reaction to crisis situations is more tangible and precise. Another means of determining the risks associated with a particular region would be the lack of such means of emergency egress. For example, an area without airports or suitable landing strips would present a risk if the need arose to get personnel out in a hurry if roads were dangerous for one reason or another, or for emergency medical evacuations. If a single roadway ties the jobsite to emergency services, and this road is frequently washed out or buried by mudslides, the risk to vehicular emergency egress is considerable. In such situations evacuations before roads are washed out or an attempt to seek alternative egress routes is advisable.

There might be a risk to personnel from a lack of sanitation in a remote area. Or a region might be home to polar bears or grizzly bears or rabies-carrying bats or disease-carrying insects or rodents. Sandstorms or windstorms, hurricanes, typhoons, or terrible air pollution might be present. Local political crises may have caused opposition or government forces to take violent actions or the area has a reputation for being especially ridden with violent crime or terrorist activities.

Risk assessments should not be taken by the same person or persons or teams all the time. To do so invites a bias to develop over time toward their particular observations, insights, and recommendations. To avoid such biases, use a different person or team to re-review what has already been assessed. See if the results and recommendations are the same or way off the mark. By doing so, the crisis management process will continue to improve and foster innovation toward a goal of life safety. In the same way, crises that have occurred in the past should be evaluated and addressed—both from the "what can be learned to avoid the issue in the future?" and "what could have been done differently in response to the crisis?" perspectives. Various operations within organizations or groups contracted as consultants or vendors to act in oversight capacities can often detect outlying events or actions or results that might be precursors to an impending crisis. Differing departments digging into details of which hidden stumbling blocks might be buried just below the surface in operational areas can sometimes discover nuggets useful for preparedness to ward off impending crisis.

Various departments or divisions within corporations should be enlisted to assess risk with regard to the potential for crisis in domestic and international operations. Legal departments need to weigh the potential for liabilities in their areas of expertise, including those of a financial and perhaps environmental nature. Insurance and risk management divisions would have access to various types of monetary and nonmonetary risk topics. Human resources might be concerned with labor laws, labor unrest, working conditions, and other aspects of employment or contracting. Travel departments would have access to information regarding airline maintenance and safety, carriers considered safer than others, visa and entry requirements, and other pertinent travel information. Financial divisions would be tasked with determining the types of risks to the bottom line and so on. Operational and process experts would be required to describe the types of resources, cycles, supplies, manufacturing, transportation, and various aspects of what will be required to achieve the goals of the organization. All should have a part in the crisis management assessment and team efforts. And, all such divisions and team members should have their own specific crisis plans in place and at the ready to activate in anticipation of the call from the crisis team.

See Appendix, "Information Collection Prior to Deployment" and "Security and Evacuation Planning" sections for suggestions regarding items to be covered with employees before deploying to risky assignments.

REFERENCES

Ripley, Amanda. *The Unthinkable: Who Survives When Disaster Strikes—and Why.* Danvers, MA: Crown Publishing Group, 2008.

Thompson, Hunter S. *Hell's Angels: The Strange and Terrible Saga of the Outlaw Motorcycle Gangs.* New York: Ballantine Books, 1966.

US Department of State. "Security Overseas Seminar." n.d. http://www.state.gov/m/fsi/tc/securitytraining/sosmq911/.

5

Preplanning and Positioning

The most fortunate of us all in our journey through life frequently meet with calamities and misfortunes which greatly afflict us. To fortify our minds against the attacks of these calamities and misfortunes should be one of the principal studies and endeavors of our lives.

Thomas Jefferson

Preplanning is perhaps the easiest thing to do concerning disaster and crisis mitigation, and yet is frequently overlooked and more often than not forgotten completely. Nothing says you care quite so much as money. Money makes the world go round, they say. Money is what most organizations are in business to make. Crisis response often requires a great deal of human capital, which requires financial capital to engage.

Preplanning is more than just having well-exercised and thoughtful plans in place. It consists of more than properly exercised and drilled response and action plans. Preplanning in this context includes having enough materiel and resources in place.

As indicated, one of the first steps in planning for crisis and developing response and mitigation efforts is the creation of a Corporate Crisis Management Team (CCMT). Formalizing this group will give management's seal of approval and show others in the organization how the company is taking the issues seriously. Highlight the efforts of this group in intracompany communications, newsletters, and postings. The group will require adequate funding to be effective, not just to pay for the hours of the participants involved, but also for training opportunities, presenters, consultants, and other costs. There might be a need for certain members of the team to travel to various locations where the plans might be implemented or to task others on the ground in these areas to report back on questions submitted.

Once established, the CCMT should consist of preselected corporate personnel and the Incident Response Team (IRT). Together, they will safeguard employees and property. This CCMT will utilize corporate crisis management plans, Local Management (LM) team guidelines, and IRT guidelines. It should conduct training sessions, at least biannually, to maintain a high level of proficiency and awareness, and utilize awareness training regarding personal safety overseas for key executives.

In one sense preplanning might include efforts to stave off emergencies or crises. For example, if the team determines a building is considered too risky for personnel to occupy based on its poor design or lack of fire detection or suppression equipment, it might make recommendations to project or senior management to move employees to another building. If transportation of hazardous chemicals via one shipping method is considered too unsafe or potentially risky, alternatives might be recommended in the same manner. Safety professionals must be part of crisis management teams, and their leadership in the areas of product and process safety will be vital to success. Many have heard the terms crisis recovery or disaster recovery. Put simply, crisis recovery consists of the steps taken in the aftermath of a crisis or disaster to begin to put the organization or corporation back on its feet, to reestablish operations to return to production or functionality. Crisis management teams might recommend a backup computer system for a corporation so that in the event of a disaster that takes out the computer room and all servers in headquarters, the crisis recovery plan implements a backed up computer system.

One item of planning that is often overlooked or not considered is finances. In times of crisis and emergency, often large sums of money are required for things such as generators; overseas flights; emergency supplies; and vehicle, air, and other transportation. Consultants or security personnel may be required to provide coverage or protection.

Money will be needed to make things happen. If your organization has put together its Emergency Operations Center (EOC) and it contains the right professionals, someone from finance will be part of the team. And, in crisis management, especially in response, it is often necessary to have funds available as soon as possible. It behooves any organization to have available enough funds, including cash for the occasional special request, especially when dealing with vendors overseas during an emergency. For example, if one were to ask for security personnel on the ground, uniformed or otherwise, to secure personnel or facilities one should be ready to sign up for weeks of coverage, 24/7, plus possibly room and board, should security personnel not be readily available in the country or region. Plane tickets and lodging, especially those purchased on short notice, will quickly run into thousands of dollars. Lodging may be at a premium or in short supply, so be prepared to have security personnel lodge with or nearby your project personnel. For security purposes, it is best if protective personnel are only minimally co-located.

Security personnel will need vehicles large enough to carry them and their equipment, as well as enough room to evacuate project personnel by vehicle should the need arise. Vehicles will be required to scout out driving routes to embarkation areas such as rail stations, ports, and airports. Vehicles rented during crisis situations will run into thousands of dollars, and some will have to be purchased to avoid exorbitant rental fees. Travel will need to be considered, whether by rail, air, or boat. So, if, for example, airline tickets can be prepurchased with no particular destination (open-ended tickets) then such reservations and tickets will need to be considered and purchased. In some situations, if commercial airlines are fully booked or blocked from flying, or airports are closed, charter aircraft may be necessary. Where is the closest airport and how will you get there? Keep in mind, helicopters have limited range and require adequate landing parameters. If you are too far from a safe airport—with safe ground transportation to get there but too far from helicopter resources, what then?

Food and water, if not already stockpiled, will need to be accumulated. Medical supplies should be collected, including an often overlooked aspect of medical care concerning required medications for personnel. Fuel for vehicles should be safely stored well away from housing. Extra batteries for phones, flashlights, and even laptop computers should be acquired.

To get back to money and preplanning: it might become necessary for someone from the expat party on the ground or back at headquarters to purchase something extraordinary at a moment's notice. It might be a generator or an all-terrain vehicle. Charter aircraft, especially during times of crisis, will run into the tens if not hundreds of thousands of dollars, depending on the number of aircraft required. The larger the aircraft, the higher are the costs.

Someone will need a credit card with a large available balance. One might consider a credit limit on more than one card of $100,000.

PREPLANNING BACK AT HEADQUARTERS

There are some critical items and provisions that are required for the successful functioning of a crisis management team. A secured room, not one that doubles as a conference room, and one that may not be reserved for non-crisis-related functions, is required. By secure is meant that the room should not be used for conference calls, or chatting up friends or colleagues on the phone, or for meetings to discuss housekeeping, or to sell products or solicit money for charities. The room should be off the grid and off limits to reservations for all meetings, and should have a card reader or closely held keypad entry. Why? This room needs to be ready at all times for emergency purposes. Employees shouldn't be stealing pens and using the computers to brush up their resumes or to rest. The room should be well illuminated (adjustable) and HVAC controlled (adjustable), with white boards, flip charts, and associated supplies. Enough laptop and desktop computers should be available for team members and support functions. Multiple data ports should be installed so that the different members of the crisis team would be able to access intranet and Internet. A secured wireless connection should be installed as well. Comfortable chairs, much like comfortable shoes, are very important.

Satellite TV in the crisis room will assist in keeping abreast of international news and events. Satellite phones will be useful for communications to employees around the world whose landlines or cellular phones may have been taken down by governments or damaged by overloaded systems. Multiple means of media connectivity—TV, Internet, even shortwave radio—are important to determine what is happening and when. A large-screen monitor with Internet, TV, and other connectivity should be one of the first purchases for the crisis room.

First, storage of the organization's crisis management plans should be reduced to flash drives that every member of the crisis team carries with him or her. Crisis plans should be loaded on secure mobile devices. Up-to-date crisis plans are better than those that list Bob from HR who left the company 18 months ago. Enough laptops with server connectivity in a wireless environment need to be in place. These laptops need to be loaded with all the applications the corporation and projects utilize in the field, including those for creating drawings and reading computer-aided design (CAD) and other much utilized databases.

Everything that requires power should be on emergency generator backup. Enough batteries need to be available for flashlights, cell phones, radios, and so on. If conditions allow, and the teams operating in the crisis team Incident Command Center are able to come and go from the building, headquarters, or wherever the command center is located, then enough refreshments and food need to be available to sustain the effort. If employees may not make it home or to hotels due to weather, road, or other conditions, cots need to be available and sleeping arrangements made on site.

For intelligence and information on locations and situations around the world there are organizations that for a fee provide intelligence and analysis from around the world. This information can be critical to planning for worsening situations or for planning well before events are set into motion. Many such groups provide suggestions for planning, for example, when to curtail more personnel traveling to a particular country or region, when to evacuate nonessential personnel, or evacuate in general. These companies do not just rely on news broadcasts or headlines. They have personnel on the ground in many areas or have contacts and people they can reach out to for timely and precise data. Companies such as these are able to pass along information such as personnel from other clients in the country/region who are evacuating or staying put, hunkering down, or using one particular means for evacuation over another. Such companies are even able to make arrangements for evacuations because they have many of these contacts in the region.

However, relying on only just one means, organization, or company for intelligence or evacuation is not recommended, as some information may not be that timely or might be based on some faulty information on the ground. It is highly recommended that US corporations take advantage of the great experience and sound judgment of personnel who operate as regional security officers (RSOs) and assistant regional security officers (ARSOs) in embassies and consulates around the world. Do not wait until crises are raging in country to contact these employees, but instead cultivate relationships as soon as you or your US personnel move into the area. By creating a cooperative relationship with your RSOs/ARSOs you will ensure that you are receiving important safety and security information in a very timely manner. This information works effectively when it is two way—that is, when corporations and employees are willing to pass along safety and security information to RSOs and ARSOs in a confidential and nonattributable manner. By making use of the knowledge and contacts of RSOs/ARSOs, which include foreign government military and police personnel, supplemented with private intelligence companies, safety and security personnel may add more tools to their repertoire.

One good advance recommendation or practice is to have RSOs/ARSOs visit your operations, your plants or warehouses, your personnel camps and housing areas. By showing them where you are located and how your operations are situated, they will get a sense of the special circumstances that might be presented to you in the way of crisis response and management. As RSOs/ARSOs are very busy people, don't be surprised if your invitation does not result in an immediate site visit. But don't be discouraged; keep trying.

In addition, by creating information-sharing relationships with corporations in country and around the region (even with competing corporations), one can sometimes—with an emphasis on sometimes—develop relationships with local law enforcement and government officials. This does not mean greasing the palms of these locals, but it does mean having met with them face to face if you are a crisis employee from headquarters, and breaking bread with them if you are an in-country manager.

Organizations will go a long way in planning for what is hoped to be a never used program or procedure if they lay the groundwork for crisis planning within their organizations, with top-down support, preparedness, and awareness and training rolled out to employees around the organization. Companies will need to broaden their nets of data collection and open up employee hotlines to receive threats or information concerning the organization and its operations. Data collection should include local/regional/national crime reports and statistics and internal incident reports. If a crisis has occurred in the past, organizations should relegate these circumstances to the training, after incident, and forwarding planning of the company. Use the historic events to plan for what might be around the corner. What worked? What did not? What could have been done better? Did the company properly concern itself with employee welfare, before, during, and after the emergency? Was counseling or financial assistance made available?

PREPLANNING IN THE FIELD

Preplanning in the field consists of many procedures and preparations. For operations within remote regions, supplies should be stocked to suffice in case of inability to obtain water and food. It might become advantageous to remain indoors, within the plant or compound. For these reasons, enough water should be on hand to last up to 30 days per person along with an equivalent amount of food. Planning should include the creation of the all-familiar *go bags*—although *going* isn't always the safest reaction to a crisis situation. Preplanning will include conversations with headquarters concerning the situation on the ground where you are operating—what the people on the ground are seeing, hearing, and experiencing. Are the news reports that are being broadcast around the world correct? Is a political party, faction, or a particular protest movement becoming more threatening and violent? Personnel in the field may have access to an expat community from different industries or to those who, with their various contacts, might provide critical intelligence and planning information.

In addition to all of these efforts, organizations will need to formalize the crisis management program into standard operating procedures and assign audit and assurance programs surrounding these efforts.

See the Appendix section "Casualty or Injury Notification Example Plan" for suggestions regarding the notification of an expat's loved ones/ friends in the event of a fatality.

6

Security and Crisis Management Plan

...in moments of crisis our thoughts do not run consecutively but rather sweep over us in waves of intuition and experience...

John le Carré (1989)
The Russia House

Terrorist groups and evildoers typically don't just happen upon targets. There is much planning and preparation involved in looking for the ideal target, or the least protected and vulnerable opportunity. Whatever the goal might be—political, ideological, fundamentalist, or financial—anyone might become a target. Explosives are often used for their obvious destructive effects and the manner in which they can be planted, such as within a vehicle or along a roadside. Sometimes, proper planning and precautions can dissuade the terrorist(s) from choosing your facility or organization for attack, or make your people and assets less vulnerable.

By having a successful, well-maintained, and exercised plan in place, your facility or project will have steady footing should an actual terrorist act or other serious man-made or natural disaster take place. Your management and all employees will be required to be involved in this effort, which includes security awareness training so that in the event of serious incidents they will know what they are dealing with, and the proper response for mitigating the effects. It is the responsibility of the corporation, Local Management (LM), and employees to provide the proper planning and preparation and to work with corporate security in this effort.

A properly crafted plan and intense preparation may reduce the risk of success of the groups who might be perpetrating the acts.

Some examples of the factors included in threat levels and terminology used by the US Department of Defense and the US military are the existence of terrorists; their capability, intentions, history, and targeting; and the security environment. The levels are

- *Critical*, which means that a terrorist group has entered the country or is able to do so. It has the capability to attack and is engaged in target selection. Its history and intentions may or may not be known.
- *High* indicates that a terrorist group exists that has the capability, history, and intention to attack.
- *Medium* describes the same conditions as high except that terrorist intentions are unknown.
- *Low* is a situation in which terrorist groups exist and have a capability to attack. Their history may or may not be known.
- *Negligible* describes a situation in which the existence or capability of terrorist groups may or may not be present.

Preparation of the ground employees and project and office managers is key to protection of persons and property in times of crisis.

Your crisis response group should see to it that LM and key employees are identified and in place. Although team composition may vary somewhat, as a minimum it should include senior local project management and senior local operational managers. It should include local finance and administration management, as well as personnel from human resources and payroll, legal, and critical management functions. Of course, security and crisis management participation is key to success, and don't overlook consultants with both regional and international experience.

Local managers and management should control and resolve all emergent situations, supported by the crisis response group in the United States, which in turn reports all actions, recommendations, and outcomes to your corporate headquarters. The crisis response group, with the approval of your corporate headquarters, may elect to send members of the emergency response team to assist the local managers in resolving an incident.

The LM consists of the predesignated senior management representatives closest to the incident. They are responsible for the initial crisis response, carrying out corporate policy, and keeping the corporate disaster recovery team advised. The local managers must keep abreast of the

APPROPRIATE US, UK, OR COUNTRY EMBASSY OR CONSULATE CHANGE IN THREAT LEVEL

Levels of Threats and Risk Conditions

1. *State of Readiness 4* applies when there is a general threat of possible terrorist activity against personnel and facilities, the nature and extent of which are unpredictable, and circumstances do not justify full implementation of High-Level measures. However, it may be necessary to implement certain measures from higher threat and risk conditions resulting from intelligence received or as a deterrent. The measures in this state of readiness must be capable of being maintained indefinitely.

2. *State of Readiness 3* applies when an increased and more predictable threat of terrorist activity exists. The measures in this state of readiness must be capable of being maintained for weeks without causing undue hardship, affecting operational capability, and aggravating relations with local authorities.

3. *State of Readiness 2* applies when an incident occurs or intelligence is received indicating that some form of terrorist action against personnel and facilities is immediate. Implementation of measures in this state of readiness for more than a short period probably will create hardship and affect the peacetime activities of the unit and its personnel.

4. *State of Readiness 1* applies in the immediate area where a terrorist attack has occurred or when intelligence has been received that terrorist action against a specific location or person is likely. Normally, this FPCON (Force Protection Condition, formerly THREATCON) is declared as a localized condition.

in-country developments in the area of international affairs and those affecting the region and US relations with the country and surrounding concerns. Changes in the local sentiment toward Americans or expats should be scrutinized, as well as any changes in the internal political situation involving the current government, challenges to the government, and other potential concerns.

Situations that may foment domestic unrest and possible protest or rioting must be followed, such as shortages or rationing of fuel, food, or other commodities; student activism and movements; and governments imposing martial law or curfews. Of course any armed warfare or external military or political threats or armed conflicts between tribes and minorities must be followed.

Terrorism is a major international concern, and threats or actions by terrorists or guerrillas warrant review of your plan. Restrictions on the press, press freedoms, communications, newspapers, and the Internet and other tamping down of liberties require attention. Military movements, exercises, and flexing of military might are sometimes pretexts to trouble, as are currency devaluations, hoarding of money, or runs on banks. Finally, departures by dependents, expats, and certainly embassy personnel are key indicators of trouble.

Evaluation of the security situation will be an ongoing function of the local managers. They should listen to area radio programs and read local newspapers to follow the security situation both in the country and in surrounding areas.

Then, contact with all appropriate embassies is needed. They will need to establish and maintain contact with the appropriate US, UK, or country regional security officer. Frequently, they host conferences with multinational companies to discuss the local security situation and the problems faced by expats. The LM leader should attend these conferences if they exist. Particular attention should be paid to the contacts the company has with the police and/or military. These contacts may be helpful in the evaluation and collection of information concerning changes in the situation.

FINANCIAL PREPARATIONS

The LM team should ensure that an adequate amount of money is available to cover costs associated with an emergency incident. The manager of payroll or human resources should be prepared to pay cash. He or she should, at a minimum, determine if blank airline tickets can be obtained from a travel agent for use in emergencies, prepare an estimate of the amount of money that he or she will need to pay for evacuation, and forward this information to company headquarters. The money should be available to the country as soon as an emergency seems likely. Credit cards for the major carriers in the country should be issued to LM members.

Consider the range of services that you could provide or arrange for, including cash advances, salary continuation, flexible work hours, reduced work hours, crisis counseling, care packages, and day care.

DEALING WITH TERRORIST SURVEILLANCE

Every effort should be made to appear too difficult a target to an adversary. The single most useful defensive measure personnel can take is to vary travel routes and times. Also, teach and remind staff to be vigilant and alert to possible surveillance. Terrorist surveillance is often so intensive that an alert person will notice something that is out of the ordinary, something that does not seem quite right. To begin to take notice of anything unusual it is crucial you first know what is normal—look around, introduce yourself to the neighbors, notice the regular shopkeepers. Avoid predictable behavior. Vary routes to work, appointments, or other engagements. Terrorists/criminals often survey their targets before attack. Being unpredictable is a very effective deterrent.

You must raise your level of awareness to a point where strange vehicles parked near your residence or place of employment are noticed and promptly reported to the authorities. This must be done immediately. It may be the first time you have seen the vehicle but it may not be the first time it has been there. You don't know what level of planning the terrorists may be in. Maybe it's only the beginning, but perhaps their planning is in the final stages. They may give you little time to act.

People standing, walking, or sitting in cars near the residence or place of employment must be noticed, especially people loitering. Be aware of someone who always seems to be around you and realize when you're being followed. If you suspect that you are under surveillance, report to the police; the appropriate US, UK, or country embassy or consulate; and/or to your LM team.

Practice and teach staff to keep track of any unusual sightings. From notes, a log can be made describing what has been seen. When recording observations of suspicious vehicles, try to obtain the make, model, year, color, license plate number, general condition of the vehicle, and the number of people in it.

If possible, get a description of the people involved; see if they are male/female, if they have any distinguishing marks/facial hair/scars, their size, or any other distinguishing features. Also look for identifying habits or movements. Does the surveillant have a limp? Nervous habit of straightening his tie, pushing glasses up his or her nose, and so on? Some distinguishing features, such as hairstyle and color, are often unreliable, because they can be changed by wigs, dyes, and so on. Make note of them anyway. Too much information is better than too little.

Don't do anything to let the surveillants know they have been detected. Do not confront suspected terrorists/criminals and ask them why they're watching, as it may initiate an impromptu attack or kidnapping.

If you suspect you are being followed by someone in a vehicle, drive normally and carefully and proceed to a safe location such as an embassy, police station, or a highly visible and/or populated area and immediately alert police, embassy staff, and/or the security network. And again, do not be predictable. Be alert for surveillance, avoid areas where you could be trapped, drive only on well-traveled streets, be on the lookout for blockades or contrived accidents, and keep staff itineraries and personal details confidential.

PHYSICAL SECURITY CONSIDERATIONS

Physical security considerations include exterior protection and perimeter security. Consider using natural barriers, fencing, landscaping, or other physical or psychological boundaries to demonstrate a security presence to all site visitors.

If the threat is considered to be high at freestanding facilities, there should be a smooth-faced perimeter wall or combination wall/fence, a minimum of 9 feet high and extending 3 feet below grade. The wall or fence may be constructed of stone, masonry, concrete, chain link, or steel grillwork. However, if area limitations and local conditions dictate the need, any newly constructed wall should be designed to prevent vehicle penetration, and should use a reinforced concrete foundation wall, 18 inches thick with an additional 1 1/2-inch concrete covering on the side of the steel reinforcement and extending 36 inches above grade. In addition, intrusion alert systems can be used to enhance perimeter security.

Consider alternative methods if the aforementioned are not feasible. Alternate methods can offer comparable protection. These alternatives should maximize the use of locally available materials and conditions to take advantage of existing terrain features. They can include the creative use of earthen berms and landscaping techniques such as concrete planters.

BUILDING SETBACK

Inside the perimeter barrier, the building should be set back on the property to provide maximum distance from that portion of the perimeter barrier that is accessible by vehicle. The desirable distance of this setback is at least 100 feet depending on the bomb resistance provided by the barrier.

Alternative methods for protecting buildings from vehicle attack (e.g., car bombs, vehicles laden with explosives) may include installing bollards (devices constructed to protect against a ramming vehicle attack). They are deployed in lines around a perimeter for anti-ram protection or to provide supplemental control of vehicle traffic through permanent checkpoints when other means are not practical or effective. Large cement planters can also be used to strengthen the perimeter boundary. Bollards or planters can effectively increase the setback of buildings. Such devices should be placed in a manner as to allow the maximum distance between the building and a roadway and/or the equal access area. They should be positioned to impede access to lobbies and other blast areas that can be penetrated by a vehicle, with low or no curb, and no glass wall or door structure between the lobby and driveway. Driveways should be designed and constructed to minimize or preclude high-speed vehicular approaches to lobbies and glassed areas (Figure 6.1).

Figure 6.1 Before the attack on the Murrah Federal Building on April 19, 1995, federal buildings around the United States had not planned extensively for vehicle-borne and other improvised explosive devices/IEDs. (Courtesy of FBI, https://www.fbi.gov/about-us/history/famous-cases/oklahoma-city-bombing.)

Figure 6.2 Blast walls, when added to a building setback, are often able to diffuse the damaging effects of shock waves from explosions.

A positive and concerted effort should be made to contact local host country law enforcement governmental authorities and request that they prohibit, restrict, or impede motor vehicles from parking, stopping, or loading in front of the facility.

In high-threat locations, if local conditions of government officials prohibit antivehicular perimeter security measures and your business/corporate building is either the sole occupant of the building or located on the first or second floor, you should consider relocating to more secure facilities (Figure 6.2).

BUILDING EXTERIOR

Façade

The building exterior should be a sheer/smooth shell, devoid of footholds, decorative latticework, ledges, or balconies. The building's façade should be protected to a height of 16 feet to prevent access by intruders using basic hand tools. The use of glass on the building façade should be kept to an absolute minimum, limited to standard size or smaller windows and, possibly, main entrance doors. All glass should be protected by plastic film. Consider the use of Lexan or other polycarbonate as alternatives to glass where practical.

External Doors

Local fire codes may impact on the guidance presented here. As decisions are made on these issues, local fire codes will have to be considered.

The main entrance doors may be either transparent or opaque and constructed of wood, metal, or glass. The main entrance door should be equipped with a double-cylinder deadbolt and additionally secured with a crossbar or sliding deadbolt attached vertically to the top and bottom of each leaf. All doors, including interior doors, should be installed to take advantage of the doorframe strength by having the doors open toward the potential attack side.

All other external doors should be opaque hollow metal fire doors with no external hardware. These external doors should be single doors unless used for delivery and loading purposes.

Should double doors be required, they should be equipped with two sliding deadbolts on the active leaf and two sliding deadbolts on the inactive leaf vertically installed on the top and bottom of the doors. A local alarmed panic bar and a 180-degree peephole viewing device should be installed on the active leaf.

All external doors leading to crawl spaces or basements must be securely locked and regularly inspected for signs of tampering.

Windows

The interior side of all glass surfaces should be covered with a protective plastic film that meets or exceeds the manufacturer's specifications for shatter-resistant protective film. A good standard is a 4-millimeter thickness for all protective film applications. This film will keep glass shards to a minimum in the event of an explosion or if objects are thrown through the window.

Grillwork should be installed on all exterior windows and air conditioning units that are within 16 feet of grade or are accessible from roofs, balconies, and so on. The rule of thumb here is to cover all openings in excess of 100 square inches if the smallest dimension is 6 inches or larger.

Grillwork should be constructed of 1/2-inch-diameter or greater steel rebar, anchored or embedded, not bolted, into the window frame or surrounding masonry to a depth of 3 inches. Grillwork should be installed horizontally and vertically on the center at no more than 8-inch intervals. However, grillwork installed in exterior window frames within the secure area should be spaced 5 inches on the center, horizontally and vertically, and set up in the manner described previously. Decorative grillwork patterns can be used for aesthetic purposes.

Grillwork that is covering windows designated as necessary for emergency escape should be hinged for easy egress. All hinged grillwork should be secured with a key-operated security padlock. The key should be maintained on a cup hook in close proximity of the hinged grille but out of reach of an intruder. These emergency escape windows should not be used in planning for fire evacuations.

Roof

The roof should be constructed of fire-resistant material. All hatches and doors leading to the roof should be securely locked with deadbolt locks. Security measures such as barbed, concertina, or tape security wire; broken glass; and walls or fences may be used to prevent access from nearby trees and/or adjoining roofs.

Vehicular Entrance and Controls

Vehicular Entrance

Vehicular entry–exit points should be kept to a minimum. Ideally, to maximize traffic flow and security, only two regularly used vehicular entry–exit points are necessary. Both should be similarly constructed and monitored. The use of one would be limited to employees' cars, while the other would be used by visitors and delivery vehicles. Depending on the size and nature of the facility, a gate for emergency vehicular and pedestrian egress should be installed at a location that is easily and safely accessible by employees. Emergency gates should be securely locked and periodically checked. All entry–exit points should be secured with a heavy-duty sliding steel, iron, or heavily braced chain link gate equipped with a heavy locking device.

The primary gate should be electrically operated (with a manual backup by a security officer situated in an adjacent booth). The gate at the vehicle entrance should be positioned to avoid a long straight approach to force approaching vehicles to slow down before reaching the gate. The general technique employed is to require a sharp turn immediately in front of the gate.

In addition to the gate, and whenever justifiable, a vehicle arrest system can be installed. An appropriate vehicle arrest system, whether active, a piece of equipment designed to stop vehicles in their tracks, or passive, a dense mass, will be able to stop or instantly disable a vehicle with a minimum gross weight of 15,000 pounds traveling 50 miles per hour.

Vehicular Control

All facilities should have some method of vehicle access control. Primary road entrances to all major plant, laboratory, and office locations should have a vehicle control facility capable of remote operation by security personnel with automated systems.

A variety of vehicle controls are available, for example

- Electrically operated gates to be activated by security personnel at either the booth or security control center or by a badge reader located in a convenient location for a driver.
- At smaller facilities, badge-activated gates, manual swing gates, and so forth.
- Closed-circuit TV (CCTV) with the capability of displaying full facial features of a driver and vehicle characteristics on the monitor at the security control center. Site security should be able to close all secondary road entrances, thereby limiting access to the primary entrance. Lighting and a turn area should be provided as appropriate. A conveniently located intercom system will enable a driver to communicate with the gatehouse and security control center; bollards or other elements may be used to protect the security booth and gates against car crash.

Control Features

Primary perimeter entrances to a facility should have a booth for security personnel during peak traffic periods and automated systems for remote operations during other periods.

Make use of sensors to activate the gate and detect vehicles approaching and departing the gate, activate a CCTV monitor displaying the gate, and sound an audio alert in the security control center. Improve or add lighting to illuminate the gate area and approaches to a higher level than surrounding areas. Install signs to instruct visitors and to post on the property as required. Construct road surfaces to enable queuing, turnaround, and parking. Also add vehicle bypass control (i.e., gate extensions), low and dense shrubbery, fences, and walls.

Security Booth Construction and Operation

As noted previously, at the perimeter vehicular entry–exit a security officer booth should be constructed to control access. (At facilities not having perimeter walls, the security officer booth should be installed immediately inside the facility foyer.)

If justified by the threat level, the security officer booth should be completely protected with reinforced concrete, walls, ballistic doors, and windows. The booth should be equipped with a security officer duress alarm and intercom system, both annunciating at the facility receptionist and security officer's office. This security officer would also be responsible for complete operation of the vehicle gate. If necessary, package inspection and visitor screening may be conducted just outside of the booth by an unarmed security officer equipped with walk-through and hand-held metal detectors. Provisions for environmental comfort should be considered when designing the booth.

Parking

General

Security should be considered in the location and arrangement of parking lots. Pedestrians leaving parking lots should be channeled toward a limited number of building entrances.

All parking facilities should have an emergency communication system (intercom, telephones, etc.) installed at strategic locations to provide emergency communications directly to security.

Parking lots should be provided with CCTV cameras capable of displaying and videotaping lot activity on a monitor in the security control center. Lighting must be of adequate level and direction to support cameras while at the same time being energy efficient and tailored to local environmental concerns.

If possible, parking on streets directly adjacent to the building should be forbidden. Wherever justifiable given the threat profile of your company, there should be no underground parking areas in the building basement or ground-level parking under building overhangs.

Parking within Perimeter Walls/Fences

All parking within perimeter walls or fences should be restricted to employees, with areas limited to an area as far from the building as possible. Parking for patrons and visitors, except for predesignated VIP visitors, should be restricted to areas outside of the perimeter wall/fences.

Garages

For buildings having an integral parking garage or structure, a complete system for vehicle control should be provided. CCTV surveillance should be provided for employee safety and building security. If the threat of a car bomb is extant, consideration must be given to prohibition of parking on the building premises.

Access from the garage or parking structure into the building should be limited, secure, well lighted, and have no places of concealment. Elevators, stairs, and connecting bridges serving the garage or parking structure should discharge into a staffed or fully monitored area. Convex mirrors should be mounted outside the garage elevators to reflect the area adjacent to the door openings.

Exterior Lighting

Exterior lighting should illuminate all facility entrances and exits in addition to parking areas, perimeter walls, gates, courtyards, garden areas, and shrubbery rows.

Lighting of building exteriors and walkways should be provided where required for employee safety and security. There should be a capability to illuminate building façades 100% to a height of at least 6 feet.

Although sodium vapor lights are considered optimum for security purposes, the use of incandescent and florescent light fixtures is adequate. Exterior fixtures should be protected with grillwork when theft or vandalism has been identified as a problem.

For leased buildings, landlord approval of exterior lighting design requirements should be included in lease agreements.

Building Access Considerations

Building Entrances

The number of building entrances should be minimized, relative to the site, building layout, and functional requirements. A single off-hours entrance near the security control center is desirable. At large sites, additional secured entrances should be considered, with provisions for monitoring and control.

Door Security Requirements

All employee entrance doors should permit installation of controlled access system hardware. The doors, jambs, hinges, and locks must be designed to resist forced entry (e.g., spreading of door frames, accessing panic hardware, shimming bolts and/or latches, fixed hinge pins). Don't forget handicap requirements when applicable.

The minimum requirement for lock cylinders is a six-pin tumbler type. Locks with removable core cylinders to permit periodic changing of the locking mechanism should be used.

All exterior doors should have alarm sensors to detect unauthorized openings.

Doors designed specifically for emergency exits need to have an alarm that is audible at the door with an additional annunciation at the security control center. These doors should have no exterior hardware on them.

Window Precautions
For protection, large showroom type plate glass and small operable windows on the ground floor should be avoided. If, however, these types of windows are used and the building is located in a high-risk area, special consideration should be given to the use of locking and alarm devices, laminated glass, wire glass, film, or polycarbonate glazing. For personnel protection, all windows should have shatter-resistant film.

Lobby
The main entrances to buildings should have an area for a receptionist during the day and a security officer at night. The security control center should be located adjacent to the main entrance lobby and should be surrounded by professionally designed protective materials.

The lobby–reception area should be a single, self-sufficient building entrance. Telephones and restrooms to meet the needs of the public should be provided in this area without requiring entry into the interior area. Restrooms should be kept locked in high-threat environments and access controlled by the receptionist.

Consistent with the existing risk level, the receptionist should not be allowed to accept small parcels or courier deliveries routinely unless they are expected by the addressee.

Other Building Access Points
Other less obvious points of building entry, such as grilles, grating, manhole covers, areaways, utility tunnels, mechanical wall, and roof penetrations should be protected to impede and/or prevent entry into the building.

Permanent exterior stairs or ladders from the ground floor to the roof should not be used, nor should the building façade allow a person to climb up unaided. Exterior fire escapes should be retractable and secured in the up position.

Construction Activities

Landscaping and other outside architectural and/or aesthetic features should minimize creating any area that could conceal a person in close proximity to walkways, connecting links, buildings, and recreational areas. Landscaping design should include CCTV surveillance of building approaches and parking areas. Landscape plantings around building perimeters need to be located a minimum of 4 feet from the building wall to prevent concealment of people or objects.

INTERIOR PROTECTION

Building Layout

The building area can be divided into three categories: public areas, interior areas, and security or restricted areas requiring special security measures. These areas should be separated from one another within the building with a limited number of controlled passage points between the areas. *Controlled* in this context means allowing or denying passage by any means deemed necessary (i.e., locks, security officers, etc.).

Corridors, stairwells, and other accessible areas should be arranged to avoid places for concealment.

Generally, restricted areas should be located above the ground-floor level, away from exterior walls and hazardous operations. Access to restricted areas should be allowed only from the interior area and not from exterior or public areas. Exit routes for normal or emergency egress should not transit restricted or security areas.

Walls and Partitions

The public area should be separated from the interior area and the restricted area by slab-to-slab partitions. When the internal area above a hung ceiling is used as a common air return, provide appropriate modifications to walls or install alarm sensors. In shared occupancy buildings, internal areas should be separated by slab-to-slab construction or as described previously.

Doors

Normally, interior doors do not require special features or provisions for locking. In shared occupancy buildings, every door leading to the interior area should be considered an exterior door and designed with an appropriate degree of security. Stairway doors located in multitenant buildings must be secured from the stairwell side (local fire regulations permitting) and always operable from the office side. In the event that the fire code prevents these doors from being secured, the floor plan should be altered to provide security to your area.

Emergency exit doors that are designed specifically for that purpose should be equipped with a local audible alarm at the door and a signal at the monitoring location.

Doors to restricted access areas should be designed to resist intrusion and accommodate controlled-access hardware and alarms.

Doors on building equipment and utility rooms, electric closets, and telephone rooms should be provided with locks having a removable core, as are provided on exterior doors. As a minimum requirement, provide six-pin tumbler locks.

For safety reasons, door hardware on secured interior doors should permit exit by means of a single knob or panic bar.

Other Public Areas

The design of public areas should prevent concealment of unauthorized personnel and/or objects. Ceilings in lobbies, restrooms, and similar public areas should be made inaccessible with securely fastened or locked access panels installed where necessary to service equipment.

Public restrooms and elevator lobbies in shared occupancy buildings should have ceilings that satisfy your security requirements.

Special Storage Requirements

Building vaults or metal safes may be required to protect cash or negotiable documents, precious metals, classified materials, and so forth. Vault construction should consist of reinforced concrete or masonry and be resistant to fire damage. Steel vault doors are available with various fire-related and security penetration classifications.

Elevators

All elevators should have emergency communications systems and emergency lighting. In shared occupancy buildings, elevators traveling to your interior area should be equipped with badge readers or other controls to prohibit direct entry of unauthorized persons into your interior area. If this is not feasible, the presence of a guard or receptionist or other means of access control may be necessary at each entry point.

Cable Runs

All cable termination points, terminal blocks, and/or junction boxes should be within your area. Where practical, enclose cable runs in steel conduits. Cables passing through area that you do not control should be continuous and installed in conduits. You might even want to install an alarm in the conduit. Junction boxes should be minimized and fittings spot-welded when warranted.

Security Monitoring

Security Control Center
If you have a security control center, it should have an adequate area for security personnel and their equipment. An additional office area for technicians and managers should be available adjacent to the control center.

Your security control center should provide a fully integrated console designed to optimize the operator's ability to receive and evaluate security information and initiate appropriate response actions for (1) access control, (2) CCTV, (3) life safety, (4) intrusion and panic alarm, (5) communications, and (6) fully zoned public address system control.

The control center should have emergency power and convenient toilet facilities. Lighting should avoid glare on TV monitors and computer terminals. Sound-absorbing materials should be used on floors, walls, and ceilings. All security power should be backed up by an emergency electrical system. The control center should be protected to the same degree as the most secure area it monitors.

Controlled Access System

This type of system, if used, should include the computer hardware, monitoring station terminals, sensors, badge readers, door control devices, and the necessary communication links (leased line, digital dialer, or radio transmission) to the computer. In addition to the normal designated access control system's doors and/or gates, remote access control points should interface to the following systems: (1) CCTV, (2) intercom, and (3) door and/or gate release.

Alarm Systems

Sensors should be resistant to surreptitious bypass. Doors in contact monitor switches should be recessed wherever possible. Surface-mounted contact switches should have protective covers. Intrusion and fire alarms for restricted areas should incorporate a backup battery power supply and be on circuits energized by normal and emergency generator power. Control boxes, external bells, and junction boxes for all alarm systems should be secured with high-quality locks and electrically wired to cause an alarm if opened.

Alarm systems should be fully multiplexed in large installations. They should interface with the computer-based security system and CCTV system. Security sensors should individually register an audio-visual alarm (annunciator or computer, if provided) located at the security central monitoring location and alert the security officer. A single-cathode ray tube display should have a redundant printer or indicator light. A hard-wired audible alarm that meets common fire code standards should be activated with distinguishing characteristics for fire, intrusion, emergency exit, and so forth. All alarms should be locked in until reset manually.

CCTV systems should permit the observation of multiple camera transmission images from one or more remote locations. Switching equipment should be installed to permit the display of any camera on any designated monitor. To ensure total system reliability, only high-quality security hardware should be integrated into the security system.

Stairwell Door Reentry System

In multitenant high-rise facilities, stairwell doors present a potential security problem. These doors must be continuously operable from the office side into the stairwells. Reentry should be controlled to permit only authorized access and prevent entrapment in the stairwell.

64

Reentry problems can be fixed if you provide locks on all stairwell doors except those leading to the first floor (lobby level) and approximately every fourth or fifth floor, or as required by local fire code requirements. Doors without these locks should be fitted with sensors to transmit alarms to the central security monitoring location and provide an audible alarm at the door location. Appropriate signs should be placed within the stairwells. Doors leading to roofs should be secured to the extent permitted by local fire code.

Security Officers

All facilities of any size in threatened locations should have manned 24-hour internal protection. Security officers should be uniformed personnel and, if possible, placed under contract. They should be thoroughly trained, bilingual, and have complete instructions in their native language clearly outlining their duties and responsibilities. These instructions should also be printed in English for the benefit of American supervisory personnel. If permitted by local law/customs, investigations or background checks of security officers should be conducted.

At facilities with a perimeter wall, there should be one 24-hour perimeter security officer post. If the facility maintains a separate vehicular entrance security officer post, such a post should be manned from one hour before to one hour after normal business hours and during special events. Security officers should be responsible for conducting package inspections, package check-in, and, if used, should operate the walk-through and hand-held metal detectors. Security officers should also be responsible for inspecting local and international mail delivered to the facility, both visually and with a hand-held metal detector before it is distributed. X-ray equipment for package inspection should be employed if the level of risk dictates.

At facilities with a perimeter guardhouse, the walk-through metal detector could be maintained and operated in an unsecured pass-through portion of the guardhouse. In addition, this security officer could also be responsible for conducting package inspections. When there is sufficient room to store packages at the guardhouse, checked packages should be stored here—new guardhouses should provide for such storage. If package storage at the guardhouse is not feasible, then it should be in shelves in the foyer under the direction of the foyer security officer or receptionist. Generally, security screening and package storage are carried out in the foyer.

Security Reinforcement

Office areas should be equipped with a reinforcement to provide physical protection from unregulated public access. Protection should be provided by a forced-entry-resistant reinforcement that meets ballistic protection standards. These standards can be obtained from your corporate security specialist. When an Access Control Manager (ACM) is constructed for security reinforcement, several things need to be taken into consideration.

Walls

Walls comprising an ACM should be constructed of no less than 6 inches of reinforced concrete from slab to slab. The reinforcement should be of at least Number 5 rebar spaced 5 inches on center, horizontally and vertically, and anchored in both slabs. In existing buildings, the following are acceptable substitutions for 5-inch reinforced concrete reinforcements:

- For sturdy construction use solid masonry, 6 inches thick or greater, with reinforcing bars horizontally and vertically installed.
- Build with solid unreinforced masonry or brick, 8 inches thick or greater.
- Use a hollow masonry block, 4 to 8 inches thick with 1/4-inch steel backing and construct with solid masonry, at least 6 inches thick with 1/4-inch steel backing.
- Construct a fabricated ballistic steel wall, using two 1/4-inch layers of sheet steel separated by tubular steel studs.
- Use reinforced concrete, less than 6 inches thick with 1/8-inch steel backing.

Doors

Either opaque or transparent security doors can be used for ACM doors. All doors should provide a 15-minute forced entry penetration delay. In addition, doors should be ballistic resistant.

An ACM door should be a local access control door, meaning a receptionist store security officer can open the door remotely. Whenever a security window or teller window is installed in the reinforcement, it should meet the 15-minute forced entry and standard ballistic resistance requirements. No visitor should be allowed to enter through the reinforcement without being visually identified by a security officer, receptionist, or other employee stationed behind the reinforcement. If the identity of the visitor cannot be established, the visitor must be escorted at all times while in the facility.

Intercom and Public Address System

A telephone intercom should be installed between the secure office area, the foyer security officer, and guardhouse. In facilities where deemed necessary, a central alarm and public address system should be installed to alert staff and patrons of an emergency situation. Where such a system is required, the primary control console should be located in the security control center. Keep in mind that alarms without emergency response plans may be wasted alarms. Design, implement, and practice emergency plans.

Secure Area

Every facility should be equipped with a secure area for immediate use in an emergency situation. This area is not intended to be used for prolonged periods of time. In the event of an emergency, employees will vacate the premises as soon as possible. The secure area, therefore, is provided for the immediate congregation of employees, at which time emergency exit plans would be implemented.

The secure area should be contained within the staff office area, behind the established reinforcement segregating offices from public access. An individual office will usually be designated as the secure area. Entrance into the secure area should be protected by a solid-core wood or hollow metal door equipped with two sliding deadbolts.

Emergency egress from the secure area will be through an opaque 15-minute forced-entry-resistant door equipped with an alarmed panic bar or through a grilled window, hinged for emergency egress. The exit preferably will not be visible from the facility's front entrance.

See the Appendix section "Hostage and Kidnapping Example Plan" for suggestions regarding the first steps to take in the event of an expat kidnapping.

REFERENCE

le Carré, John. *The Russia House*. London: Hodder & Stoughton, 1989.

7

Crises and Response

A crisis is an opportunity riding the dangerous wind.

Chinese proverb

Crises require proper preplanning and response. One of the best reasons for having a properly thought out, planned, vetted, and exercised plan is to avoid the "take charge herd mentality" most often exhibited by someone, often a senior member of management or a division head of engineering, operations, or any one of a number of functions. It is often someone who has "been there"—worked or lived in the country, or someone who simply feels empowered. He or she might not come right out and say "I AM IN CHARGE HERE!" but might just as well.

This is where subordinates might develop the *herd mentality* or cower in a corner and let Mr. or Mrs. In Charge take over the meeting and obliterate months or years of crisis planning. Typically, this leads to rush judgments such as "We have to get them out (evacuate)." One phrase that is less seldom uttered is, "We need them to hunker down where they are (shelter in place)." A chief executive officer (CEO) might utter the famous words, "I WILL GO THERE AND GET MY PEOPLE." Often in such cases, little or no solid information has been ascertained. No hard facts have been determined. The conference room crowd and the world, for that matter, are relying on some utterings from a media-appointed *expert* on the situation or unattributed reports from the country as a journalist stands with a flak jacket on a balcony of a hotel in the country capital. All of this, of course, comes from the warm, latte-festooned, glowing television set about 3000 miles from Ground Zero.

So, here in our theoretical conference room, Legal and HR, Safety and Security, Travel, Operations, Engineering, and the CEO are present. After hearing the CEO put forth the edict, "We WILL get them out," someone has the idea to charter planes. One person rushes out of the room to call his friend in Travel, who knows a guy who knows a guy who charters planes. Someone from HR starts dialing her friend with an airline, at which the airport has charter plane services. And now, at least two and soon to be many more noncorporate personnel know you are thinking of evacuating your several hundred or thousand employees. Soon, someone from the travel company or the charter service contacts a local news station. Reports surface that XYZ Corp., in downtown Los Angeles, has employees in harm's way in Stanistan. Local news trucks arrive, and soon the cable news networks air the live feed. In a country far, far away, a local warlord sees that XYZ Corp., which had been on his radar for several years, has 40 expats who are awaiting evacuation. And, incidentally, he controls ALL roads leading to the airport, the ports, and the highways. So, unless they can hurriedly arrange a helicopter evacuation (not likely because the closest helicopter is 1500 miles away) this might be a long day and night. A discussion in a conference room in Los Angeles has now led to a potential hostage taking, or worse, scenario. Crisis communications just took a giant leap backwards.

Seem far-fetched? Such occurrences are not uncommon at all. Many security and crisis professionals have experienced well-meaning people causing great harm to befall their employees by either allowing employees to *self-evacuate*—advising them to "get out as best you can"—or by rushing to hire a group of ex-Special Forces to get to the expats and get them out as they see fit. Both scenarios can lead to tragic outcomes, although one group traveled to Iran and reportedly made it work at the behest of Ross Perot. If charter flights are the way to go, why not move cautiously, yet expeditiously to line up availability and costs? What are other companies operating in the area doing? Does your company have business partners or contacts with these and other entities whereby one might share the load of planes, trains, boats, or other means? Why are we even discussing getting people moving if moving is not the best alternative?

Harnessing the successes, strategies, synergies, and experiences of human resources professionals, the corporation's lawyers, VPs of operations, security and safety personnel, and travel and benefits specialists makes a great deal of sense in many ways. Having these professionals operate on their own and without a common cause or purpose makes a difficult situation extremely risky. Corralling these individuals into one

CASE STUDY   THE STOLEN SECRETS

The company had been through months of wrangling and tough negotiations. The acquisition had been hard on everyone, but now it was time to celebrate. The social events were held around the globe, at each company's former corporate headquarters. Many speeches and toasts to success would follow. Employees from the organizations began to exchange visits and hold meetings, in person or via the Internet. It was all coming together very nicely. Then, late one evening, the phone rang at one of the headquarters' senior management offices. It seemed there had been a fire at a research park, and although there didn't appear to be much in the way of property damage, something more interesting had been discovered.

As the scenario was laid out to the senior manager, her apprehension quickly grew to fear and then outrage. It seems that the fire appeared, at least from initial fire department observations, to have been deliberately set. Furthermore, in an attempt to view which files might have been damaged by fire or heat, smoke, or water, three research file cabinets were found to be completely empty. The senior manager reached for her purse, realizing that she had quit smoking. But, she considered now as good as a time as any to start again.

The file cabinets had contained the research for the company's next iteration of widgets, one that would create such a demand it would launch sales into the stratosphere. With all of that research gone, what would happen next? To make matters worse, the corporate officer's phone rang again. It was their lead contractor on the research project. He told her that his office had been broken into, and persons unknown were seen to be taking boxes from the office and building. What a day! She'd need to stop to buy a carton of cigarettes before this was all over.

The officer contacted senior counsel, who contacted the CEO, and the CEO contacted three vice presidents. The six of them would meet late into the night to discuss their options. It was decided that the legal department would begin to look into the matter, and much time was spent checking out and acquiring representative legal counsel on the ground at both the city of the distant research

71

facility and the contractor's office location. As it was the weekend, and with one preferred counsel on vacation for several days, hours became days, and roughly six days after the event corporate security was contacted. The fact that the crime, alleged crime, or whatever had taken place happened six days prior made saying the trail was now cold a huge understatement. There were conflicting reports from everyone involved or whoever might have witnessed something.

It was unclear if one man or 50 had been observed carrying items from the contractor's office complex. And, when asked to produce records of which research might have been taken, the contractor could produce nothing for the materials supposed to be contained at his location, or what he had been working on where the fire had occurred. Corporate security began to add 2 plus 2 but it wasn't equaling 4. Something didn't seem right. The contractor was unavailable for the legal department to speak with him, either on the phone or in person. His office staff was unaware of his location other than that he was most likely traveling with his new wife. Security asked for permission to travel to the location of the fire and the contractor's office, which were separated by approximately 100 miles. However, being halfway around the globe, senior management was still attempting to engage local counsel there to help with the matter.

A call was set up, and the senior officer, legal counsel, and local counsel were conferenced in with corporate security. Corporate counsel seemed reluctant to include corporate security from the outset, but the senior officer and the in-country counsel agreed that having this department included made sense. When allowed to speak, security asked what should have been an obvious question from the outset. When could anyone verify the research data were last known to be at the office where the fire took place, and the location of the contractor? No one could produce the answer. Security asked if, during the course of the acquisition, someone had been tasked to assess what information was on hand, what assets, and would research of this nature be considered an asset, and if this had been verified by the audit team, which had all the correct clearances and had signed all the requisite nondisclosure forms. It became clear by the silence that no one had verified the existence or the location of the research for quite some time. It wasn't known if the acquired company had ever verified the existence of the research, which seemed totally implausible. The researcher had been trusted with various projects before, and had never let the company down.

The senior officer asked corporate security to proceed as quickly as possible to visit the research facility and the contractor's office, and to meet with the contractor as well. Corporate security asked if the crisis management team should be *stood up*, and the senior officer quickly shot down the idea. So, the security officer left for the facility, having had at least enough time to coordinate with a security firm in country to provide logistical and language assistance. The contractor was eventually located and he agreed to meet with the security officer alone. Sweating profusely, the contractor proceeded to spin a tale about corrupt officials and law enforcement who might have been involved in stealing the crown jewels of secrets. Did he have proof of the research being under his care to begin with? Of course, he stated, but those records had been taken as well. The more he spoke, and perspired, the more the security officer felt that old feeling of doubt and sensed the unmistakable scent of fabrications.

To add to the mix, now it appeared that investigating in this country would require a payment or gratuity made to law enforcement. The company would not do so due to anti-corruption laws. Had the due diligence not attempted to account for assets such as research?

The research was never found. One can wonder whether or not it ever existed. The situation never reached the light of day outside of the group that worked on the issue—luckily, it would seem, as knowledge of such a blunder would have hurt the corporation immeasurably. And the corporate security officer and others would have benefited, one might argue, from the help.

room during a crisis is very smart. Allowing them to work alone from their offices makes little sense at all. In a situation such as that described in the case study that follows, thinking of the *what if's* in advance in a case involving corporate secrets or sensitive information involves the need to collect many factions and functions within a corporation.

HISTORICAL PERSPECTIVE

We can learn from history how great leaders handled grave crises.

> Kennedy knew firsthand of war's futility. He had been there, and it had shaped him and his enduring impression of the world. When a reporter once asked him about his experience in the Depression, Kennedy concluded that as a rich man's son he knew nothing of it until he read about it later at Harvard. "War is my experience," he said. "I can tell you about that." In the agonizing days ahead (of the Cuban missile crisis), he often convened his inner circle, the men he trusted to give him advice and not to leak it to the press, to consider his options... (p. 97)
>
> Mark Updegrove (2009)
> *Baptism by Fire: Eight Presidents Who Took Office in Times of Crisis*

Kennedy had learned in the military that during times of crisis advice from others can be very beneficial. Crisis, of course, goes along with the office of the presidency.

> On December 20, 1860, a little over a month after Lincoln's election, the South Carolina legislature, in secession convention in Charleston, declared "the union now subsisting between South Carolina and other States under the name of the United States of America is hereby dissolved," raising the din in the drumbeat for secession in the Deep South followed... (p. 97)
>
> Mark Updegrove (2009)
> *Baptism by Fire: Eight Presidents Who Took Office in Times of Crisis*

Kennedy surrounded himself with a staff consisting of successful business and military men respected in their various fields who brought with them divergent backgrounds and viewpoints. He realized that his own perspective on domestic and foreign policy, on the military, on all things of importance to the country and his presidency had been skewed by his privileged upbringing. If you want to have an organization that functions much like you think, surround yourself with like-minded people, correct?

74

President Abraham Lincoln utilized former political rivals who could unite different factions and concerns while providing sound judgment during difficult times. One might feel like Lincoln if placed into a position of planning a session or the first meeting of a corporate crisis planning team. There are competing interests and concerns, and those who want to take charge and those who want to kick back and do nothing. Some might not want to be there at all, and have no interest or understanding of crisis management. Such situations exist in many corporations, and, unfortunately, it often takes a real crisis or tragedy involving employees to shake people out of their indifference.

Without a plan in place, a crisis plan that has had the buy-in of corporate functions ranging from Operations, to Logistics, to Human Resources, to Legal and Safety, your organization could itself slide into chaos and crisis, right there in the conference room. Without a vetted, planned, rehearsed, and exercised procedure, developed before the hopefully not-too-soon-to-arrive day, a type A personality in your group will take charge of this crisis, make it his or hers, and possibly place people and assets in great jeopardy. I have witnessed this myself on many occasions, before I had a voice in the matter. I have seen well-meaning and intelligent individuals take an already bad situation and propose actions that would make it much worse. I have been present as senior management ordered people to drop everything and jet off to far-flung locations (no volunteers in this man or woman's army!). It's like rushing into a room full of noxious fumes and chemicals. Now, instead of having one victim, you have two. There is nothing worse than a well-meaning executive, CEO, or vice president who storms in and demands to be seen, heard, and to *take charge*.

The most effective way to handle an emergency or a crisis situation is to have a well-crafted, well-vetted, rehearsed, and understood response plan ready in advance. The opposite of allowing the bellowing senior manager to *take charge* is to have seasoned, trained, and drilled professionals handling their own respective areas of expertise. When the puffed up manager states he or she will "GO THERE AND GET MY PEOPLE," he or she can be told by the logistics specialist that there is no way to get a commercial flight anywhere near the incident, and no one would be allowed into the area should the manager be able to do so. The manager can be advised that the military of Country XYZ has not been able to reach the area and begin a search and rescue, so it might be best if he or she leave the room and begin to make him- or herself useful, such as calling other companies that operate in the area to see what they are doing and how they might be able to help (it would be advantageous to provide such a manager with a list and contact information of companies and personnel). Such a plan shouldn't lie on a shelf or remain on a hard drive, waiting to be pulled out. For all of the aforementioned reasons, the crisis management plan must be a living, breathing document. People, companies, phone numbers, and responsibilities change—constant updating and checking are required to keep a plan functional and current. Corporations and organizations whose crisis management decision making is hijacked by one person within an organization, or companies that leave their crisis management planning to one person, run the risk of failure from not taking advantage of the true benefits of delegation and cross-functional experiences and talent.

REPORTING EMERGENCIES TO THE CORPORATE CRISIS MANAGEMENT TEAM

In the highly volatile situations that require a report to the Corporate Crisis Management Team (CCMT), it is essential that the initial message provide as much information as possible. The team will need several key pieces of information. First and foremost is the type of emergency. You will need to let the team know if it is a terrorist attack or a state of war. Describe any civil unrest or anti-American/anticompany demonstrations that are happening. Alternatively, if it is a natural disaster you are faced with, tell them about it and what is going on. Also be sure to report who declared the emergency and who received the information—was it an ambassador or representative of the host government or the project manager/deputy declaring the emergency, and who in your organization did he or she notify and how? Be sure to convey the date/time the emergency was declared and what areas/regions are affected—best to use local time and the 24-hour time clock. To convey urgency and what is at stake, be sure they know why the emergency is being declared—is there an immediate danger to life or property or is it a precautionary measure to protect either/both of those? (Refer to the Appendix section "Security and Evacuation Planning" for a check-off list for this protocol.)

This book does not just focus on the *response* piece, because, as you may realize, this is not the only make or break action for security and crisis practitioners. Breaking down the aspects of crisis response, there is, of course, the first aspect of planning—the response, or mitigation, by identifying the risk. Risk is evolving; it is often nebulous but sometimes it is staring you right in the face. It sometimes lies beneath the surface, simmering and yet ready to explode.

For some organizations, doing the right thing with crisis management will mean summoning up the will to do so. Companies will be required to establish a new mindset, to embrace crisis management. The terminology and phrases, the training and characteristics of crisis planning and planners will need to become part of the corporate DNA. Personnel will need to be cultivated and sent to workshops and seminars on the theory and processes of crisis management. This will provide opportunities for persons within and from outside of the organization to become more proficient or to pass along advice and considerations. As previously mentioned, with the backing and support of senior management, and if required of the board of directors, employees will feel the importance of such programs and understand that the organization cares about their well-being.

Crisis rooms and equipment vary depending on the nature of the organization's/company's operations. For example, if the corporation is involved only with domestic operations, a national map will suffice. Planning would then incorporate procedures for those states/provinces, and so on where employees are located. Many corporations, unfortunately, deal with multiple locations in multiple nations and regions around the world. For this reason, communications will be key to success in all aspects of crisis operations.

There is almost always a failure of communications, due to either an overload of mobile phone towers or the deliberate taking down of communications networks by governments or antigovernment forces. Or there are natural causes such as damage due to earthquakes, hurricanes, cyclones, or other disasters. When crisis communications fail, your plans must operate on autopilot with the ability to move forward without a reliable means to contact regional managers or personnel at headquarters if this is out of the country or some distance away. Headquarters must have confidence that the personnel on the ground and in country will follow the crisis plan and not deviate from this planning unless absolutely necessary. By absolutely necessary one should believe that the personnel covered by the crisis plan should do exactly what the crisis plan dictates unless and until it is dangerous to do so.

By having on the ground and in-country management buying into and adhering to your crisis plan, things will operate in a more successful manner. Some examples include: If it becomes necessary to *bug out* to evacuate and grab your *go bag*, where are you going to go? Will you go to one of a few safe houses or predetermined destinations where headquarters knows to contact your group or look for you? Or, will you run off to where no one has much hope of determining your whereabouts or safety? Headquarters will expend valuable resources and time looking for you and your group if they don't know where you are.

TO LEAVE OR NOT TO LEAVE, THAT IS THE QUESTION

Much can be said about whether to evacuate personnel, or not, during an emergency. Some might say by remaining and not evacuating personnel you are placing them at risk because the *bad guys* or government forces no doubt know where they are. This might be true, but if past experience is any indicator, evildoers and criminals are opportunistic and never cease to come up with surefire means of monopolizing a crisis situation.

One method of doing so is the ubiquitous *government roadblock* that pops up within a moment's notice in various locations. Government troops, police, or supporters stop traffic ostensibly to *check IDs* or "conduct vehicle searches" but instead these often become shakedowns for money or expensive items, including the vehicles in which the victims are driving, or simply a way to wage violence against anyone. Arrests often take place if vehicle occupants give these forces any trouble.

Other types of roadblocks might include forces opposing the government, who might, for example, see any foreigners as working to support the government. Or, the sole intention of erecting roadblocks might simply be to steal and rob unsuspecting victims. Traveling by road during political and man-made crises can be very risky. Traveling by road during natural disasters can be equally risky for obvious reasons, such as unsafe atmospheric conditions, flooded roadways or crossings, mudslides, lava flows, rockslides, and any number of issues.

Traveling under dangerous conditions should not be undertaken unless the alternative is much more risky. In many cases, to stand fast or remain where one is would be the preferable mode of action. If an alternative site must be moved to, it should be to an area or site for which a route has been scouted and deemed to be safe for travel. There are companies that provide emergency medical and security evacuations, but in most cases, an airport or at the very least a suitable airstrip is required. Helicopters are hard to find in most circumstances and have a limited operating range. Keep in mind, if evacuation is required, it should be kept as a last resort because there might be more danger on the road than remaining where one is located.

To evacuate or not evacuate is one of the most important decisions to make during a crisis. Often, personnel on the ground might be hearing or seeing things that have not made it to the media, government, private sources, or media markets around the world. In-country personnel might therefore be in a better position to determine if it might be necessary to evacuate, or if conditions have broken down so badly that to evacuate would be placing employees and dependents directly in harm's way. On the other hand, managers and specialists back at headquarters half a world away might be receiving reliable information such as warnings by government sources for all expats to make their way to airports or designated transfer points. Such routes of travel would often be protected by government and military forces. If conditions are such that the streets and cities are in utter chaos, with no sign of police or military for the safety of expats, perhaps hunkering down and remaining where one is might be the best solution.

BACKUPS TO THE BACKUPS OF YOUR BACKUPS

Anyone who knows a great deal about planning can tell you that plans do not always go as well as expected. There can be many reasons for plans falling apart or failing to achieve the goals set forth. Planning can fail to take into account all of the human foibles.

Think of it this way: the least reliable aspect of crisis management in a real situation is communications. As previously indicated, governments or natural disasters can quickly smash or disable phone and Internet networks. Satellite communications can be used as a standby, but atmospheric and other conditions might render such efforts moot. Batteries lose their charge, phones break or are lost, and handheld radios are limited in range. Communications can be fleeting during the early stages of a crisis and then vanish in a puff of smoke.

Transportation might be available for expats and then be unavailable in an instant, such as in the case of an airport being closed, seaports being shut down, or train services being canceled. If evacuation plans don't take into account the possibility of one method of evacuation being unreliable, and another type of transport might not be acceptable or available, employees might be left to use automobiles and trucks as transport. If your plans call for contacting one particular host or home-based government agency, and that agency is unavailable for contact due to communication failures or possibly evacuation of their own personnel, another source to turn to for information or safety must be planned for.

Government resources might be limited even in normal situations, depending on your location, remoteness, geography, climate, weather conditions, or any number of concerns. To come to rely solely on these resources during a crisis situation is risky in and of itself. Private resources, examples of which include emergency medical and security evacuation services, security protection teams, private chartered aircraft landing at private airfields, and alternate means of ground transportation should be contracted with in preparation for that day when you're all dressed up with no way to get there. For example, if you have one primary means of hiring local ground transportation resources, and they are unable to assist, what are your options? What are the options if you discover the airports and other means of transportation have been closed or unusable? Is there a port where ocean or even river transportation can be purchased? If airfields and landing strips are closed or not possible to reach, is there a helicopter company that could charter you in or out?

Many organizations that have emergency security and medical evacuation contracts with providers don't back up these providers. But what happens if the national airports are closed and travelers are left stranded at the airport? What if roadblocks are set up and your personnel are unable to reach departure locations? What if a mass evacuation has the emergency evacuation vendor so overwhelmed that your personnel will be on the third flight leaving in two days? Backing up everything comes from the knowledge that during bad situations, not everything goes as planned.

See the Appendix section "Travel Safety and Security Information" for suggestions regarding travel tracking and intelligence programs.

REFERENCE

Updegrove, Mark K. *Baptism by Fire: Eight Presidents Who Took Office in Times of Crisis*. New York: Thomas Dunne Books, 2009.

8

Mother Nature Strikes Again
Planning and Preparation

Thank Heaven! the crisis,
The danger, is past,
And the lingering illness
Is over at last—
And the fever called *Living*
Is conquered at last.

Edgar Allan Poe
For Annie

Nothing quite so completely challenges the nerve, cunning, planning, and tenacity of crisis managers like non-man-made disasters. Mother Nature can surprise like no other and change direction like a dragonfly. While weather is becoming easier to predict, hurricanes in particular, earthquakes and wildfires often strike out of nowhere. The following case study is one of many that the author could cite wherein the hubris of those who dare to test the fury of Mother Nature creates a fast-moving and very dangerous situation for employees, families, coworkers, and organizations.

On October 29, 2013, a storm took a left turn (according to scientists, a storm such as this would occur once every 700 years) and hit the New Jersey coast dead center (Pesce, 2013). Hurricane Sandy, as it was called, proceeded to kill 159 people and cause more than $65 billion in damage. Sandy—the name would be retired from use in naming hurricanes

CASE STUDY   JOE VERSUS THE VOLCANO

Joe was an expat with a multinational corporation, and was a well-respected geologist in his company and in his field of expertise. He was a loyal and dedicated company and family man. He loved all things geologic. And, he loved the game of golf. So, when the opportunity presented itself for him to take his family to an exotic location to combine two of his favorite things, the temptation was too great. There just happened to be a golf course south of his project office that bordered and was overshadowed by an actual volcano. In fact, the grounds of the course were warm from the geothermic activity.

The volcano had been noticeably active recently, and the crisis management team had sent a notice to Joe and his team that seismologists and volcanic experts had warned that the big one might be on its way. But it was vacation time, and Joe and his happy family were all set to play some golf, lie in the sun, and enjoy some mai-tais. "Joe," the crisis management team asked, "Please don't go. Delay your game and R and R." Joe replied, "Nope. I have had these tickets for months. Not going to happen."

The crisis management team implored senior management, who stated they were not about to impinge on someone's free time, especially that of someone as important to the organization as Joe. Joe was advised to take a satphone, as communications in the southern area were known to be shaky even during optimal times. Joe demurred, stating that he was going to relax and didn't want calls about the project.

Readers could probably guess or write the next few paragraphs. Yes, the volcano did erupt, and it was a big one. Major highways leading into Joe's vacation site were blocked by land and mudslides. Boulders rained down on the vacation region, no doubt canceling a few rounds of golf, or at the very least interfering with some scores. Poisonous volcanic gases killed one entire herd of livestock. Communications dropped like a bad habit; no calls were coming out or were going in. The in-country project and headquarters worried about Joe and his family. Joe was worrying about his family which he had arranged for their travel to meet him. No one in the company knew his family was flying from overseas to vacation with Joe. But Joe was stuck in his hotel. Joe and his family were safe but had no means to communicate this to anyone.

> For three very long days, no one heard from Joe. The crisis team made every attempt they could muster, even reaching out to embassies and consulates. But there was simply too much confusion and disruption to get any word in or out. Finally, Joe made it to a regional hospital while his family remained at the hotel. He assumed the hospital would have communications and he was correct. He then telephoned the in-country project and headquarters to let them know he and his family were safe.
>
> Joe had ridden out the volcano, but he would never travel unprepared again.

because of the destruction it left in its wake—caught many emergency and crisis planners by surprise.

The case study that follows describes the experience of a company expat employee whose request to travel to a region prone to volcanic activity for a leisurely weekend reached my desk. I had already been viewing and reading news reports of impending seismic and volcanic activity affecting a wide area. But the dangerous conditions were far from the city where the company had stationed expats and their dependents. However, this employee wanted to visit a resort and take along his family. The employee was insistent, and in spite of much cajoling and warning by my office and others, he traveled to the area along with his family. As you might expect, the seismic and volcanic activity increased.

Disasters come in various forms—natural or man-made—to cite the long-standing conventional wisdom. Natural disasters are easy to categorize; these consist of earthquakes, hurricanes, volcanoes, and tsunamis. During the twenty-first century, however, the world has seen an increase in the number, size, and variety of natural disasters. These occurrences include flooding, snow, cyclones, tornadoes, and severe weather in general. There have been a variety of instances such as emergencies involving nuclear facilities, chemical facilities, forest fires, water emergencies, and power outages (Figures 8.1 and 8.2).

Man-made disasters have been on the increase, one could argue, with conflicts ranging from the Arab Spring (see Chapter 12) to coups and additional civil unrest. To say the corporate crisis manager or consultant has to remain abreast of current events around the world is an extreme understatement. He or she must have a broad-ranging network of public/private intelligence and news sources.

Figure 8.1 On January 17, 1994, Californians experienced the devastation of a large quake in a major metropolitan area. (Courtesy of FEMA, https://www.fema .gov/media-library/assets/images/36990/.)

Figure 8.2 The proliferation of land mines around the world makes land travel in several regions dangerous and unpredictable. (Courtesy of C-52 of 3/2 Stryker Brigade Combat Team, http://www.army.mil/article/26877/rethinking -ied-strategies-from-iraq-to-afghanistan.)

In planning for such a wide variety of natural and man-made potentials, the corporate professional must consider risk potential, potential outcomes, and mitigation potentials.

The potential for risk from naturally occurring events concerning expats in a particular region depends on the environmental possibilities for consequences to humans. For example, as we read in Chapter 1, if one considers the placement of expats in Japan, risk varies if the expat is to be posted in Tokyo versus Fukushima, scene of a nuclear accident in March 2011 after an 8.9 magnitude earthquake and tsunami (Mendick and Ryall, 2011). In the Japanese disaster, more than 18,000 people died (McCurry, 2011). In 2004, the earthquake and tsunami in Sumatra killed more than 230,000 people (Mills, 2014).

One might say, therefore, that the risk potential for persons living and working in the Fukushima and Sumatra areas would be that of susceptibility to earthquakes and tsunamis, not because of incidents that happened 50 to 100 years ago, but instances within the past few years. The risk potential would be for loss of life or property and failure of infrastructure—to include the power grid, communications, roads, bridges, airports, trains, mass transit, and others.

So, if one were to place expats in the regions surrounding Fukushima or Sumatra, these past occurrences must be considered. How does one plan for an earthquake or a tsunami? A company certainly would not want its expats living or working in low-lying areas or structures. Ensuring structures are built to earthquake tolerances and strengths might be another mitigation tool. Finally, early warning systems and services, both government owned and private, would be a recommendation to make to senior management in such circumstances.

Potential outcomes given the aforementioned disasters might be

- Loss of life
- Injuries
- Loss of communications
- Loss of property
- Food and water shortages
- Lack of medical care
- Lack of transportation

Obviously, emergency services will be a while in arriving. And, depending on the location or region, they may have difficulty in reaching the scenes. In some regions around the world, first responders would

85

be quickly overwhelmed and would rely on the world to supplement or mount rescue efforts.

What might some mitigation potentials consist of? As previously mentioned, if flooding, coastal or otherwise, is a concern, not situating plants or housing in low-lying areas would be advisable. Planning for and training with personnel on escape routes to high areas would be another option, as well as ensuring there are backup means of communication to landline and mobile phones and Internet. Satellite phones might be utilized.

Emphasis might be placed on arranging go-bags with water, food, and medical and other supplies. Maps and foreign currency, candles and matches, GPS devices, meals ready to eat, batteries, and light sticks are the standard fare. Training employees in or providing for professional medical services is something that is undertaken by many organizations around the world. Knowing that medical services, even with prearranged emergency evacuation or response arrangements, may be some time in coming necessitates that medical efforts to stabilize patients be put into planning efforts.

As much as possible, it will be necessary to preplan and preposition such supplies and ensure they are not expired or depleted. It will be incumbent on those charged with protecting the security and safety of the expats located in foreign locales to consider all possibilities of what could go wrong, what bad things could happen. It will be necessary to become a history major (or at least a minor) to delve into what has happened recently and not so recently in the area or region from an emergency or disaster standpoint.

If a volcano erupted in Java, near Krakatoa, in 1883 and is estimated to have killed more than 37,000 people primarily from the resulting tsunami hitting nearby islands (Australian Government Bureau of Meteorology, 2016), is there a reason to be on high alert in Sumatra, Indonesia in 2014? I would argue there is not. However, volcanic activity can be slow in developing. That is to say, as with Krakatoa in 1883 and Mount Saint Helens in Washington State in the United States in 1980, there are buildups and warnings. Technology and science are better today in warning of impending volcanic eruptions. So planning for natural disasters may be as easy or as time consuming as consulting the Internet, history books, or regional records. But, with changing weather and atmospheric patterns, with seismic and volcanic activity popping up in new regions, a little bit of science goes a long way. Watching hurricanes form is a common activity for security and safety personnel with offshore or coastline operations likely to be affected by them.

Having backup contingency plans is especially important when dealing with Mother Nature. Backup plans are required because you can easily plan for a hurricane or typhoon making landfall in one area, and then be dismayed at its arrival on an opposite coastline.

One of the most important things to do during natural emergencies and crises is not to panic and put personnel at risk by having them evacuate to unsafe areas or by unsafe means. But, if evacuations are started and are considered the safest route, these should be undertaken with great care. Protocols for evacuations and training for these procedures will be critical to your success.

See the Appendix section "Emergency Equipment and Supplies" for ideas on some emergency supplies to keep on hand for crisis events.

REFERENCES

Australian Government Bureau of Meteorology, Commonwealth of Australia. The eruption of Krakatoa, August 27, 1883. 2016. http://www.bom.gov.au/tsunami/history/1883.shtml.

McCurry, Justin. Japan quake death toll passes 18,000. *The Guardian*, March 21, 2011.

Mendick, Robert and Ryall, Julian. Japan earthquake: Tens of thousands missing as full devastation emerges. *Telegraph*, March 12, 2011.

Mills, Allison. Benchmarks: December 26, 2004: Indian Ocean tsunami strikes. *Earth Magazine*, December 26, 2014. http://www.earthmagazine.org/article/benchmarks-december-26-2004-indian-ocean-tsunami-strikes.

Pesce, Carolyn. Millions on east coast brace for Sandy. *USA Today*, October 29, 2013.

Poe, Edgar Allan. "For Annie," *The Works of the Late Edgar Allan Poe* by Rufus Wilmot Griswold. Blakeman and Mason, 1859.

9

Health Crises, Epidemic, Pandemic, and Outbreaks

Any idiot can face a crisis, it is this day-to-day living that wears you out.

Anton Chekhov

Much has been written and considered since the worldwide pandemic scares of 2009. At the time this book was being written, another health scare—that of ebola—was grabbing international headlines. And although ebola and the flu are as dissimilar as the sun and the moon, much of the preparatory activity for dealing with them both involves some of the same components. Even given what has taken place over the past several years, there is still debate in many organizations about the necessity of having a pandemic plan in place and whether or not critical resources, such as time, money, and supplies, should be devoted to this as a bona fide risk. The fact is that outbreak pandemics with novel outbreaks are recurring events. They are unpredictable and result in serious health effects to a large proportion of the population with significant disruption to the social, economic, and security concerns of the community.

Not having a pandemic plan in place is not the equivalent of the Y2K debacle—remember that? How many of us gave up our New Year's Eve in 2000 because the data world was going to crash? A pandemic plan is not the twenty-first-century equivalent of that mistake. A pandemic plan continues to be a tool everyone should have in place and ready to roll out.

Even if you never use it, it would be an exercise in emergency planning that could benefit you in the long run.

If you are working in volatile areas, the impact of a pandemic may be more severe. Due to the lack of a plan or the inability of the community, or even national health services, to respond appropriately, the local populations of the countries you are working in may be greatly, quickly, and severely affected.

As a result of the press coverage in 2009 concerning the avian infectious outbreak of disease H5N1 and the belief by many experts that the outbreak could mutate into a novel outbreak and then make the jump to humans around the world, the World Health Organization (WHO) has convinced me that the discussion among security professionals and their corporations should not be about how likely such an event is to occur, but about actually planning for one to take place. The WHO has encouraged countries, states, cities, and organizations to prepare for such an event. How governments, businesses, corporations, and citizens prepare for a global pandemic is critical due to the projected impact of such an event.

Consequences of an outbreak may include employees calling in sick, either too sick to work due to their own illness or caring for a friend or family member. In the actual occurrence of a pandemic, it is estimated that up to 25% of the workforce may be affected initially, and many of them will die, further impacting the workforce. Reduced numbers of employees slows throughput and output, and production suffers. The number of employees who are willing to travel on commercial carriers to work on overseas or national projects will suffer. In order to protect employees, corporations may begin telling employees they cannot travel, or travel will be severely restricted. *Business critical* is the term used to explain this curtailment of travel. The goods and services companies provide will be consumed or purchased less and be less in demand due to growing economic and societal health issues. Emergency responders will be fewer, and infrastructure support employees will be diminished. Hospitals, clinics, and doctors' office employees will be impacted as will public utility workers. One can lay out scenarios in which shortages of deliveries to grocery stores, staff to stock the groceries—even production workers to produce the foodstuffs—cause angst in the general public. What spark would be required to set off a panic or violence among the populace?

According to scientists in 2009, the avian outbreak spread throughout Asia, Europe, and parts of Africa (Engel, 2009). Many believe the outbreak is changing and reshaping in its genetic structure. Many wonder if the availability of vaccines can keep up or if the correct vaccines are even being produced.

Corporate security managers and others within corporations, such as safety and human resources employees, who track and are responsible for dealing with the threats, risks, and responses to such events must be aware of where outbreaks or similar occurrences have taken place. Business intelligence sources, such as travel tracking and intelligence vendor and the WHO website (www.who.int), can greatly improve your vision of risk. A proper planning program, procedures, and training are required by and for your organization's employees who act in emergency planning roles, for example, if you have an emergency action plan team or committee for disaster response and recovery. Internal working groups of cross-functional disciplines are necessary to provide the depth and correct skills for effective response. All emergency response planning for the offices, facilities, and projects around the world need to have sections dedicated to this effort.

Your plan should have a backup for your backups or alternates due to the nature of the potential problem and the likelihood of many people becoming affected. All the staffing requirements for your plan should include a depth of qualified staff who are capable and trained in all aspects of the plan. Your planning and response documentation is intended to provide a platform from which you can continue to operate your business and still respond effectively. It should be procedural in nature. The plan must instruct those who are part of your emergency and crisis teams in the methods and procedures required. The plan must provide for deployment and initializing your teams. The term *business continuity* could not be more important or critical to this type of planning process. Communication, as always, will be critical, including developing *phone trees* and lists of employees and their backups and how you advise employees of what your company is doing and what they need to do. A large portion of the planning document should be educational in the sense that it can provide employees with important health information and prevention and treatment support. And, finally, as with any such documentation, people will need to have the response plan down on paper, the result of a process that has been thoroughly discussed and rehashed.

In addition, it is incumbent upon planners to have the plan endorsed and supported by the highest levels of the organization. Senior management is the only group that can drive this effort. As with any such program, you will need to enlist the support of all the business units within your company and the corporate departments that provide support. The pandemic plan or program should be a part of your overarching emergency preparedness and crisis management program, and it must include the best medical information that is currently available. As such, mention of a pandemic as a possible occurrence to which you will need to devote time and resources is essential to success.

Your plan should begin as any emergency response document does: with the onset of a domestic or global outbreak. Your company and its employees around the world need to have a uniform set of guidelines for response. There are phases to a flu pandemic, and your program should mesh with the recommendations and specifics provided by the World Health Organization. Your plan and response should mirror the advice of the WHO.

Company planning may include the purchase and storage of antiviral treatment medications if the project or office is remote enough that medical resources may be lacking or at a great distance. In such situations, dependents may be in immediate need of the prophylactic resources provided by these antivirals. If the project, office, or facility has engaged the services of an appropriate medical clinic or medical personnel, such as project doctors, these services must be stocked with antiviral and antibiotic medicines. It will be necessary to assess the local medical resources to see that these are adequate and have the ability to handle a pandemic or outbreak situation. Resources, such as a medical review by International SOS, will enable corporate management on the ground to have expert opinions as to the emergency medical capabilities of local medical facilities and staff.

Security managers should realize that due to the nature of pandemics, it may not be possible to immediately bring employees out of a particular country because of the host nation's health policies, which may include shutting down people traveling outside the country if they might have been exposed to a highly contagious outbreak. WHO requirements may also mandate border and travel closures and restrictions. The same conditions and preclusions would apply to dependents. Employees may find themselves in a position in which government and WHO rules would apply. The services of an International SOS could be called on when an employee is going to need medical services that are beyond the capabilities of local medical services and professionals. An International SOS would know the closest qualified medical resources and the legalities and current restrictions, or lack thereof, for travel. It may become corporate policy that employees are allowed to transport their dependents or leave projects or offices on their own if conditions warrant or allow. It may become necessary to provide employees with access to countries to which they could or could not relocate, depending upon local health conditions, for example, if that country is affected by the same viral outbreak.

In communicating with your planning team and employees, it should be clearly stated that while the continuation of business and the preservation of operations and delivery of products and services is ongoing, the most important aspect is the protection of employees and any dependents who might also be affected by a pandemic. Your corporation should communicate that it will work as hard as possible to reduce the risk of spreading an outbreak and will prevent an outbreak whenever possible. Such an effort should be part of the corporate policies of your company. The policies and priorities, again, should be supported vociferously from the top down. The policy statement should be part and parcel of your emergency and crisis response plan for a pandemic.

INITIAL RESPONSE AND MITIGATION, RECOVERY

Once an outbreak or report of a serious incidence of disease is received, the crisis management team (which will most likely be located in the country or location of the outbreak) should be required to delve into the issue and determine whether or not the emergency operations center should be convened and staffed. It may be necessary to immediately determine the need for an alternative location if the current location of the emergency operations center might be at risk or compromised by the outbreak.

Whether or not the emergency operations center is opened and staffed, the crisis management team must be advised of any incidence of the outbreak or impact on any international office or facility. The crisis management team would be looked upon to provide the advice necessary for on-the-ground management and determine which type of assistance in personnel or materials would be required. As with any such crisis, an outbreak might be a long-running incident, so plan accordingly for staffing and backup of normal duties for those staffing the crisis management center. If the location of the crisis management team is within an affected pandemic area, care should be taken, including the use of video or other standard phone teleconferencing, to reduce the risk of spreading the outbreak. Each team member must have assigned duties as outlined in your hard copy of the crisis management plan.

As with any crisis management plan, it will be critical to designate and break down key employee positions and responsibilities in order to determine, outline, and provide resources for someone backfilling the position if key employees are infected. This may be termed *analyzing the impact upon your business.*

If the WHO announces a change to the global phase of a pandemic, your company should enact an emergency declaration. Such announcements will typically be made by the chief medical officers of the countries affected: the Surgeon General in the United States or ministers of health in other nations. The WHO will have advised or will be advising these countries on the response steps to be initiated. This might be your first indication of trouble.

It is also likely in the United States that the departments of Health and Human Services and/or the Centers for Disease Control will issue guidelines and recommendations. Your yardstick and the international organization that should be followed, however, is the WHO.

If the WHO indicates that an epidemic or the pandemic has reached Phase 4, the company should activate its crisis management team and emergency operations center. The team shall determine the level of the crisis and how this crisis will affect company employees and operations. Immediate steps should be taken to reduce—in whatever ways are immediate and possible—the impact upon the business. Your crisis management team and senior management will be faced with serious issues, decisions, and responses to be implemented.

With the level of decision making necessary in order to adequately protect the company's people, assets, and business, again, approval must come from the president/CEO and the board of directors. You will be declaring a disaster situation, requiring the implementation of quick decision making and expenditure of great amounts of time and, possibly, money. The levels of emergency situations and an explanation of each reads as follows:

In a level one pandemic/epidemic situation, there is no immediate threat to life or property, but the situation can grow in breadth and magnitude. Your crisis management team will most likely be located in the country, city, or region of the outbreak and will, in turn, be notifying and working with your emergency operations center. The emergency operations center will be monitoring and communicating frequently with the crisis management team and all areas of the company that might be affected. Preparation should be made for the activation of the emergency operations center and determining if the emergency operations center will remain where it was initially planned to be or will be relocated in addition to the need for the possibility of evacuation and other developments. In a level one situation of a pandemic or epidemic, there may be an outbreak in a local area but one in which your company has no or very few employees who may be affected. In this case, there is no immediate impact to your business operations, facilities, and offices within the country, region, or area that is reported to have had an incident.

During a level two pandemic/epidemic situation, it may become necessary to move, relocate, or evacuate employees located in the country, region, or affected area. Your crisis management team may then deem the situation a disaster, requiring the ramping up of your company's emergency operations center. The emergency operations center should continue to monitor the situation closely at this level with the knowledge that the current level might further escalate into a level three occurrence. Level two may be declared by emergency officials operating in regions around the country, by city emergency officials, or those in state and federal governments, and it may affect your local projects and facilities due to a local outbreak or occurrence. The situation may prompt the closure of your operations by official acts and orders of local governments. During this phase, many employees and/or their dependents may be affected by the outbreak.

The occurrence of a level three situation may be identified as a situation in which your offices or facilities may have or will require evacuation. Your company resources will be taxed to the point at which you might require assistance of local first responders, government agencies, or third-party vendors. Local authorities or governments or regional national entities may declare an emergency situation. Your emergency operations center should now deem the situation a disaster, and appropriate recovery and response steps should ensue. The situation of pandemic or epidemic will have affected serious numbers of the employee workforce and the world. At this stage, the WHO may announce or declare the probable occurrence of a pandemic, which is global in nature, or an epidemic, which would refer to a local occurrence.

In the event the WHO announces an impending pandemic (global outbreak) or epidemic (local outbreak), the crisis management and emergency operations team should consider this a level four situation, requiring the immediate and ongoing staffing of both of these support mechanisms.

Your corporate senior leadership should, of course, be involved with decisions made concerning the operations of your company in the midst of a pandemic or epidemic. The information needed to make these decisions will be relayed to senior leadership via the crisis management team and emergency operations center. The crisis management team on the ground in the location(s) affected will be called on for continuous updates in order to justify decisions and additional steps to be taken. Daily meetings and updates will be required. The teams, as mentioned previously, will need to remain fresh with backups and shift work or staffing. The jobs of those employees on the teams will need to be backfilled during this time frame. Prioritization and formalizing of duties and recording of all decisions and steps taken will be required. Going forward, a strategy to tackle local issues from a local perspective will be most beneficial in the long run. Corporate resources are always available should local management and local crisis management teams be overwhelmed.

One very important aspect of your response plan to a pandemic or epidemic is communicating your plans and the expectations of your company to and for your employees. For example, employees should be directed to advise their managers if they are ill and not to report to work while they are ill. Local health departments and the WHO can provide your company with information you can package into training programs about basic hand washing and hygienic techniques for the workplace. Managers should be kept up to speed on the corporate response to issues so that they can pass along this information to the workforce. Consider publishing all appropriate information on the corporate website or special links to health and emergency response information. If media requests are received, these should be routed to the corporate communications professionals for comment.

Hygiene information should include advising employees of the installation by the company of hand sanitizers in restrooms and instructions for actions, ranging from proper cleaning of restrooms to sanitizing telephone handsets after another person has used them. The levels of absenteeism should be tracked and charted. Monitor levels of sickness absence. Assign employees to be tasked with maintaining contact with local state and federal health officials, government ministries, and other appropriate liaisons.

Pertaining to the national and local government agencies, the possibility of a pandemic or epidemic can be a very effective argument for maintaining good relationships. Not only will you be kept up to date on the latest health intelligence and response information, but you could also ensure that proper response and treatment options are open to your employees should the need arise. Whenever possible, the active support of government health services (such as clinics, offices, warehouses, technical, and even financial assistance) should be provided.

As mentioned previously, the implementation of crisis management and business continuity plans needs to be mandated and also directed by the highest levels within the organization. Corporate division senior management needs to ensure that the proper contingency plans are enacted.

Such planning will include authorizing overtime and shift work; closing down or shutting down segments, production lines, or some projects; or reducing workforce size. It may be necessary to make due with the staff that is capable of working and cut out all other work that is not critical to the company. Obviously, travel needs to be curtailed or halted. Meetings involving the general public should be stopped for fear of the outbreak being passed on. Teleconferencing would be an adequate alternative.

One critical internal representative and member of your crisis management decision-making and response team will be that of your travel department representative, whether this is an employee or contractor to your company. These travel agents can issue travel advice and ensure there is compliance with your corporate policy, such as restricting travel to various regions. A travel tracking software and management program would allow for security managers to be advised of anyone who has booked travel to regions or countries that might become affected after tickets have been issued. These employees could be contacted to cancel such travel. Updated travel policies and restrictions should be kept current on internal corporate websites. Travelers should always be advised to check and maintain their vaccinations as current for safe travel. If travel is deemed business critical to areas that might be of concern, proper authorization at senior management levels must be undertaken.

Proper staffing for your emergency operations center will be just as critical as the proper response effort. Care will need to be taken if the emergency operations center would be within an area that is affected by the pandemic or epidemic. Teleconferencing of the emergency operations center should be considered an option. The emergency operations center leader should be given the authority to request additional resources and personnel as required.

In order to respond adequately to a pandemic or epidemic, the corporation should determine, on a department-by-department basis, those critical functions, employees, materials, equipment, and supplies required to do the job and do it in a safe manner. A business impact analysis is an excellent way to start this process. Part of a realistic assessment would be to ask how your operations would continue should between 25% and 50% of your workforce be ill as some estimates would project. What if they remained off work for up to four months?

There will be certain departments, locations, facilities, and assets that would be essential to continuance. These must be identified. The priorities of your company might shift given a loss of production capabilities, and what would these be? If your business products are critical to the government for national security or infrastructure purposes, will the government step in to shore you up in order to continue? Finance departments will need to be focused on time-driven reporting and payment considerations. Orderly shutdown practices and procedures need to be developed. The proper personnel required to safely and efficiently operate the corporation must be identified, and these employees must have alternatives to back them up. Breaking employees into teams and otherwise maximizing your experience is another option. If critical outside temporary staffing may be trained and brought in, would this be useful? Supervision should be trained on how to spot and react to and report employees who appear to be or have called in sick.

A key consideration concerning those companies that supply your operations with materials and services is that during a pandemic or epidemic you will need to contact them and assure the flows of these goods in coordination with your operational priorities. Your suppliers and vendors may be forced to provide you with less due to their own circumstances. You will need to plan for these eventualities. Once your products or services are ready, there may be less demand for these, again due to the circumstances of customers or end users. Your operations will need to analyze the needs for support of your production, including how you will transport critical employees, communications necessities, food and water supplies, and other demands if employees must *hunker down* at one facility. Similar concerns will include deciding if employees will telecommute and work from home, requiring that they be supplied with the proper computer and communications equipment and connectivity, or if your operations could, in fact, be located physically at some alternate location. Concerning information technology, the company's needs for backing up and storage of critical data will not cease due to a pandemic or epidemic, and the same people will require access to data in order to do their jobs. Your human resources and benefits employees may want to consider the staffing and special provision of mental health services to allow employees to cope with stress. Security managers should work closely with those in occupational health and safety, who will be experts in dealing with the prevention and treatment response in pandemic and epidemic situations.

Corporate communications and other departments will be necessary to provide ongoing WHO updates and issuance of warnings and other critical data. They can help you craft the manner of how this should be passed on to employees. Your communications employees should be critical members of both the crisis management teams and emergency operations center staffing.

Concerning foreign governments and pandemic or epidemic notifications, they will follow the lead of the WHO. In the United States, the Centers for Disease Control (CDC) will follow the protocols set forth by the WHO. Other sources for United States recommendations and responses include the US Department of Health & Human Services and state departments of health and human services. Your local crisis management teams should be responsible for communicating with host government health agencies under the guidance and support of the emergency operations center.

If your crisis management team is advised that an outbreak, pandemic, or epidemic has taken place, your facility should begin to place written notices at every point your employees are entering buildings and facilities advising everyone that they should not enter if they have or suspect they are feeling symptoms associated with the outbreak. Make use of bulletin boards and points of prominence (including restrooms) to post information concerning how employees can work to reduce chances of transmission.

If multilingual resources are necessary, this needs to be taken into consideration. Tips on hand washing, covering one's mouth when sneezing, and use of hand sanitizers (made available) should be covered and demonstrated if necessary. Those charged with the responsibility of responding to emergency situations involving a pandemic or epidemic should be equipped with appropriate personal protective equipment, such as microfilter masks, as recommended by the WHO. Supplies should also include recommended cleanup kits and materials. Minimizing entry and exit points into the facility wherever possible or practical is important. The actual number of entry points should be limited to reduce the chances of persons slipping in without noticing the posted materials and in order to adequately comply with these standards. Hand sanitizers should be placed at entry points, and special trays or kits for sanitizing footwear should be made available.

Another means of controlling the spread of an outbreak is referred to as *social distancing*. This is the practice of basically limiting exposure of people to other people, thereby increasing their chances of not contracting the disease. Most people will view this as the practice of avoiding a baseball game, concert, or even visiting the mall, but social distancing is also applicable in the workplace. Some of the ways to limit contact and exposure between employees have been mentioned, such as holding conference calls for meetings even to the extent that employees in the same building or facility hold a virtual telephone meeting or conference. When meetings face to face are required, the larger the space and the more

DESCRIPTIONS OF PHASES AND RESPONSE
(PER WHO GUIDELINES)

The first two phases can be referred to as the Interpandemic Period.

Phase 1: No new infectious outbreak or disease subtypes detected in humans; such a subtype may be present in animals, which has caused an infection in humans; however, the risk of infection or disease in humans is considered to be low.

Company response: Monitoring of situation with understanding that CDC and WHO are doing the same while working toward the development of new treatment vaccines.

Phase 2: An animal outbreak subtype is present and animal-to-animal contagion is experienced; no such subtypes have been reported in humans.

Company response: Monitoring of situation, checking on CDC and WHO updates.

The next three phases can be referred to as the Pandemic Period.

Phase 3: There are human infections resulting from a new subtype, but the occurrence of human-to-human transmission is not reported or is reported only on rare occasions with very close contact.

Company response: Begin close review of pandemic/epidemic response plans; working up of various communications to be issued to employees as warranted.

Phase 4: Human-to-human spread has been reported, but this is occurring in centralized, localized clusters, which leads experts to believe the outbreak is not as contagious at this point.

Company response: All crisis management and emergency operations team members should be made aware of the escalation; continued monitoring of WHO information and compliance with recommendations; redoubled effort to have communications ready for employees if it becomes necessary.

Phase 5: Human-to-human spread of outbreak is growing in numbers but is still centralized and localized; there is some evidence that the outbreak is adapting to be more easily spread between humans, but it has not achieved this level of success (whereupon it would be deemed a substantial pandemic risk).

Company response: Continued monitoring of the situation and readying of communications plan.

Phase 6: Outbreak has adapted, and there are confirmed reports of an ongoing transmission of the outbreak to the general population.

Company response: Serious thought and discussion should be given to ramping up the crisis management teams; if the decision is made, immediately implement crisis management plans to ensure proper response and recovery in countries or regions that have been impacted.

employees are spaced apart, the better. Some experts recommend about three feet between participants.

Avoid having employees eating together, such as in company cafeterias or lunchrooms, will prove difficult unless employees are able to eat alone in their own space. If this is not possible, lunch breaks can be timed so as to reduce the numbers of people in the same place at one time by setting firm times. The same would apply for break rooms, in which collecting in groups should be discouraged. As with business travel, if meetings, training, and speaking engagements outside of the workplace are not required, these should be canceled or postponed. Make use of flex scheduling to reduce the number of employees on site at any given time. Telecommuting, if at all possible, will assist you in these efforts and will provide employees with more comfort and the ability to check on loved ones or friends from their homes and lodging.

Strict communications should be made to employees, and the proper method of communicating by employees to their managers should be in place. If employees are feeling sick, they should not be at work. Ensure this is communicated clearly and multilingually. Employees who get sick at work should report this right away and should be sent home with proper instructions and resources or references, including where to go for help. If any employees have worked immediately around other employees who call in or go home sick, you should pass along how they should be mindful of feeling any symptoms and the information about where to get treated if necessary.

RESPONSE METHODOLOGY OVERVIEW

Your corporate team of crisis management and response should consist of your crisis management team and your overarching management center, which would be the emergency operations center. Supporting the entire mechanism are the local crisis management teams with the various members in support functions. All functions and processes should be clearly spelled out in your crisis management plan. The crisis management team is designed to assist in immediate response to on-site emergencies. This team provides whatever support is necessary and ensures that these situations are managed effectively and efficiently. If the situation is deemed to be severe enough, the crisis management team would ask that the corporate emergency operations center be convened and stood up. The emergency operations center is dually charged with evaluating the response to emergency situations and events and assessing what additional resources are required or steps to be taken. It provides the vehicle or conduit for communicating the needs of the crisis management team to the rest of the company. Major decisions affecting the policies, direction, and operations of the corporation are made via the emergency operations center with the support and involvement of senior management. Successful operation of the emergency operations center will require continuous and effective communications with all business divisions and senior management contained within each segment. Emergency operations centers require continuous staffing and must be staffed as quickly as possible. In the event that first-line members are unable to participate or continue, backups and alternates must be ready and equipped to step in. Clearly spelled out roles, leadership, and functions must be in writing and drilled in advance with tabletop exercises. One note of caution: There can only be one emergency operations center leader.

Your divisions or business units should have identified recovery teams of specialists designated to attend to the functions required to get the operations back on track. These teams will have backups and alternates for each primary member. Their functions include assessing any additional needs for recovery, which would then be relayed to the senior management of each division and then on to the emergency operations center. Think of the emergency operations center as the mother ship, providing resources that can be airdropped to whomever is in need.

Good luck.

As important as pandemic plans are, another resource that should not be overlooked includes that of having your professionals visit qualified

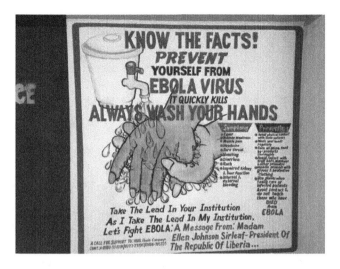

Figure 9.1 *Pandemic* is not a word many schoolchildren or adults were familiar with a few years ago. Planning for pandemic should now be familiar for crisis managers. (Courtesy of Center for Disease Control, https://www.google.com/search ?q=CDC+photos+from+Africa+hand+washing&biw=1920&bih=963&tbm=isch &tbo=u&source=univ&sa=X&ved=0ahUKEwiQ65S7q9fKAhUrx4MKHafAAK8Qs AQIIw#tbm=isch&q=CDC+free+photos+ebola&imgrc=ljYavqsfnRy7iM%3A.)

health care professionals who deal with preparing individuals who are preparing to travel to far-flung reaches of the globe. Travel vaccination specialists provide travelers with pretrip briefings on everything from keeping healthy wherever they are traveling to what vaccinations are suggested, recommended, or required. Such clinics and specialists can recommend prophylactic care for travelers (Figure 9.1).

REFERENCE

Engel, Mary. New bird flu cases revive fear of human pandemic. *LA Times*, January 4, 2009.

10

Crisis in the Workplace
Violence and Bullying

The crisis of today is the joke of tomorrow.

H. G. Wells

People being violent toward others in the workplace is not a twenty-first or even a twentieth-century development. Violence in the workplace has been around since cavemen grouped together to break rocks. According to the Bible, Jesus entered the temple and overturned the tables and wares and chased away the merchants and customers.

Was he *acting out* in the workplace? Was he an *active assailant*? Did Jesus *just snap*—to use the popular vernacular? In feudal Japan, the term *hostile takeover* meant a group of samurai had attacked and defeated a rival. *Bringing in consultants* referred to the use of ninja to inflict *market pressure* or *leverage*. In the China of the twenty-first century, much as in the first century, workers might surround a factory or work site and hold the managers or owners hostage or worse while they seek to have their demands and grievances addressed.

Wherever people gather together to work—in every culture and every country on Earth—there exists the likelihood of violence taking place. Add to the work mix various cultures, religions, nationalities, values, norms, behaviors, lifestyles, and tolerances and combine these with life stressors such as job cuts, layoffs, plant closings, acquisitions and mergers, salary freezes and cuts, terminations, outsourcing, divorce, breakups, boyfriend or girlfriend issues, loss of loved ones, health concerns, or substance abuse, and sparks may quickly become raging wildfires.

Policies and procedures can be effective means of first identifying and dealing with situations before they turn violent and become crises. By considering what is going on with the interpersonal relations among workers and each other or workers and management, the tide against a violent act might be stemmed. Situations often have two sides; the side that is presented by the evidence may seem clear, but what has led to this action or reaction? What is at the root of the difficulty? Consider the female employee who reported being harassed by a particular male coworker numerous times to her supervisor. The behavior consists of the male employee making obscene gestures and sounds directed at her in the presence of others. Management has failed to act quickly or appropriately, and the woman is pegged a *troublemaker* or *itching for a lawsuit* or *she dresses like she wants the attention*. The actions by the male worker are deemed to be normal give and take between male and female members of the workforce. Then, one day, she and the male coworker find themselves alone in the box-folding room performing normal duties, and he grabs her hard by the ankle as they are ascending a stairway. She breaks free and throws a box cutter at him, which sticks in his chest. The police and paramedics arrive to stretcher the man away as he is gasping for air from a collapsed lung and walk the female employee out of the plant in handcuffs. But who is to blame? Who was the attacker? Who is the perpetrator, and who is the victim? What could have and should have been done differently? What are the liabilities for the company for not having a program and policies in place to deal with such things taking place?

According to the Bureau of Labor Statistics in 2012, of the 767 US workers who were victims of violence in the workplace, 463 were homicides and 225 were suicides. Eighty-one percent of the homicides were shootings, and in the case of workplace suicides, the percentage of those who died by gunshot was 48%. Of the 2012 total of 338 women killed in the workplace, 29% died as a result of homicide (Bureau of Labor Statistics, 2013).

What statistics and many studies don't take into account are the unreported instances of workplace violence, both physical and the nonphysical—what some might call *practical jokes* or *taunting*, which, in fact, is more akin to *bullying*. As in the case of students who have endured bullying and taunting to the point at which they decide they will no longer be the victim and will instead seek out their own victims, so have employees taken matters into their own hands.

What government agencies and statistics don't track is the number of companies that wait until an extreme or severe incident of workplace violence takes place before developing or seriously considering a workplace violence plan. As stated, workplace violence plans should not just be thought of as a plan to be carried out once an incident takes place. Such a plan is, in fact, a means of predetermining or identifying potential employee areas of violence and dealing with them effectively in a manner and method that might prevent or predict a violent occurrence down the road. No one can know how many incidents of workplace violence might be prevented by the proper application of counseling or discipline upon an employee before he or she inflicts violence upon a coworker.

Of equal and appropriate mention is the necessity of employees to feel comfortable and obligated to report to their supervisor or manager security issues they are experiencing that might affect their workplace. These situations include violent or abusive relationships in which a current or former boyfriend, girlfriend, spouse, etc., has harmed or threatened them and the potential of a violent incident or harassment to exist at their place of employment. Any outside threats that might be manifested upon individuals in the workplace must be reported to the appropriate levels of management, which must act on these accordingly.

Businesses must have a policy that is enforced, communicated, and touted from senior management on down through the organization against bullying and violent behavior. Employees are encouraged to report any harassment, threats of intimidation or acts of violence (verbal or physical), concerns of potential violence, or violent behavior to their supervisor. Persons engaging in such acts are subject to sanctions and disciplinary measures up to and possibly including discharge of employment. In addition, the possession of firearms at work should be strictly prohibited.

Organizations must have mechanisms and protocols in place for the reporting of threats and the immediate communication of incidents taking place. Overheard threats or comments must be first reported to a supervisor or manager or someone in human resources. If an organization has a workplace violence committee or group or an employee assistance plan helpline, these methods must be communicated to employees as valid means of communicating concerns. Limiting the number of locations or setting up any barriers to threats being communicated overlooks the fact that unhappy employees often express dissatisfaction or make comments or verbalize threats in advance of actions taken.

SAMPLE WORKPLACE VIOLENCE
RESPONSE AND PREVENTION PLAN

The following is an outline of XYZ Corporation's workplace violence response plan. Decisions for implementing any or all of the following measures will be made jointly by the workplace violence committee and XYZ Corporation management with the input of the affected individuals when possible.

Before action can be taken, the threat must be reported. All threats and harassment should be taken seriously. Although we do not want to overreact, we must not ignore potential situations either. Once a situation is reported, as a supervisor, you will work with the committee to carry out the following response plan:

1. If the committee believes that a workplace violence incident is reasonably possible, the following precautions should be taken:
   a. Contact security.
   b. Gather all available information about the potential offender:
      i. Name.
      ii. Address/phone number.
      iii. Date of birth, social security number.
      iv. Vehicle description and license plate number.
      v. Personal information and photograph, marital status, children, financial status, names of friends, relatives, coworkers.
      vi. Check prior criminal record and civil records.
   c. Determine potential targets of violent acts and establish level of security for them.

   The following actions may be selected at the discretion of the committee and management:
      i. Twenty-four-hour watch on home of targeted employee.
      ii. Guards at work entrances.
      iii. Parking privileges for employee(s) near building entrances.
      iv. Send targeted employee(s) away from the area for a short period.

108

2. If a direct or overt threat of workplace violence is made or if an incident appears imminent, implement checklist (I) and do the following:
   a. Alert security-related employees:
      i. Receptionist.
      ii. First, second, and third shifts.
      iii. All various departmental shifts.
      iv. If agreed upon by the committee and management, a statement may be made to employees in an area where an incident could occur.
      v. Data security (to limit computer access and monitor) if necessary.
   b. Contact local police.
   c. Contact legal department for legal assistance, restraining order, and/or filing of charges if necessary.
   d. Distribute photograph of potentially violent individual (access card photo) to all security shifts.
   e. Contact employee assistance program (EAP) (does your EAP handle this?) and provide them with information about the individual so that they can estimate his or her potential for violence.

      In addition, the following actions may be selected at the discretion of the committee and the management:
      i. Place threatening individual under surveillance.
      ii. Counsel targets on security precautions.
      iii. Provide security service to potential target.
3. During a workplace violence incident:
   a. A crisis manager will be assigned (the security manager will be the primary crisis manager) followed by the
      i. Security coordinator.
      ii. Vice president, corporate operations.
      iii. Vice president of human resources.

      The crisis manager will coordinate all actions with outside authorities and XYZ Corporation employees. The crisis manager should go to a safe area or outside the building in a protected location to work with local authorities/police.

b. The director of corporate communications or his or her delegated staff will coordinate all communications with the press. At no time during an incident shall the press be permitted on XYZ Corporation (private) property. The communications department will use all available resources (police on site, etc.) to keep press off company property.

c. The crisis manager or the local authorities may use the public address system to warn employees about what is taking place and what to do.

   Specific communications may include the following:
   i. Evacuate the building believed to be the location of the attacker, if known.
   ii. Take cover under furniture, etc.
   iii. Specific details of the attack or attacker.

4. Postincident recovery:

   a. Depending on the magnitude and effect of a workplace violence incident, some or all employees may be dismissed for the day or longer.

   b. Contacts will be retrieved to notify family members of any injured or deceased employee(s).

   c. If the facility is closed as the result of an incident, individual department managers will be apprised of the situation and told when employees may report back to work. Department managers will maintain home phone numbers of employees and contact them with this information. The phone list should be kept at home so that it is available if the facility is closed.

   d. Any damage to the property resulting from the incident will be repaired immediately after authorities approve. Property operations will be responsible for renovation of the facility prior to reopening. The intent will be to erase all traces of the incident and, to some extent, change the environment enough to minimize reminders to employees returning to work. The renovation should be completed as rapidly as possible so the facility can be reopened quickly.

e. Depending on the magnitude of an incident, within 24 hours after an incident, XYZ Corporation's EAP may conduct an incident debriefing for affected employees. This may be followed a week later with a second debriefing.

f. An additional debriefing may be conducted for all other interested employees within 48 hours of an incident.

g. The crisis manager is responsible for a complete documentation of the incident, including all dates and times. Copies will be provided to XYZ Corporation's district manager, deputy district manager, general counsel, human resources officer, human resources supervisor, and public information officer.

Of course, the time has long since passed for employees or supervisors to overlook verbal messages by employees that can be construed as threats. Everyone has bad days, but threats and altercations, such as acting out like a child, must be corrected. Often issues concerning interrelationships between coworkers or managers and supervised employees can and are diffused short of a violent outbreak or the loss of an employee's job. As mentioned, a top-down approach to an effective workplace violence program is necessary because it works toward assuring employees that the company takes the matter seriously. It is important, and some would argue critical, that employees understand that there will be no adverse actions taken against anyone who reports incidents of harassment or bullying. And, to the extent possible, all such reporting will be treated in strict confidence.

When a supervisor, manager, human resources specialist, or a member of a workplace violence committee or an Employee Assistance Program (EAP) helpline call taker are informed of a threat or an incident, he or she should gather all pertinent information regarding the threat, incident, or observation. Such information includes names, dates, locations, the type of threat (or bullying), details of the threat, and names of any witnesses. The reported information must be documented, and an immediate investigation must be launched. All witnesses and those providing information must be treated with respect. The person who has been reported as exhibiting concerning behavior must be treated with respect. Those investigating must keep any personal biases and judgments in check, and if they

111

are unable to do so, another investigator must step in. All sides must be heard and be allowed to provide their observations, details, and opinions. If the information leads the investigator to determine the reported acts or behavior actually took place, immediate actions must be taken, such as recommendations for persons to have counseling, reassignment of personnel, disciplinary actions, or dismissal.

SPECIAL NOTE ON EMPLOYMENT TERMINATIONS

Loss of employment may be traumatizing. Employees should be treated with dignity during this often painful process. Include your HR officer in the termination meeting to help support your action. In all cases, notify the security officer and retrieve all company property, access cards and keys from the employee. Consideration should be given to changing locks. If the employee is threatening or abusive, call security. The police may be called to stand by as a precaution in extreme situations.

REFERENCE

Bureau of Labor Statistics. National census of fatal occupational injuries in 2012, http://www.bls.gov/iif/, 2013.

11

Demonstrations, Protests, Work Stoppages, Plant Seizures, and Strikes

These are times that try men's souls. The summer soldier and the sunshine patriot will, in this crisis, shrink from the service of their country.

Thomas Paine

Demonstrations and protests vary around the world. Sometimes, a perceived slight at work becomes a labor dispute, which leads to strikes against a company's operations and facilities. In some areas, workers might rally against supervision and management and, in effect, take plants and managers hostage. At times, demonstrations and protests are not directed specifically at the corporation or facility but against the country from which the corporation hails. At times, protests might not have any agenda at all except anarchist goals and diatribes. Political rallies, protests, and demonstrations may evolve quickly or have a slow burn of intensity. Government and police forces may force peaceful demonstrations to turn violent through their actions. Cultural and ethnic differences may cause tempers and hostilities to flare.

All around the world, from Kansas City to Cairo, businesses and employees are susceptible to and at risk from gatherings of people for political, social, and other collective reasons. As has been witnessed in the Middle East with the Arab Spring of 2011 and similar occurrences, people can be injured, property destroyed, and governments toppled by demonstrators and protestors. Businesses might merely be inconvenienced by traffic jams and blocked infrastructure during protests. In some cases, however, governments—in reaction to demonstrations and demonstrators—might employ widespread violence, disrupt telecommunications and commerce, close banks and government offices, implement curfews, or other severe retaliatory measures. Demonstrations might turn on foreigners or foreign-owned businesses.

Organizations in at-risk areas or industries must prepare for the minor and major crises that may erupt given demonstrations, protests, strikes, or riots.

The following information is intended as a basis for minor to major labor disturbances and is applicable and usable for demonstrations and protests in general. When dealing with intense hostilities and demonstrations in foreign high-risk areas, government and private sector security consultations would be necessary to bolster plans and mitigation.

Special circumstances require special planning and preparation. Preparation for the potential of mass strikes and demonstrations may take an inordinate amount of time and attention to detail. There are some things to look for among those gathering in protest and those grouping for the purpose of hearing speakers or other circumstances. There are some concerns and observations that will be critical to successfully planning and preparing. First, understanding needs to be acquired surrounding the dynamics and workings of group mind sets.

Political or issue-minded groups of protestors are rarely spontaneous or unplanned. Groups might have organizers or representatives present on the scene or during preplanning sessions, and these people will instruct those participating on how to conduct themselves. This coaching will include how to react or act toward the media, the press, military, government representatives, opposing groups, and others. You should anticipate damage to the vehicles of your company or corporation if driving in or around the demonstrators. Vehicles may be obstructed by barriers or numbers of people or by persons walking or standing in front of vehicles. Participants will feign injuries by brushing against or appearing to be struck by moving vehicles. Methods of damage to tires and vehicles will include roadway nails, welded spike tire shredders, glass and car scratching, spray painting, tire cutting, denting from thrown objects, spitting on vehicles, throwing sugar water on vehicles, and throwing flammable liquids. Parked or moving vehicles known to belong to companies, corporations, or employees will be targeted. During the initial and perhaps ongoing stages of protest and demonstration, there may be use of intoxicants, which may occur if the protestors have vehicles nearby at night. The discharging of firearms during the night may take place. Any employees or persons crossing into the property will be targeted for obscenities and challenged to engage in violence. The period of late evening and early morning presents the greatest risk of harassing behavior.

Telephonic or e-mailed, texted, mailed or tweeted bomb threats may be directed at the company. Suspicious packages must be reported to law enforcement. Management or other employees may receive telephone or other forms of threats. Any corporate security personnel will be harassed. From the outset, the initial protest activities may be similar to a campus festival complete with speakers and possibly music. As mentioned, initially such gatherings may be more of a rowdy party. Protestors may exhibit an indestructible attitude, which has been instigated by political, social, or religious representatives. Violence-prone protestors often are able to provoke normally calm employees. These individuals are generally *hard core* protestors who are more prone to violence. Activities described as being directed against employees will also be focused upon vendors or contractors attempting ingress or egress. The initial protest euphoria will generally subside in a few weeks.

Security and management should be aware of observations or reports of protestors or demonstrators accumulating or carrying rocks, bricks, sticks, or bottles, which could be used for bludgeoning or throwing. Others may be seen carrying baseball bats, tire irons, knives, swords, hammers, or rebar. Bricks or stones may be observed being prestaged in piles for throwing. Protestors carrying spray paint cans are an indication of the intent to spray paint signs and buildings. Demonstrators may be observed carrying nails or caltrops/cheval traps for the purposes of damaging and deflating vehicle tires. Demonstrators may be carrying bolt cutters for the purpose of cutting gate padlocks or cutting holes in fencing. Fireworks, flares, smoke bombs, homemade and improvised devices, or Molotov cocktails may be seen in the crowds.

Often, demonstrators carrying out violent acts will change articles of clothing in order to thwart law enforcement and government observers from identifying them for detainment or arrest. Gas masks provide similar concealment and protection from smoke or chemical agents used by authorities. Trash-can lids or other types of metal or plastic shields may be carried by those seeking to confront security or police forces. Trash cans, mailboxes, newsstands, and bicycle racks may be used for barricading demonstrators from authorities.

Security and management will need to attempt close coordination and cooperation with local law enforcement and/or government agencies to protect corporate employees. Special planning needs to be directed at executive protection, incident reporting, contracting security services, and conducting security awareness training for employees.

In order to adequately document violations of local laws, it is imperative that trained personnel capable of using video and still photography be available to respond to locations for the purpose of documenting any violations or destruction of property.

Camcorders have proven to be the preferred method of documenting protest activities. This is due to their mobility and flexibility. Camcorders record the language and threats used as well as the act.

Objectives of protest documentation:

a. Prosecution of criminal violators.
b. Developing and preserving evidence of ongoing misconduct, thus enabling the company to obtain legal assistance, limiting the activities of protestors.
c. Developing and preserving evidence of protest misconduct.
d. Documenting activities of company employees and guards. Protestors will often make false claims of assault, harassment, etc., toward company employees, agents, and customers.
e. Serve as a preventative tool in that individuals prone to commit illegal acts are more reluctant to do so when they are aware they are being filmed.

Management must be informed of anticipated protest activities and advised accordingly of security requirements and/or operational charges. Employees must be instructed as to their expected conduct, incident reporting, procedures, and documentation measures.

Physical security enhancements must be enacted at residences of management members that may include the following:

- Improved lighting, including motion lighting
- Deadbolt locks on doors with a minimum inch and a half throw bolt
- Securing windows by drilling and pinning sashes or installing security locks
- Using timer lights when away from the residence
- Parking vehicles inside of garages
- Testing alarm systems or installing alarm systems, including alarm contacts on all doors and windows (or motion detectors within windows)

- Duress code emergency notification button on alarm panel
- Battery backup of alarm system
- Burying or shielding telephone lines or installing line loss alarm notification
- Caller ID for telephones
- Using a telephone recorder and allowing the recorder to answer the telephone
- Program speed dial *911* into telephones
- Cellular telephone for home telephone backup and vehicle assistance
- Varying routes to work
- Taking security measures if persons believe they are being followed
- Advising trusted neighbors to watch residence
- Request law enforcement patrol
- Survey exterior of home before exiting vehicle to enter home or enter vehicle
- Report any unusual or suspicious activities to law enforcement and security manager immediately

A corporate protest command needs to be implemented in the country, at the protest location, and back at HQ. The protest command center (PCC) will be based at the main office with 24-hour international telephone capabilities and will be staffed effective around the clock should a protest take place. The PCC will be staffed 24 hours a day. Security management may be provided by in-house security, consultants, contract security, off-duty police officers, and others as required or allowed.

During a protest, it is critical that serious matters be dealt with effectively and quickly. The PCC should be contacted if a member of management cannot be located. Every officer, department, and regional, area, or branch manager must be made available to be reached during this labor situation.

In the event that protestors or demonstrators attempt to block ingress or egress from the facility by placing vehicles or objects at entrances, the following sequence should be followed:

a. Video documentation.
b. Notification of police department, military, government and request that the vehicle(s) or object(s) be towed or removed.
c. If there is no police response to a towing or removal request, and with company management approval, towing companies or other resources may be contacted.

Every effort will be made to document such activity with camcorders while ensuring the following sequence is initiated: (1) removing company employees to an area of safety if necessary; (2) notifying police, fire, emergency medical response—if required—and ensuring that police reports are made of incidents; (3) preserving evidence (i.e., recovered nails, spikes, statements, etc.) and maintaining chain of custody; (4) obtaining written statements from victims and witnesses; (5) obtaining a police report; (6) notifying company management of the incident; and (7) logging the sequence of events and responses in a daily log book.

Key facility and corporate contact telephone numbers, e-mail addresses, and other contact information needs to be available to the PCC and other team members at all times. There must be addresses, maps, and directions to homes or lodging.

It may be necessary to work with government or law enforcement liaison to determine availability of parking areas if laws permit the use of off-duty police officers. It would be beneficial to advise local prosecutors' offices and emergency responders. Local law enforcement must be continually updated as to developments that may affect the duration, length, or extent of the protest or demonstration.

Mobile lighting unit(s) or the ability to obtain units will be useful in the case of areas with poor lighting or power outages. Property lines must be established and legally defensible (clearly marked with spray paint on paved surfaces and in the presence of law enforcement), such as a snow fence on paved and other areas, if necessary, and/or placing PRIVATE PROPERTY—NO TRESPASSING signs along the fence line and in front of the building(s).

Repairs of the fence line should take place by re-strapping and replacing three-strand barbed wire. If appropriate, concertina or razor wire may be added for high-security fencing concerns. It is recommended that locks to all critical operational and equipment areas be rekeyed with high-security locks and maintained as continuously locked at all times. These areas include telephone rooms, computer rooms, engineering and equipment areas, human resources records, and gate locks. All gates must be secured to eliminate gaps. All exterior doors with key hardware must be rekeyed. If time allows, all exterior doors should be equipped with alarm contacts. Overhead doors must be padlocked when not in use. Keys must be checked out, controlled, and audited.

Closed-circuit television cameras and monitors must be maintained or improved for optimum performance. Videotapes of activities prior to and during the strike must be collected and maintained in a secure location by management. Cameras should be added to sensitive areas.

For windows, three-quarter-inch plywood cutouts for front windows (or Plexiglas) will protect windows from projectiles. In addition, awareness training should take place for all management and administrative employees.

Lighting should be improved to add 500- or 1000-watt lighting near the main gate. There needs to be a determined effort to plan the amount of work in process or at deadline along with a determination of production capacity and scheduling with the available work force. Determine any alternative producers to assist with production to meet the needs of sales. What maintenance concerns are there for heating, cooling, power generation, water, etc.?

During protest and demonstration activities, travel and outside purchases must be given special attention. General and field travel as well as outside purchases should be eliminated or minimized, and equipment deliveries should be delayed if possible.

Provision will be made for accessing vendors or deliveries and pickups at the facility. Prior notice must be given to vendors when possible to describe the labor situation and expected conduct of delivery or pick-up personnel. Notify trash haulers and delivery services, such as UPS and FedEx. Provision will be made for access for construction personnel in the facility only if necessary. The press should be politely directed to contact the media designees or the plant or facility manager. If asked for a statement, the standard reply should be, "You will need to speak with our media representatives." The plant or facility manager must approve all communications.

Utilize any slow and non-busy security time for training, catching up on projects, etc.

Paychecks will be mailed or electronically deposited for those not reporting to work due to the protest. Only the plant or facility manager may give the official notice at the end of the protest or shutdown. Recall procedures will be issued by the appropriate officer.

When conditions warrant, the protest or demonstration response team needs to be activated by contacting members and giving them the preassigned time and location for meeting. If conditions warrant, an alternate meeting site should be activated. Arrange for transportation of team members if conditions are unsafe for operating motor vehicles. The team should discuss operations and deployment and the types of equipment to be disbursed. The security team then deploys and takes up positions. Crisis mode access control and monitoring procedures will be initiated, and any special transportation requirements put in effect.

Planning and discussion needs to take place surrounding who will be in charge of security services as to the contract security provider; security consultants, if any; and who directs the corporate security functions and response. Communications will be required with these persons 24 hours a day. Security management and officers will coordinate their presence with company management.

It will be the responsibility of security officers to ensure proper access control procedures are followed and maintained. Security will be responsible for the protection of employees and assets and for coordinating emergency response and incident response procedures. Security will assume duties, including recording, documentation, and investigation of incidents and accidents. Security will maintain government and law enforcement liaison. Security will be in charge of the supervision of contract security forces. Contract security will be utilized for main gate coverage and perimeter patrol of critical areas, such as the main gate and the interior perimeter; for shuttle driving and backup; and for parking pickup locations if necessary. Such officers will be utilized for residence patrol.

Contact should be made with local police, fire, and emergency medical agencies prior to any expected protest. A primary contact should be established with company security designees. Efforts should be undertaken to establish a method for quick identification of vehicles and owners through license number verification.

Safety professionals will ensure that any radio or cell phone communication requirements during the protest or demonstrations are met and will establish contact with a telephone service provider to ensure that the lines are protected and secure and to coordinate with the phone company to provide tracing services for harassing phone calls at the plant or managers' homes. Recorders should be placed on those phones through which calls will be routed.

Legal resources need to be at the ready with corporate and local country counsel on notice. Counsel will make contact with local prosecutors. If misconduct is evident, it is the management's intent to bring charges. There is a need to develop procedure or policy for disciplinary action against employees engaged in protest or misconduct. Legal counsel must give an opinion on property line boundaries where protestors can form areas of protest lines.

If a pickup point is to be utilized for the transportation of employees to and from facilities, a list must be prepared indicating the names of those persons to be picked up to ride the shuttle vehicle. As each employee enters the shuttle, his or her name must be checked off.

Employees will be met at the shuttle vehicle by a security representative, who will request that identification be produced prior to employees boarding. (This may be waived if no replacements are transported.)

A security representative will accompany the employees to and from the facility. Boarding procedures will be repeated at the plant prior to reboarding for transport to the pick-up locations. Departure and loading schedules must be established and strictly maintained. Carpooling is strongly recommended to off-site parking.

The shuttle vehicle will pick up employees at a designated site and drive to the facility. The shuttle will enter the main gate. The gate will remain closed until the shuttle approaches. Radio communication from the shuttle will alert security personnel of their arrival. Depending on the situation, an alternative gate may be used. The gate will remain open only long enough to allow the shuttle vehicle ingress and egress. Employees will disembark and load at a side entrance away from the view of protestors. All employees will enter the facility through the north maintenance door to the training room. The employees will then proceed through the training room to the maintenance employee locker room. The employees will exit the maintenance employee locker room into the east hallway. The employees will then proceed to the second floor of the facility by utilizing the central staircase. Employees will be required to wear identification badges while on company property. Access into restricted or rekeyed areas will require issuance of numbered keys to authorized employees. Key audit procedures must be maintained.

All vehicles must enter and exit the employee parking lot through the main gate entrance. Employees driving into the lot must keep their windows rolled up and doors locked. Employees must not stop near the protest line while entering or exiting the parking lot. Employees are prohibited from bringing alcoholic beverages or controlled substances onto company property. Employees are prohibited from bringing firearms or other weapons onto company property. Employees must wait inside of their vehicles until the shuttle van picks up employees for transportation and await transportation from the plant to the parking lot. Employees must not speak to or engage in any harassment directed toward protestors. Such harassment includes use of profanity, obscene gestures, threats, or taunting of any manner.

Employees who engage in threatening or taunting or any unacceptable behavior will be subject to termination. Employees must report any harassment or threats they receive. Employees not adhering to any of the above requirements may be subject to termination.

Upon arrival at the main gate or other designated gate, visitors or vendors will be required to wait while the contact is notified. Once approval is granted, the name, company, time, and vehicle description must be recorded. Prior notice provided to security of the person or visitor arriving will facilitate a quicker entry. Any visitor, vendor, or delivery person granted entry must be met and escorted while on company property. The employee authorizing the visitor must notify security officers when the visitor is exiting the property. The exit time must be recorded. Vendors doing business with the company on a routine basis must be advised of the situation and their expected conduct.

Unusual activity must be reported to your local police departments. Unusual activity would include the following:

- Known or strange cars driving past your residence or parking outside your residence
- Known or strange persons walking past or loitering at your residence
- Encounters with strange or known persons at public places, such as grocery stores, malls, etc., where threats are made
- Strange or obscene, threatening, or harassing telephone calls to your residence or relatives
- Receiving strange packages, letters, or harassing and threatening mail

Any protestor who engages in any harassing, threatening, abusive, destructive, or intimidating behavior perpetrated upon any employee or vendor of the company living in any city is engaging in criminal activity.

After you have notified law enforcement, contact any investigator on duty to report the incident.

Do not talk about the protest with persons in public places. Do not talk to protestors. If you are questioned about your employment with the company or about the protest, consider this an attempt to harass or threaten you and walk away—get out of the situation. Avoid places where protestors are known to congregate or frequent. Do not wear apparel that indicates you are employed with the company.

If your vehicle is followed by persons you believe to be protestors, utilize a cellular telephone to contact the police department. Obtain the license number and vehicle description if you may do so without jeopardizing your safety. Drive to your police department while the vehicle is following you, or drive into a public place, such as a fire station, drive-through bank, fast-food, etc., and request that law enforcement be contacted to report the incident. Keep doors and windows locked.

When you drive into the parking lot at the shuttle pick-up location, you will park along the back side of the lot. You will then wait alongside your car while a company shuttle vehicle picks you up to take you to the plant. At the conclusion of your shift, you will be picked up and driven back to your car. When you drive into or out of the lot, you must keep your windows up and your doors locked. Do not stop to talk to any protestors while you are driving into or out of the lot.

You must not engage in any conversation with protestors at any time. You must not make any obscene or threatening gestures toward any protestors at any time.

HANDLING BOMB THREATS

Emergency planning for the potential of bomb threats must be initiated. This includes caller ID for the main switchboard if available. Telephones used for receiving calls must be equipped with recording equipment. Check on any call-tracing capability with your phone provider. If a threat is received during business hours, the switchboard operator (or employee taking calls) will complete a bomb threat checklist form. The operator activates a tape recorder, and the call recipient notifies management. After doing so, the operator or recipient notifies the security director. The security director contacts the police department and requests a bomb dog be dispatched and directs responders. The security director then contacts the fire department to stand by. The security director initiates contacts with the Federal Bureau of Investigation (FBI), Legal Attache (LEGAT), Regional Security Officer (RSO) offices. The security director initiates call trace procedures and meets with management in the command center. The security director collects a bomb threat checklist form and any recordings to provide to law enforcement. If the decision is made to search or evacuate the facility, security personnel assist in the process of ensuring the interior is secured. Security officers hold all incoming traffic. The building exterior is searched and secured. The security director coordinates with management and law enforcement on issuing *all clear* and reoccupying the facility. The security director and management meet in the command center upon reoccupying the facility.

If a bomb threat is received after business hours and the facility or facilities are occupied, the call recipient completes the bomb threat checklist form and notifies security personnel or the director, and the same procedures are followed. If a bomb threat is received after business hours and the facility or facilities are unoccupied, the call recipient completes the bomb threat checklist form and notifies the security director. The security director/personnel pages the facility or facilities and repeats three times, "May I have your attention please. Please proceed to security muster points." The security director and personnel respond to move persons to these security muster locations. The security director contacts police department emergency number and requests a bomb dog be dispatched and directs responders after which the security director initiates call trace procedures.

Bomb threats and dealing with bombs require specific planning and procedures. Bomb threats come in a variety of forms as indicated: telephonic or electronic, sometimes merely scribbled on a mirror. Brick-and-mortar facilities require procedures geared toward preventing access to those who would wish to plant bombs. Search and evacuation are primary concerns for such institutions. In areas plagued by improvised explosive devices, route planning and intelligence are equally as critical.

BOMB THREAT PROCEDURES

To handle bomb threats when a telephonic threat is received, the caller should be kept on the phone as long as possible. The bomb threat caller is the best source of information about the bomb. The caller should be asked to repeat the message. Every word spoken must be written down. If the caller does not indicate where the bomb is located or the time the bomb will explode, make sure to ask these questions. The caller should be advised that the building or facilities are occupied and that detonating a bomb could result in the death or serious injury of innocent persons. While listening and speaking with the caller, special attention must be paid to any background noises or sounds heard from the caller's location, such as music playing, machinery running, traffic or other location noises—anything that might provide a clue to their location. Listen to the male or female voice closely, does he or she sound calm, frightened, slurring, or excited, and is there an accent or some type of impediment? While noticing all of these special circumstances, complete the bomb threat checklist. When the call and the form are completed, please provide the form to security and make yourself available for any subsequent interviews.

When a written, mailed, e-mailed, or electronically received threat or suspicious package arrives, notify security immediately and save all materials, including any envelopes or containers. Further handling of these items must be avoided.

If a suspicious package is observed, it must not be moved or touched.

Specific actions should be taken when a bomb threat is called in. One crucial action in this situation is the call recipient completing a bomb threat checklist form and notifying security. Security will notify the appropriate member of management and make any necessary additional first responder contacts. Management will meet the initial call recipient in a conference room or private room and will interview the call receiver in order to determine the next course of action to take. The bomb threat checklist will provide useful information and will be reviewed and discussed.

Management will make its decisions based upon factors such as if the caller is an adult. An adult caller is deemed to have more capabilities as opposed to a younger person who might want out of school on the first warm spring day, for example. Did the caller give a specific time of detonation? A specific location? Management would more sensibly decide if there would be adequate time to conduct a search in such area, such as a locker room versus an auditorium. By making statements such as, "The bomb is in the C301 training room," if one actually exists, further credibility is ascertained. The caller may state a reason for planting a device, political goals or a monetary aim, which adds some concern. It may seem impossible, but some callers actually identify themselves and, more often, a group to which they are associated.

If the caller states that the time of detonation is 30 minutes or less and has indicated a specific location of the bomb and the reason for placing the device, evacuation must proceed immediately. If the answers are *no* to these factors indicated, the caller's comments must be evaluated, and an investigation or search must commence.

In either case, the police and authorities MUST be contacted IMMEDIATELY.

Concerning evacuation, in the absence of the plant manager, a designated member of management will authorize and conduct the evacuation procedure. A trained, volunteer bomb search team may be deployed while other employees evacuate. During the search, two-way radios and cell phones must be turned off. An overhead paging system or desk phones may be utilized. As indicated, employees will utilize routes and assemble at designated collection points. Team members assist evacuation. The search team will require flashlights, stickers or electrical tape, blueprints of the facility, and a roster of phone numbers, including home phone numbers.

The following is a suggested course of action and duties for members of the bomb threat response team.

Responsibility	Action
Security	Investigates and confers regarding threat
	Initiates emergency contacts
Officers	Directs emergency responders
	Holds and stages all vehicle and pedestrian traffic with the exception of emergency responders
Evacuation team	Using voice commands, evacuate all employees to the designated parking area
	Position to ensure a safe exit and reentry of the facility
	Sweeps the area to ensure all are accounted for, does a head count at the collection area, and uses a phone to advise the command center when evacuation is completed
Search team	Conduct a search, beginning with the most accessible areas
	Use the phone to communicate and to advise when search is completed
	Evacuate no later than 15 minutes prior to detonation time
	Assemble in preassigned areas and with team captain
All employees, visitors, vendors	Leave building through exits as designated by the evacuation team
	Wait for further instructions
Incoming visitors and vendors	Held at front gate area
	Wait for further instructions
Maintenance employees	Shut off main gas valve and fuel lines at main valve
	Ensure fire system is operational
	Search areas, such as HVAC or other equipment locations
	Shut down appropriate equipment
	Evacuate with search teams
	Do not use radios
Member of management	Makes decision to evacuate
	Remains while building is occupied
	Receives updates on search and evacuation teams

The following search technique is based on the use of a two-person search team. There are many minor variations possible in searching an area. The following contains only the basic techniques.

When the two-person search team enters the area to be searched, they should first move to various parts of the area and stand quietly with their eyes closed and listen for a clockwork device. Frequently, a clockwork mechanism can be quickly detected without the use of special equipment.

Even if no clockwork mechanism is detected, the team is now aware of the background noise level within the area itself.

Background noise or transferred sound is always disturbing during a building search. If a ticking sound is heard but cannot be located, one might become unnerved. The ticking sound may come from an unbalanced air conditioner fan several floors away or from a dripping sink down the hall. Sound will transfer through air conditioning ducts, along water pipes, and through walls. Background noise may also include outside traffic sounds, rain, and wind.

The individual in charge of the area searching team should look around the area and determine how it is to be divided for searching and to what height the first searching sweep should extend. The first searching sweep will cover all items resting on the floor up to the selected height.

The area should be divided into two virtually equal parts. The equal division should be based on the number and type of objects to be searched and not on the size of the area. An imaginary line is then drawn between two objects and understood by both team members.

FIRST AREA SEARCHING SWEEP

Look at the furniture or objects in the area and determine the average height of the majority of items resting on the floor. In an average room, this height usually includes table or desktops and chair backs. The first searching height usually covers the items in the area up to hip height.

After the area has been divided and a searching height has been selected, both individuals go to one end of the area division line and start from a back-to-back position. This is the starting point, and the same point will be used on each successive searching sweep. Each person now starts searching his or her way around the area, working toward the other person, checking all items resting on the floor around the wall area of a room. When the two individuals meet, they will have completed a *perimeter sweep*. They should then work together and check all items in the middle of the area up to the selected hip height, including the floor under rugs or mats. This first searching sweep should also include those items that may be mounted on or in walls, such as air conditioning ducts, baseboard heaters, and built-in wall bookcases if these fixtures are below hip height.

The first searching sweep usually consumes the most time and effort. During all the searching sweeps, electronic or medical stethoscopes might be used on walls, furniture items, and floors.

SECOND AREA SEARCHING SWEEP

The individual in charge again looks at the furniture or objects in the area and determines the height of the second searching sweep.

This height is usually from the hip to the chin or top of the head. The two persons return to the starting point and repeat the searching technique at the second selected searching height. This sweep usually covers pictures hanging on the walls, built-in bookcases, and tall table lamps.

THIRD AREA SEARCHING SWEEP

When the second searching sweep is completed, the person in charge again determines the next searching height, usually from the chin or top of the head up to the ceiling. The third sweep is then made. This sweep usually covers high mounted air conditioning ducts and hanging light fixtures.

FOURTH AREA SEARCHING SWEEP

If the area has a false or suspended ceiling, the fourth sweep involves investigation of this area. Check flush or ceiling-mounted light fixtures, air conditioning or ventilation ducts, sound or speaker systems, electrical wiring, and structural frame members.

Utilize a sign or agreed upon marking (such as a piece of green duct tape) to indicate that a room or area has been searched. A piece of tape should be placed on the floor across the entries to searched areas or on the doorjamb approximately two feet above floor level.

The area searching technique can be expanded. The same basic technique can be applied to search any area.

In conclusion, the following steps should be taken in a search for an explosive device:

1. Divide the area and select a search height.
2. Start from the bottom and work up.
3. Start back-to-back and work toward each other.
4. Go around the walls and proceed toward the center of the area being searched.

It is imperative that personnel involved in a search be instructed that their only mission is to search for and report suspicious objects. Under no circumstances should anyone move, jar, or touch a suspicious object or anything attached to it. The removal or disarming of a bomb must be left to the professionals in the bomb and arson squad.

When a suspicious object is discovered, report the location and an accurate description of the object to the search team captain. The team captain should relay this information immediately to the emergency control center, which will notify the police officer in charge. Members of the search teams locating the device should be assigned to meet the bombing and arson squad officers and escort them to the scene.

In the meantime, evacuation team members should create clear zones of at least a 300-foot radius around the suspicious object and on the floors immediately above and below the object.

The decision to evacuate or not evacuate should then be made based upon information provided by the police officers on the scene.

Do not permit reentry into the building until the device has been removed/disarmed, and the police bomb and arson unit has declared the building safe for reentry.

Report any unusual, suspicious packages received via mail or courier to law enforcement.

Reoccupation	
Responsibility	**Action**
Member of management	Makes decision to reoccupy with input from emergency responders.
	Enters building first and occupies conference room adjacent to main office.
	Receives report from all involved team members.
Security	Second person to enter the facility to ensure areas are secure and report to conference room.
	Re-assumes post and ensures area is secure.
Evacuation team	Enters facility in preparation of assisting employees entering building.
Search team	Enters facility in preparation of assisting employees entering building.
All employees, visitors, vendors	Allowed to continue their activities.
Maintenance employees	Powers up all equipment.

129

Threatening Phone Call

Date threat received	Time	Address threatened	Phone # received from	Phone # received on

Be calm and courteous. Listen carefully. Don't interrupt. Turn on the tape recorder.

Write down exactly what the caller says. Ask the caller to repeat if necessary. Ask the following questions that apply. Use the back if needed.

Caller's name and address? _____

Why are they upset? _____

Where is the bomb located? _____

When will the bomb explode? _____

What kind of bomb is it? _____

Why was the bomb placed here? _____

What will cause it to explode? _____

What does it look like? _____

Mark all that apply.

___ Sex M or F   ___ Approx. Age   ___ Race B/W/O

Attitude
___ Angry   ___ Coherent   ___ Crying   ___ Excited   ___ Irrational   ___ Righteous
___ Calm   ___ Incoherent   ___ Disgusted   ___ Intoxicated   ___ Laughing

Speech
___ Accent/Foreign   ___ Fast   ___ Slow   ___ Distinct   ___ Distorted   ___ Deep breathing
___ Accent/not local   ___ Loud   ___ Soft   ___ Familiar   ___ Nasal   ___ Stutter
___ Accent/local   ___ Pitch high   ___ Pitch low   ___ Lisp   ___ Raspy

Background noises
___ Airplanes   ___ Car motor   ___ Noisy   ___ Static   ___ Factory
___ Animals   ___ Dishes   ___ PA system   ___ Street   ___ Office
___ Booth   ___ Household   ___ Party   ___ Trains
___ Clear   ___ Music   ___ Quiet   ___ Voices

Language
___ Well-spoken   ___ Uneducated   ___ Obscene   ___ Reading   ___ Taped

Report call immediately to: Farmland Security   **Phone Number: 816-459-6900**

Fill out completely, immediately after the threat.

Date _____ Your phone number: _____   Position: _____

Your name _____   Address: _____

131

Emergency plans are different from crisis plans in that these are designed to be utilized and implemented during a variety of circumstances, ranging from a medical emergency or fire to trespassing persons on the property. Emergency plans are such that exercises and drills—especially drills—are necessary to keep employees and others sharp and focused in the event of such an occurrence.

Such a plan might be one that applies to the company's staff who are working for Company XYZ or any subsidiary company of Company XYZ in a dangerous, hostile, or volatile region.

The plan might apply to regular expat employees (office- and site-based) and family who are residing in the particular country or region or expat employees (office- and site-based) and family who are visiting the region for short periods of time on project-related business. Finally, the plan may apply to local employees working in the offices of Company XYZ in the regional building or plant building only.

The objective of this plan is to provide a document that can be referred to by staff should civil unrest occur in the country or region.

ESCALATING PRECAUTIONS

The plan should become a consideration, for example, when civil unrest has occurred previously, and it is possible that further unrest will occur. Should this occur, avoid crowds and demonstrations. If there is harassment of foreigners, stay at home or in your hotel and go out as little as possible, especially after dark.

The country director will advise all staff covered by the plan as to the level of alertness in place as staff arrive or if there is a change from one level of alertness to another (refer below for the levels of alertness adopted for this plan).

Should staff wish to monitor any situation over and above the level of support offered by this plan, they should contact their embassy, monitor embassy websites, or listen to broadcasts on the BBC World Service on the hour at most hours. A listing of embassy phone numbers and websites should be provided as part of the plan. Should staff be concerned about the current status of alertness or they suspect changes have occurred, they should contact the country director (CD) or the office manager (OM) with any pertinent updates.

STAFF COVERED BY THIS PLAN

A list of staff covered by this plan will be kept by the OM. The staff list will be updated by the OM as new staff are employed or when visiting staff enter or leave the region or country. All staff will be provided a copy of this plan when they first visit the country or region. A register will be kept by the OM to indicate when staff were provided copies of the plan. All staff will be required to confirm that they have received and read a copy of the plan, and they have been informed about the current level of alertness.

LEVELS OF ALERTNESS

The following four levels of alertness will be adopted.

- *Level 1*: Register staff, monitor staff whereabouts, and have passports ready.
- *Level 2*: Purchase airline/rail or safe transportation tickets and secure accommodation.
- *Level 3*: Demobilize nonessential staff and dependents.
- *Level 4*: Demobilize all staff and secure office.

The change in the level of alertness will be made by the country director in consultation with company management. The country director will have the discretion to move from one level to another should consultation not be possible in the time required. The actions of each level shall be treated as cumulative as the level of alertness is increased.

Level 1: Register Staff, Monitor Staff Whereabouts, and Have Passports Ready

All regular expat staff are to be registered with their embassy (country nominated on passport) by the OM. Changes in address should be updated as they occur. The office secretary is required to monitor the staff whereabouts by sending out travel rosters on a daily basis. The travel roster will include the traveler's details (to include current and/or future, that is, the next day and beyond within 365 days). The daily roster is supposed to be cumulative of the data of each day and gets repeated daily and removed only when the travel is done. Through this, staff movements and updates of emergency medical/security evacuation vendor cards issued by the Company XYZ head office will be easily monitored via the existing quarterly reporting structure managed by corporate security, safety, etc.

Action	By Whom	When
Register regular expat staff and family	Office manager	New regular expat staff arrive in the country
Update country movements of staff movements as they occur	Country director	Daily

The CD is to be advised of all regular and contract expat staff visiting the country. In the majority of cases, the CD will be aware of visiting staff because they will be working for projects managed by the CD. Other Company XYZ staff outside the control of the CD must advise the CD about their trip if they wish to be covered by this plan. A note will be sent to all staff and key US and UK staff alerting them of the fact that they should be advising the CD before visiting the country.

OM to maintain a register of the location and contact details (office and accommodation location) of all staff in the country, and a mobile phone is to be issued to a nominated staff member at each project site. Visiting staff is to advise the OM of the duration and anticipated movements while in the country. Any changes to the initially notified itinerary are to be immediately sent to the OM by the respective staff member.

All passports are to be valid and exit/entry visas up to date. Any processing of new visas is to be completed in as little time as possible.

Action	By Whom	When
Advise of level 2 alertness to staff, key US/UK contacts	Country director	Change from level 1 to 2
Maintain staff register	Office manager	During level 2 alertness
Advise embassy of staff	Office manager	Upon entry and exit of staff from the country
Valid passports	Office manager	During level 2 alertness

Level 2: Purchase Tickets and Secure Accommodation

The OM is to purchase open, three month-duration, fully refundable return tickets for all expat staff and family to travel to the country. The OM is to check that all visiting staff have tickets that can be changed at short notice. New three-month duration, fully refundable, return tickets are to be purchased for visiting staff to their desired point of disembarkation if the tickets of the visiting staff cannot be easily changed.

At the same time, an amount of US$10,000 shall be withdrawn from the company accounts and held within the safe at the office.

Staff shall be relocated to secure accommodation. The assessment of secure accommodation will be made on a case-by-case basis by the CD in consultation with corporate security, security officials, and embassy officials. Staff on site may be recalled to stay in a secure hotel in a safe location.

New visits by Company XYZ staff are to be discouraged during level 2 alertness.

Action	By Whom	When
Advise of level 2 alertness to staff and key US/UK contacts and that travel to the country is to be discouraged	Country director	Change from level 1 to 2
Purchase tickets	Office manager	Change from level 1 to 2
Withdraw cash	Office manager	Change from level 1 to 2
Staff advised to move to secure accommodation	Country director	Change from level 1 to 2

Level 3: Demobilize Nonessential Staff and Dependents

All nonessential staff will be evacuated from the country in close coordination with embassy requirements and guidelines. Secure transport to the airport is to be preorganized by the embassy or the CD. Staff will be advised as to when and where they will be picked up. All coordination is to be done via the CD.

New visits by Company XYZ staff are not permissible during level 3 alertness unless prior consent of country director has been obtained.

Action	By Whom	When
Advise of level 3 alertness to staff and key US/UK contacts	Country director	Change from level 2 to 3
Nonessential staff advised of evacuation	Country director	Change from level 2 to 3
Outward tickets confirmed	Office manager	Change from level 2 to 3
Safe transport organized in consultation with embassy	Country director	Change from level 2 to 3

Level 4: Demobilize All Staff and Secure Office

All expat staff are to be demobilized from the country. Essential office information and equipment is to be stored in a safe location. All software and working files are to be backed up and a copy taken out of the country by the CD (possible to have files copied to CDs).

The office is to be made secure by

- Removing any signs that indicate the office is foreign owned
- Doors to be secured as well as possible by boards or chains to make entry as difficult as possible

The transport of the expat staff to the airport is to be arranged in close coordination with embassy staff. Where possible, embassy convoys are to be used. Regular local employees are to be sent home.

Action	By Whom	When
Advise of level 4 alertness to staff and key US/UK contacts	Country director	Change from level 3 to 4
All remaining staff advised of evacuation	Country director	Change from level 3 to 4
Outward tickets confirmed	Office manager	Change from level 3 to 4
Office secured	Country director and office manager	Change from level 3 to 4
Safe transport organized in consultation with embassy	Country director	Change from level 3 to 4
Regular local employees sent home	Office manager	Change from level 3 to 4

EMBASSY TELEPHONE NUMBERS

- *British Embassy:*
  - Address/phone
  - Website: www.britishembassy.gov.uk/XXX
- *American Embassy:*
  - Address/phone
  - Website: www.XXX.usembassy.gov/XXX
- *International Emergency Medical/Security Evacuation Vendor Inc.*
  - Phone/e-mail

Evacuation Route Map

Post evacuation roads, with alternatives, muster points, and locations.

12

Political Crisis

The whole life of an American is passed like a game of chance, a revolutionary crisis, or a battle.

Alexis de Tocqueville

In the careers of many security and crisis management professionals, political crisis presents one of the more difficult challenges. Political crisis can escalate quickly and strike in the middle of the night while many nations and professionals sleep. One singular event, seemingly insignificant and perhaps not even noticed, can ignite a country into turmoil and chaos. Political crisis can blow up and quickly vanish from the scene, or it can linger and be present until governments fall and nations are destabilized. And you—you, the intrepid crisis manager—must juggle the objects of mitigation while keeping your eyes firmly focused upon your one main goal: that of life safety.

Political crisis is a difficult barometer from which to gauge necessary planning and preparation. Suffice it to say that security and crisis professionals and practitioners must be ready for quickly developing and potentially very dangerous situations. On the lower end of the threat spectrum, political crisis might be of the nonviolent/nonthreatening type, such as mass nonviolent protests or nationwide strikes. Protestors might be singing and holding hands; the event might have a festival atmosphere. But, suddenly, riot police move in and start cracking heads, clearing the square, or gathering on point. There may be mass arrests and detentions. Property may be seized and rights trampled. In reaction, the formerly nonviolent protestors push back, policemen are beaten and stoned, fires are set, and the chaos grows into a violent frenzy.

In Tunisia, police actions against a fruit vendor led to the Arab Spring. It began in the following manner: On December 17, 2010, an unlicensed fruit and vegetable seller in Sidi Bouzi, Tunisia, Mohamed Bouazizi, went about his daily trade of hawking his wares. A city inspector approached Bouazizi and attempted to confiscate his illegally peddled apples. As Bouazizi tried to take back an apple and struggled with the inspector, the inspector slapped him. Estimates are that roughly 40 people witnessed this disgrace to Bouazizi.

Witnesses reported that two people accompanying the inspector beat Bouazizi. Shortly after the inspector and companions took the fruit he was selling, Bouazizi approached a municipal building to demand the return of his goods. He was refused and reportedly beaten again. Later, at approximately noon, Bouazizi stood in the middle of the street and doused himself with paint thinner outside the governor's office. A little over two weeks later, Bouazizi died in the hospital from burns over 90% of his body. Violent protests ensued after the first reports of Bouazizi's self-immolation. Ten days after Bouazizi died, Tunisian President Zine el-Abidine Ben Ali fled the country.

On January 25, 2011, protestors by the thousands filled Egypt's Tahrir Square. By February 11, President Hosni Mubarak resigned and handed power to the military, which announced plans to hold elections. And by July 2013, Morsi was forced out of power again by the military.

By August 22, 2011, plans were being made for the new Libya following the ouster of strongman Muammar Gaddafi.

Demonstrations in Egypt seemed to be on a fast track. In roughly 18 months, Egypt experienced one political strongman step down due to violence in the streets, followed by an elected leader who faced his own round of street protests, followed by threats from the military to step down, and, eventually, for all intents and purposes, a military push for his removal. During this period of upheaval and uncertainty, many expats in Cairo and other locations around Egypt were faced with angry mobs upon the streets that set up roadblocks around city streets and beat many people. At one point, thousands of prisoners escaped from Egyptian jails, adding to the fear and panic of a nation that, only months before, had seemed to welcome international businessmen and -women. International corporations were left with the following dilemmas and the need to prioritize:

1. Ensure all dependents leave the country as soon as possible (arrange for Human Resources and the Travel Department to assist).
2. Determine best source of credible information on the ground.

3. Establish agreed-upon *tripwires,* which will be used to determine next actions.
4. Establish criteria for determining if evacuation or *standing fast* is the safest course.
5. Check airport routes and arrange for security at living quarters and ground transportation security. (If you haven't vetted and identified security professionals on the ground, now is the time to do so.)
6. Ensure proper communications between HQ/Security and Expats (SAT phones, mobiles, radios).
7. Ensure all offices, living quarters, and facilities are secured (interface with plant/living quarter security).
8. Assemble regular telephone and in-person meetings to discuss the crisis at hand.

I hope you never have to set forth down the pathway of the aforementioned checklist. I can tell you that in the case of Egypt, in particular, even companies that had crisis management plans in place experienced many difficulties. Some difficulties that immediately arose in the case of Egypt, especially Cairo and Alexandria, were the lack of reliable communications. That is, telephone and Internet services were cut to avoid the world seeing what was really going on and to limit protestor forms of communications. Once the government learned it was losing the upper hand and that the military could not be relied upon to back up the police in putting down protests, it cut these forms of communications.

Satellite phones remained an option, but for companies that did not have satellites already in place in Egypt, there were provisions in place by the Egyptian government for inspecting and sometimes delaying or denying the import of such devices, especially given the government's attempts to limit all forms of communication in general. For companies that had good relations with the Egyptian government and direct shipping practices in place with established Egyptian business entities and projects, satellite phones could be obtained.

Tunisia was fresh in the minds of many protestors in January 2011. On January 28, the Egyptian police prepared their customary riot response tactics. What some observers had gathered from the January 25 actions was that the police tactics had not dispersed or turned away the large crowds of protestors. On January 28, one could argue, the protestors stood their ground and caught the world's attention—a significant event of protestor bravery. (January 25 was a commemoration of Police Day, 1952, when Egyptian security forces disobeyed directives from the British to leave Isma'iliyah; 43 police officers died at the hands of the British and 43 were wounded; Danahar, 2013, pp. 89–90.) January 28 was deemed the *Day of Rage* by the protestors. Many protestors would die, but by evening, those who had been beaten and shot had the police on the run (Danahar, 2013, pp. 93–95).

On January 28, with unrest and protests growing, President Hosni Mubarak imposed curfews around the country. By January 31, the Mubarak regime knew that its attempts to gather support from the military were failing. And, on that day, it sent *goons* into Tahrir Square, some mounted on camels and horses, to wade into demonstrators with clubs, rocks, pipes, and machetes (Wickham, 2013, pp. 164–165).

The streets became urban battlefields. The extent of the mayhem was not reported by many in the media, who were focused on Tahrir Square because of the sheer visual weight of the images of men on horses fighting against police in riot gear.

Given these events and circumstances, an organization that had failed to lay even the most rudimentary groundwork would have a difficult, if not impossible, time catching up.

But, when it comes to politics, every situation cannot be planned for. In October 1962, President John F. Kennedy faced a political crisis when he learned that the Soviet Union had placed offensive weapons (medium- and intermediate-range ballistic nuclear missiles) in Cuba, 90 miles from the United States. Prior to this, the Soviet Union had placed 150 jets, 350 tanks, 700 antiaircraft units, and 20,000 troops on the island (Updegrove, 2009, p. 204).

The troops and nonoffensive weapons were known about, but it was secret that the United States's secret U2 spy plane flights had confirmed the placement of missiles. President Kennedy had some forewarning, in the form of intelligence, of an impending crisis. What would become known as the Cuban Missile Crisis held the world at the brink of nuclear war and possible shared annihilation. Within the Kennedy administration, Bobby Kennedy recalled, it was decided that, if the Soviets were "...willing to go to nuclear war over Cuba, they [the United States] were ready to go to nuclear war, and that was that..." (Updegrove, 2009, p. 206).

No crisis plans existed for such a scenario. No one had foreseen how cavalier and careless the Soviets would be concerning the idea and placement of offensive, nuclear-capable missiles on the United States's doorstep. The options for crisis response included invading Cuba and destroying the missiles, which would have surely have led to the death of Soviet troops and advisors, or allowing the missiles to remain and bowing down to the Soviet Union, which would have led to President Kennedy's political defeat and the United States being held hostage to the Soviets. Kennedy chose a third option: a naval blockade of Cuba, which was presented to the United Nations as a *quarantine* to forestall the delivery of any more missiles to the island.

The ability to think quickly in political crises is not an easy commodity to acquire. The information required to detect and plan for political crises is not gathered in an easy manner either. It takes trustworthy private and government intelligence sources, along with 24-hour news on satellite TV and the Internet to ascertain such critical data. Sources with trusted governments may provide news of what risks are present and the steps that expats need to take for their safety. These sources can even arrange for evacuations in some cases.

Political crisis planning and forecasting do not require one to have a degree in foreign or international relations, political science, or sociology. It does require a network that includes public and private intelligence sources, such as those maintained by liaison with US government agencies and business colleagues. It might include intelligence paid for from travel or security intelligence firms. Being glued to the 24-hour news machine is no way to plan for crisis, even with the immediacy of instant communications around the globe. Crisis planning for political turmoil does require the resources, cooperation, and networks of corporate individuals such as those working in security, safety, travel, human resources, legal, finance, insurance, and risk departments; senior management; and many others.

REFERENCES

Danahar, Paul. *The New Middle East*. New York: Bloomsbury Press, 2013.

Updegrove, Mark K. *Baptism by Fire: Eight Presidents Who Took Office in Times of Crisis*. New York: Thomas Dunne Books, 2009.

Wickham, Carrie Rosefsky. *The Muslim Brotherhood*. Princeton, NJ: Princeton University Press, 2013.

13

Drills and Exercises
What Works and What Doesn't

The world is indeed full of peril, and in it there are many dark places; but still there is much that is fair, and though in all lands love is now mingled with grief, it grows perhaps the greater.

J. R. R. Tolkien (1954)
The Fellowship of the Rings

Drills and exercises have been the corporate mantra of many organizations for decades. For others, these are more recent occurrences due to regulating of various industries—such as when the US government began requiring or suggesting emergency and crisis drills for chemical and port facilities. Drills are often called for or mandated by US government agencies for US corporations operating within the United States. What is not regulated or required is such practices for organizations operating overseas. I cannot stress enough how critical it is for crisis management professionals to suggest and gain approval for plans and processes to be initiated for circumstances around the globe, which can quickly spiral out of control.

"Practice makes perfect" is an age-old adage that couldn't be more true with crisis planning. But here is where some disaster planning becomes a bit constrained and can even work against the planners and those the plan is intended to protect. Typically, disaster management or crisis management teams consist of the same personnel, albeit with backups if they are out of the office. The team might include security and crisis managers, along with Human Resources and Legal Department employees. Frequently, the team members are midlevel management, not at the top of lower echelons, but possessing decision-making responsibilities.

Disaster and crisis teams often include managers from travel, relocation, benefits operations, information technology, finance, and other disciplines. Meetings are often held quarterly, with biannual exercises and drills. With the same group meeting and discussing the crisis and disaster management planning, the methodologies, procedures, and responses can become restricted in breadth and imagination. Team members might dominate discussions and planning, and many are used to always getting their ways or have a great deal of practice in heavily influencing other participants. Similarly, the crisis management exercise planning can become influenced by thinking and procedures that become routine, predictable, stale, nonreal-world, and less than versatile.

So, what can and should be a vital part of any crisis management plan can become an exercise in back-slapping and self-congratulation if there is no outside review or exposure to differing ideas and assessments. One easy way to ensure that a plan has not become inbred and inefficient is to have employees within the corporation who are not part of the crisis management team review the plan and give honest, unbiased assessments. Give such employees copies of the plan and see what they make of the flow, viability, and thinking. It is important to choose employees who will not be influenced by members of the crisis team, and these employees should have little interaction until they have completed their plan review and are ready to present their findings. This should be done at a special crisis management team meeting convened for this purpose.

Training and drills can be repetitive and boring, and they can engender ridicule from senior management. Lost time at work is not something that senior management is enthusiastic about condoning. Properly conducted drills and exercises, even tabletop exercises, cost time and money and end up taking people away from their jobs and true specialties. Time and time again, however, the role that drills and exercises play in successful crisis management plays out in the real world. Think of it this way: Employees and personnel are building up their muscle memories (more mental exercise than muscle training, but then again, the brain needs a workout too!) with regard to how to respond in crisis situations. Drills can point out disparities or areas in which planning is lacking. Drills and exercises, if done properly and with enough frequency, can build up the muscle memory it takes to be in the right places, such as muster points; to go to the right places, such as the stairwell instead of the elevators; and to do the right things while doing both of these activities.

Richard Rescorla was the head of security for Morgan Stanley Dean Witter when terrorists struck the World Trade Center. Before the 1993 attack on the parking garage at the Center, Rescorla preached the mantra of drills to get Morgan employees familiar with how to evacuate their floors and the gigantic tower. He was often made fun of and people didn't pay much attention, but they grudgingly participated. Over the next eight years, Rescorla continued with the drills and exercises, never giving up on training and advising people that "They're going to get us [World Trade Center] again. By air or the subway," and he was proven correct on September 11, 2001. After having successfully evacuated a large number of employees, Rescorla was last observed heading up the stairway due to a report that an executive had not left his office and was still on a telephone (Ripley, 2008, pp. 206–210).

What has been made light of by many, what has been drilled and exercised until completely bored employees said, "But, we have done all this and nothing has happened," can turn to lethargy and stagnation in many organizations. Not every facility is the World Trade Center. Not every enterprise resides in a building that has been hit once by terrorists and is reportedly still in their sights. But, what crisis and security professionals can and must rely upon is a realistic assessment of risk. Such an assessment is critical to achieving success in crisis management. If a facility resides within a stone's throw or inland of the beaches in Sumatra, Indonesia, or Northern Japan, planning and drills shouldn't focus on responding to and surviving blizzards and avalanches. It wouldn't be worthwhile to lay on a supply of snowshoes and parkas for your employees in these regions. Hopefully, in the aftermath of an event such as a tsunami or earthquake in such regions in Indonesia and Japan, it would be much easier to convince employees and senior management to plan for such events. But, as you might have experienced, or as has been pointed out in this book, even when buildings have been previously struck by terrorists, employees and management can begin to become complacent and develop the second deadly sin of naysaying crisis planning and management: "It can't happen here again."

So, from reports of eyewitnesses and participants, we know that more people survive disasters and crises when there is a plan present. And, we know that plans are more effective when there are drills associated with these plans. Athletes train for performance, and people who golf for fun or for business or hobbies visit the driving ranges to work on and improve their skills. Key personnel in emergency planning might be out of the country, no longer with the company, or incapacitated. Planning, drills, and exercises must be kept current for these reasons.

A word or two concerning communications and crisis management: Many groups and consultants deal with the specifics of training organizations for what to say and do during a crisis. Such training is critical for the education and development of crisis management teams. Much of this training takes place during and in the aftermath of crisis management exercises and drills when organizations realize their shortfalls in the areas of communications during crises. Organizations steeped in the methodology of crisis management would be expected to have a communications professional trained in these areas referred to as the public information officer, or PIO. Often, this is someone from the Corporate Communications or Marketing Department. These employees are frequently able to deliver training based upon recommendations of crisis management consultants or companies directed at providing teams with things to do or not to do during a crisis. What might not be so common are efforts by corporations to deal effectively with local or regional governments, cities, communities, or cultures in opening up the lines of two-way communications and information sharing. Local communities might provide useful or lifesaving information during man-made or natural disasters. And, occasionally, local leaders in the community might have to be advised of issues with an organization that might affect them. Dialogue should be established between local and home-turf government security agencies, police, fire, emergency services, and others, for example. Headquarters or project-based communications personnel can assist with these efforts.

For the most part, I feel that tabletop exercises are good for only one real purpose: initial introduction of and discussion about the crisis management plan. It is not that these exercises are unnecessary; they can be beneficial from a discussion standpoint. But, from a practical application, tabletops are comparable to dancing with your sister—it's nice, but it's just not the same. Tabletops are often check-the-box exercises, and one might argue that these are not exercises to begin with—especially if one considers exercising to be using one's muscles. (OK, the brain can be exercised during a tabletop, but is the brain a muscle?) Tabletops might consist of the right people who would be called on during an actual emergency and crisis being gathered together. And, there might be a very sexy scenario written for all to view and become actors within.

These tabletops often begin in a way similar to the following:

- At 10:30 p.m. cryogenic tank #20 in the Tallahassee production facility develops a leak.
- At 10:35 p.m. security officers on mobile rounds notice a vapor cloud rising from the cryogenic farm area and alert the Control Room.
- At 10:36 p.m. the Control Room alerts Facilities Maintenance of a suspected vapor cloud and begins a systematic pressure check on control panels/screens.
- From 10:36 p.m. to 10:40 p.m. Facilities Maintenance dons protective gear and begins to make their way toward the cryogenic farm area.

And on and on it goes.

Oooooh! The personnel gathered in the training room almost get goose bumps reading these cue cards!

Right away, people start pulling open their crisis manuals (which everyone was asked to bring to the training session) and start familiarizing themselves with their procedures and steps to take. The leader or moderator or trainer calls on the participant from Engineering: "Frank, when you receive the call from the Control Room, what are you going to do as the lead engineer on duty?" Frank glances at his crisis manual and replies, "Well, Nancy, I am going to log into the operating system and begin pressure checks!"

Nancy turns to the rest of those seated in the conference room and gushes about Frank, "That's right, Frank, very good!" Nancy tosses a candy bar at Frank, who catches it like a seal at SeaWorld feeding time.

Frank has proven two very important things to those seated in the conference room:

1. He brought his crisis manual to the exercise.
2. He can read and speak English.

Before the first break, the participants scoot their chairs together in functional areas as each *team* nominates a spokesperson for their group and delves into their response descriptions. As runners hand these groups their *exercise injects* of new information, the team members giggle and joke about what the next steps might mean. There is no pressure, just good clean fun.

Waste of time? Not entirely. You will quickly find out those who have no idea what they need to do in an emergency situation. But, having the manual right in front of them allows some casual participants the opportunity to *fake it*. Manuals are a cheat sheet. They are a crutch for the uninitiated and for those who have no interest in remembering what to do or why to do it during an emergency. Manuals are the Bible for a flock that hasn't memorized any of the Psalms, Gospels, or Proverbs.

Tabletops most generally and without too much prodding quickly evolve into quick fire gabfests of "Here is what I would do" or "Here is what you would do" and jump to too many conclusions. Tabletops make assumptions as to who will do what, how they will do it, and why. Resources and materials appear out of an imaginary warehouse of availability. Fires are quickly extinguished. Flood waters recede in minutes. Power is restored in milliseconds. Casualties get up and walk like at a cheap tent revival. Before the first break, many crises have been solved and the teams are conferring on where they will have lunch. Tabletop exercises are mental masturbation.

The only worthwhile types of tabletops are those that begin with people seated at tables, and these people quickly get off their butts. In more pronounced and aggressive scenarios, the participants know they are there for a crisis management exercise, but of course don't know the nature of the exercise. There are moderators and observers who push the participants where they need to go. With a little coaxing and cajoling, a successful moderator (backed up by additional participants) may inject twists on the scenario that cause the teams to pack up and move to different locations, such as the Emergency Operations Center, or storage warehouses, or additional operational areas. Vans and vehicles are waiting to take the team members—who, when exiting the facility, are confronted by media shoving cameras and microphones in their faces (consultants hired to make the exercise more successful). There is no excuse for having a tabletop exercise with a mature, professional, practiced and ready crisis management team. Tabletops are a colossal waste of time. First you walk, then you run, then you sprint. Have faith in your team; don't coddle and baby them.

Tabletop exercises often become social time as groups become lost in their own little worlds of chit chat or sidebars. Much time is wasted in discussion or argument, rather than in actually responding to the crisis. It is too easy to say, "Well, this is what we would do," or "Whatever it says in the crisis management book," or "When faced with this roadblock, we would just do the following." Nonsense. Not in the real world. In the real world, one of the first things that goes away is communication. During a tabletop exercise, participants often yell across from one table to another, "Hey, Finance Department, I am calling you for some money, pick up the phone." But, as we know, phone lines, texting, mobile phones, Internet, and even satellite often fail or are overloaded when crisis strikes. Persons, divisions, departments, and groups need to find ways to activate and utilize their plans with little or no communications, as if they are acting within a vacuum. This is a concept one can speak of in a tabletop, but it is best understood when the groups return to their respective buildings, facilities, or countries.

REFERENCES

Ripley, Amanda. *The Unthinkable: Who Survives When Disaster Strikes—and Why.* Danvers, MA: Crown Publishing Group, 2008.
Tolkien, J. R. R. *The Fellowship of the Rings.* United Kingdom: Houghton Mifflin Harcourt, 1954.

14

Management Duties during Crisis

Every little thing counts in a crisis.

Jawaharlal Nehru

The exact duties of a company local manager (LM) will be coordinated with the corporate crisis management team (CCMT) in the event of a crisis incident.

Upon being advised of a crisis situation, the LM will meet as soon as possible after immediately notifying the CCMT. Once the CCMT is notified, there are several things that need to happen.

First, select a secure base/premises to be used by the LM. Once the location has been established, management should communicate the rising tensions to the CCMT for analysis.

The LM should then establish and maintain a reliable source of communications with the CCMT. A secure telephone line, which should be manned 24 hours a day, must be kept exclusively for communication with the CCMT. In case there should be a loss of primary communication at any point, the LM should also establish an alternate means of communication with the CCMT as a backup.

Management will also need to initiate a 24-hour *incident log* to record all relevant detail.

Throughout the crisis, management and the CCMT will stay in touch using the established means of communication, documenting all communication along the way. They should be kept informed of local events and

State Department personnel, like the US Embassy, for example. The most important thing here is to keep the CCMT informed!

Of course, paramount in a crisis is that management and the CCMT account for all personnel. Management should establish a tracking procedure to locate all personnel, at all hours, and should ensure that any involved personnel are briefed on the need for strict security. Personnel should be instructed (by management) to maintain a low profile. Management must ensure the security of all employees by taking appropriate steps to protect personnel from possible aggressors.

Management will make tentative travel arrangements (open airline ticket reservations, etc.) for employees and dependents and arrange alternate modes of transportation out of the country in the event the initial plan is impeded. It is critical to ensure that all personnel have compiled important personnel documents (passports, records, and other travel documents), in the event that an evacuation becomes necessary and that personnel know the best way to the airport, including alternate routes. It's also a good idea to instruct that personnel have a suitcase prepared with a maximum of 66 pounds per person to avoid any delays. If there is a bit of extra time, management should also consider making arrangements for the storage of personal belongings, luggage, and portable household items.

Consider also how the office should be prepared. For example, identify documents being removed/destroyed, disposition of outstanding contracts/accounts, handling of inventory and its storage. It is important to protect sensitive information from unauthorized access.

Note: Any time there is liaison with corporate CCMT, provide accurate, timely, objective, and unbiased information to the CCMT to ensure effective coordination between all the participants.

As directed by the CCMT, and through the medium of an authorized spokesman, control media statements, as well as their contents and timing. Establish contact with friendly journalists who may be prepared to assist in inserting helpful articles in the media. No media comment should be made unless authorized by the CCMT; all media inquiries should be referred to the authorized spokesperson. With CCMT direction, prepare a press statement, as a contingency, to handle possible media inquiries. Initiate detailed examination of legal implications to include company liability and consumer and client contracts.

Advise the CCMT on the possible liability of the company in connection with the medical and legal consequences following the injury or arrest of personnel. Consider the implications of liaison with other interested companies, clients, unions, etc. Consider communicating with other foreign companies in the area to share intelligence and resources.

Prepare a position paper for CCMT, listing the nature of the threat, what actions have been taken to date, and any policy inputs and requests (of the company or company personnel). List if there is any legal exposure for the company, what your policy for liaison with government and law enforcement should be, and any recommendations for public relations work.

Upon receipt of notice that a serious incident has occurred, the initial CCMT coordinator (corporate security manager) will immediately start notifications. He or she will alert the CCMT chairman and ascertain a meeting time and location. The next step will be to notify all CCMT members of the incident and meeting time and location. Following this, it will be necessary to alert other senior management or environmental resource personnel, as directed.

- Activate a 24-hour secure command center to receive, evaluate, and pass on information to the CCMT.
- Contact all appropriate LM (if not originally contacted by the LM).
- Begin to maintain a 24-hour incident log.
- Establish a secure telephone and/or cyber link with incident location to acknowledge all messages.
- Ensure the appropriate LM is convening and taking appropriate action until CCMT can provide guidance.
- Alert the Incident Response Team (IRT), as directed by the corporate crisis management team.

The CCMT's general responsibilities upon convening include those of legal concerns; that is, they are responsible for advice and information on all legal aspects during and subsequent to a crisis occurring. Legal concerns might involve liability such as a lawsuit brought about by shareholders or brought by others affected by the incident. Those who might be injured, detained, or prosecuted based upon the actions taken by the corporation might file suit. Legal concerns include any issues that might result from members of the team or expats contacting or sharing information with law enforcement agencies. Legal should call the shots on what to do with sensitive company or documentary records during a crisis.

Corporate Finance will have the responsibility of determining what shall or shall not be done regarding financial aspects of the crisis response.

These concerns include the origin of crisis funds and how and where these are to be drawn upon, and by whom. A decision by Finance will decide which branch or by what means funds may be withdrawn, if the funds will be in cash, and, if so, in what denominations. Funds should be withdrawn discreetly and with strict security precautions. International monetary restrictions and rules must be accounted for and, in certain situations, special couriers might be required.

Human Resources in the corporate headquarters will be responsible for advice and recommendations involving personnel considerations during the crisis. HR will assist in deciding who remains and who stays put during the crisis, whether additional personnel might be required, how to assist with the dependents of expats back home, etc. There may be certain considerations involving pay and insurance for personnel now working in high-risk areas. The Public Relations Department will handle and advise management and personnel on all aspects involving information flow during the crisis. PR will designate a spokesperson to be the face of the corporation to the media. They will decide what to say and when to say it and will be shepherding the communications to family members and other dependents of the expats in the crisis situation. They will field all press and media inquiries.

During the crisis, corporate Security and Safety Departments will handle the aspects of keeping all personnel on the ground, as well as those who will be dealing with the crisis, safe in all manner of operations. They will coordinate contacts and liaison with security and safety personnel, any law enforcement or regulatory agencies, and any designated contractors and vendors involved in operations.

Government and international affairs departments will interface with governmental and regulatory agencies to ensure that cooperation between the corporation and these agencies remains intact.

INCIDENT RESPONSE TEAM

The IRT consists of the company's Global Corporate Security Team with the background and experience to assist the LM in resolving major incidents at the convenience of the CCMT. They are responsible for providing regional/country data, formulating plans as part of the CCMT, deploying within four hours of notification, assisting/supporting the LM while in country, and acting as the liaison for all kidnap/ransom (K&R) initiatives.

The IRT will provide the following:

- Monitor the crisis situation.
- Provide in country, firsthand analysis of the crisis.
- Advise the CCMT and LM on appropriate actions.
- Assist in the gathering of crisis area intelligence.
- Serve as liaison between government officials, hostile groups, aggressors, protestors, embassy personnel, and evacuation elements.
- Assist in coordinating the safety and security issues in the crisis.
- Provide physical protection for the senior company executives.

In the aftermath of the crisis, the executive team will evaluate all facets of the crisis—those managed successfully, as well as those that require improvement.

The crisis management team will meet shortly after the crisis to compare notes and make recommendations to strengthen the existing procedures. Later, new pages and recommendations can be distributed to appropriate managers for inclusion in their copies of the crisis management plan.

It is imperative that the global offices or headquarters has properly directed the establishment and maintenance of communications that are critical to rapid and safe implementation of the plan. The LM operations leader will have overall responsibility for establishing communications system/procedures and ensuring that the available equipment is operational. The LM should have a variety of communications equipment available. CB-type radios are frequently installed in vehicles and homes; portable satellite telephones have proven to be reliable for *in extremis* communications, and single side band (SSB) radios may be used in offices and by employee ham radio operators. Local telephones will probably be available, although their performance may not be dependable, especially for communications with the appropriate US, UK, or country embassy or consulate. Verify the country's legal requirements for using any radio to ensure compliance with local laws.

There are several different types of communications networks that should be established:

- *Local company to the CCMT.* This link may be difficult to maintain because of its dependence on telephone service, which may be easily disrupted. Portable satellite telephones, electronic mail, or fax may be more dependable. The LM leader should be given the authority from the CCMT to unilaterally decide to implement the

emergency evacuation plan. The tenuousness of the communications link with the CCMT demands that the LM team leader be
able to act without directives from the CCMT, if necessary. The
LM operations leader should determine if communication with
other company global offices in the geographical area is possible
through a type of long-range communications. If this link can
be established, plans should be made for the neighboring global
offices to relay messages to the CCMT.

- *Local office to the embassy or consulate.* This is regardless of citizen-
  ship, which will usually support all expatriates of a US company
  or other foreign national company employees. The embassies and
  consulates maintain a close watch on political/military events
  in the country and have plans for the evacuation of expatriates.
  The establishment of a reliable communications channel with the
  embassy is thus of great assistance to the local company emergency evacuation plan. The principal communications link with
  the embassies and consulates will probably be telephone. The
  individuals responsible for evacuation planning in the embassy
  should be identified and a list of their telephone numbers stored
  with other emergency and evacuation (E&E) documents. If there
  are disturbances in the phone system, the operations officer
  should arrange for the company to become part of the emergency
  radio network of the embassy.
- *Face-to-face meetings with the embassy security officer.* This could
  be hazardous if there are demonstrations in the vicinity of the
  embassy, and the team leader must make a decision concerning
  this option based on assessment of the situation.

Inside the company, communications are necessary to announce the
decision to begin evacuation and to coordinate its implementation. CB
radios, SSB, and satellite/cellular telephones may all be used to establish a
link between the global offices and other locations. All systems should be
periodically tested to determine which provides the greatest quality and
dependability. In times of instability, the link should be monitored on a
24-hour basis.

The means of communication between company offices and the individual homes can be CB radios, portable radios kept in individual homes,
and/or satellite/cellular telephones.

SAMPLE CRISIS MANAGEMENT CHECKLIST

Each global office must

- Have a contact list in place of all LM members.
- Maintain a contact list of all CCMT members.
- Maintain a list of contact numbers of the IRT members, including the 24-hour emergency number.
- Maintain a contact list of all in-country personnel.
- Maintain a contact list of embassy and consulate support personnel.
- Establish secure and reliable communications with corporate headquarters (CCMT), to include an alternate means if the common source fails.
- Maintain a contact list of transportation resources out of the country to include alternative modes if common methods are not available (e.g., aircraft, boat, vehicles).
- Obtain a list of alternate airports in the area, including small airfields (their capabilities and contact information).
- Have personnel information sheets on all in-country personnel (such as next of kin and other emergency notification information).
- Maintain up-to-date personnel files on all expatriate personnel and their dependents.
- Have on hand any risk analysis and vulnerability assessment reports/results of in-country facilities.
- Have on hand the established emergency evacuation plan.
- Establish a safe haven and stock it with emergency supplies/provisions and periodically check the freshness and quantity of supplies.
- Have emergency funds available (cash).
- Provide a layout of the facility/facilities, including the surrounding area, to the CCMT and IRT.
- Establish a procedure for accounting for personnel when a crisis develops or an evacuation becomes necessary.

ESTABLISH AN INCIDENT REPORTING PROCEDURE

In the highly volatile situations that require a report to the CCMT that a state of emergency exists, it is essential that the initial message provide as much information as possible. Messages should:

- Describe the type of emergency and if it is a terrorist attack, state of war, due to civil unrest, anti-American demonstrations, anticompany demonstrations, or a natural disaster.
- Indicate in the report who declared the emergency, such as the host government, the ambassador or his or her representative, or a project manager or his or her deputy.
- Report who received the notification within headquarters, such as the general manager, an office manager, a secretary or receptionist, another employee, or a local national employee.
- Report how the notification was conveyed, such as by telephone, messenger, public broadcasting, private sources, or personal observation.
- Report when the emergency was declared (Give the time/date groups in local time using the 24-hour clock (e.g., 1500 hours/May 20, 2001).
- Report where the emergency has been declared. Is the emergency countrywide or in certain states, provinces, regions, or cities?
- Report why the emergency was declared. Is there an immediate danger to life or an immediate threat to property? Are the actions part of a precautionary measure to protect life or property? How imminent is the threat?
- Report what measures have been taken by the host government in the face of the emergency that might influence evacuation or other actions. Some examples are airports being closed to civilian traffic, setup of roadblocks on major arteries, or commercial communications being curtailed or cut off entirely. There could be a curfew in effect or public gatherings may have been prohibited. Take an assessment of those kinds of limitations and the general feel of the environment.

- Report what actions have been taken by embassies in the area, such as expats being ordered to immediately evacuate or place-in personnel on *alert* status. Are personnel being recalled from outlying areas? Are documents being destroyed? In some circumstances, governments will order their citizens to move to collection or evacuation points.
- Report the action that appropriate embassies and the embassy or consulate recommend, such as awaiting instructions, remaining indoors, assembling at collection points, or destroying equipment and records.

Be aware of the typical currency details such as weight/cubic size/ amount/denomination/pounds/ounces/inches/centimeters.

The safety and security of those affected by security threats is of primary importance, whether in a foreign country or in any environment characterized by potential terrorist/criminal threats.

Avoid predictable behavior. Vary routes to work, appointments, or other engagements. Terrorists/criminals usually survey their targets prior to attack. Being unpredictable is a very effective deterrent.

You must raise your level of awareness to a point where strange vehicles parked near your residence or place of employment are noticed and promptly reported to the authorities. This must be done immediately. It may be the first time you have seen the vehicle but it may not be the first time it has been there. You don't know what level of planning the criminal or terrorist may be in. Maybe it's only the beginning, but perhaps the criminals' or terrorists' planning is in the final stages. They may give you little time to act. People standing, walking, or sitting in cars near the residence or place of employment must be noticed, especially people who are loitering. Notice someone who always seems to be around you and realize when you are being followed. Don't do anything to let the person doing surveillance know that he or she has been detected. Do *not* confront suspected terrorists/criminals and ask them why they're watching. This may initiate an impromptu attack or kidnapping. If you suspect you are being followed by someone in a vehicle, drive normally and carefully and proceed to a safe location, such as an embassy, police station, or a highly visible and/or populated area and immediately alert police, embassy staff, and/or your security network.

In robbery circumstances, never resist an armed robbery, as resistance usually leads to violence. In fact, it is helpful to consider in advance the possibility of being robbed so that you can think through reactions and thus be better prepared.

In any conflict with political implications, do not take sides. Plead ignorance of local politics and express only the desire to contact the appropriate US, UK, or country embassy or consulate embassy or consulate for the purpose of being reunited with your family back home.

If disturbances erupt and prevent evacuation and the outside environment seems dangerous, stay in your hotel or home. Try to contact the LM; if you're unsuccessful, try to contact the CCMT. If you're still unsuccessful, contact the IRT. If all that fails, try to contact the appropriate US, UK, or country embassy or consulate by telephone. If that doesn't work, try to contact other friendly embassies by telephone or note (e.g., Canada, Germany, etc.). If you can't get through to anyone, try to hire someone to take a note there for you.

If disturbances erupt and prevent evacuation but the outside environment does not seem dangerous, contact the LM for instructions. If unsuccessful, try to contact the CCMT. If unsuccessful, contact the IRT or the appropriate US, UK, or country embassy or consulate by telephone. You may attempt to contact other friendly embassies by telephone or note (e.g., Britain, Canada, Germany, etc.). If unsuccessful, try to hire someone to take a note there for you.

Do not attempt to circumvent roadblocks or document checkpoints, as you are likely to be shot. Stay away from the scene of disturbances. Consider it a life-threatening situation—not an attraction. If you hear gunfire or report of hostilities, take shelter inside a neutral building, meaning one that is not a military target. Government facilities of any sort are likely to be military targets, as are television or other communications centers.

It may be inadvisable to leave a safe harbor, assuming it has sufficient food and water. This would not be prudent, unless there is immediate danger of it becoming engulfed in hostilities or taken over by a military force. Otherwise, a safe harbor should only be left if evacuation is offered by an embassy or humanitarian organization or authoritative communication indicates that hostilities have been suspended or terminated.

If it is necessary to move out of a safe harbor, it is generally best to move in a direction away from hostilities—away from troops, tanks, or circling helicopters.

Under most circumstances, it is inadvisable to make a run for the airport with hostilities still in progress. The airport probably will be closed.

Moreover, it will likely be a magnet for fighting or military positioning, and, in any case, your path to it will likely be impeded by military roadblocks.

If stranded in your hotel, seek out other guests and organize the group to take care of housekeeping chores and create an emotional support base. Do not watch activity from your window, particularly if sniper fire is being directed from your hotel or the area. Sleep in the area offering the greatest protection against gunfire from the outside. Move to a room that is not exposed to the area of gunfire. Know your escape routes in case of fire.

Never do anything that would give a hostile intelligence service reason to pick you up. But, if you are detained by a foreign intelligence, first ask to contact the American embassy. You are entitled to do so under international diplomatic and consular agreements, to which most countries are signatories.

Phrase your request appropriately. Your request is more likely to succeed in a Communist country if you present it as a demand. In Third World countries, however, making demands could lead to physical abuse.

Do not admit to wrongdoing or sign anything. Part of the detention ritual in Communist countries is a written report, which you will be asked to sign. Decline to do so and continue demanding to contact the embassy or consulate.

Do not agree to *help* the hostile service. The hostile service may offer you the opportunity to help them in return for releasing you or your forgoing prosecution. Either refuse outright or delay a firm commitment by saying that you have to think it over. Either action often leads to release.

Report to the embassy or consulate and the LM as soon as possible after such an incident. You should then request assistance in departing the country. Departure is generally possible with embassy assistance. However, you will risk rearrest on future visits or may be denied future visas.

Report to your corporate supervisor immediately upon return to the appropriate US, UK, or country embassy or consulate. This is especially important if you were unable to report to the embassy, consulate, or in-country manager.

Every year, thousands of expats are arrested abroad—many on drug charges. The experience of being arrested overseas is notably different from being arrested in your home country:

- Few countries provide a jury trial.
- Most countries do not accept bail.
- Pretrial detention may last months, often in solitary confinement.
- Prisons may lack even minimal comforts of bed, toilet, and washbasin.
- Diet is often inadequate, requiring supplements from relatives and friends.
- Officials do not speak English.
- Physical abuse, confiscation of physical property, degrading or inhumane treatment, and extortion are possible.

KNOW YOUR RIGHTS

If you are arrested, ask permission to notify the nearest appropriate embassy or consulate. This is particularly important in countries with which the appropriate US, UK, or country embassy or consulate has status-of-forces agreements. Under international agreements and practice, you have a right to get in touch with the consul. If you are turned down, keep asking, politely but persistently. If you are unsuccessful, try to have someone get in touch for you.

WHAT THE APPROPRIATE EMBASSY OR CONSULATE CAN DO

Consular officers will do whatever they can to protect your legitimate interests and ensure that you are not discriminated against under local law. Consular officers can

- Provide lists of local attorneys.
- Help find adequate legal representation.
- Visit you in jail.
- Advise you of your rights according to local law.
- Contact your company, family, and friends.
- Arrange for transfer of money, food, and clothing from your family and friends to prison authorities.
- Try to get relief if you are held under inhumane or unhealthy conditions, or if you are treated less favorably than others in the same situation.

WHAT THE EMBASSY OR CONSULATE CANNOT DO

Unfortunately, what American officials can do for you overseas is limited by foreign laws and geography. The embassy or consulate *cannot*

- Get you out of jail by posting bond or bail.
- Pay your legal fees or related expenses, serve as attorneys, or give legal advice.

Travel security requires some special considerations and planning. Travel plans should be treated as *need to know* information only. Those who are not part of the team, management, or work teams should not be privy to the destinations or itineraries. Especially if such regions are prone to the threat of kidnapping or terrorist activities, you are unaware of whose comments might make it into the wrong hands. Administrative assistants, telephone operators, and others should not advise callers of the employee's travel plans. While traveling, employees should remove any luggage identification in plain sight and opt for those that cover name and address, etc. The address and phone numbers used should be the company's; however, as mentioned, don't use the company name or logo. Room security is very critical, and anything of value should be kept with you while you are away from the room. This does not include expensive jewelry or watches, which are bad-guy magnets, but rather things such as your passport, wallet, and credit cards. Contrary to popular belief, your passport should never be kept in a room safe or a front desk safe; instead, it should be on your person when you take day trips, go to the jobsite, etc.

Your security department or consultants should have warned you ahead of time about the risks of walking alone, areas to avoid, and the general risks of *tourist* activities. In some countries—and this is the age-old dilemma of security professionals—it is simply too risky for employees to walk or even drive about. As mentioned previously, travel security is a tough gospel to preach, as many *world travelers* will roll their eyes or take security and safety recommendations as talking down to their knowledge and abilities. Keep a mobile phone/mobile device that works within the country with you and know the emergency phrases required in order to ask for police, medical, fire, etc., assistance.

"Do you mean to say that when I am riding my bike, working out, jogging, etc., I need to carry my ID and my passport with me?!" Yes, dear sir/madam, you are correct. If you come upon a military or police official, a roadblock checkpoint (what were you doing running/biking with roadblocks about?), etc., or you and every other expat must suddenly leave the area/country (why weren't you aware of impending trouble?), do you think in such cases they won't ask you for identification? Do you think if you are a foreigner without your passport, they will allow you to go and get it? Dream on. And keep your entry visas or stamps, etc., with you inside your passport as well. Because of the proliferation of excellent—really excellent—pickpockets (or those who lift valuables, steal purses, briefcases, backpacks, mobile phones, iPads—you name it), men should keep wallets in front pockets. Don't keep your backpack unzipped or fail to pay attention to who is hovering next to you, behind you, etc.

15

Realities of Crisis Management around the World

The time is out of joint. O cursed spite that ever I was born to set it right!

William Shakespeare
Hamlet

Most crisis management experts agree upon some truisms with regard to crisis planning and execution. There is the planning which takes place within organizations. Someone, somewhere, at some point has convinced, or in the case of insurance companies, required the organization to develop crisis management policies and procedures. Following this, exercises and drills are engineered and conducted. Often, organizations turn to template and *canned* procedures and even exercises in order to *check the box* for this task. Like security programs, crisis management plans are not a one-size-fits-all endeavor. Organizations come in all shapes and sizes, from local to regional to international in location, size, and scope. For these reasons, not every plan will suffice from one group to another. While emergency plans are straightforward and drilled into our heads from early childhood (from duck and cover from the 1950s and 1960s to school fire drills and code blue drills), crisis planning seems a bit of a reach for most employees, students, or others.

Many organizations have robust, well-disciplined, and funded crisis management teams. These teams might have Six Sigma black belts as part of their leadership. The team might use certain weekends to rappel from the tops of a campus tallest buildings. From all appearances, this group and organization stand ready for everything. However, one opinion to be offered from an outsider looking in is that this organization might be all talk and no action, "all hat and no cattle." Some consider plans and charts to be simply that, unless and until the organization and the group have attempted to or put these into place during an actual crisis. And, to be clear, an emergency is not always a crisis. Having a string of emergencies, such as fire alarms going off and evacuating a high rise or a medical emergency that requires getting help to an employee on the 57th floor, is not a crisis management badge of accomplishment. No, crisis management is most often not a one-time event or occurrence. Incidents take time and often have days or weeks of buildup in the case of man-made crises. Mother Nature sometimes makes her presence felt in drawn out actions such as flooding, ice and winter storms, or earthquakes, followed by shortages, fire, famine, etc. (Figure 15.1).

Crisis management is more than some flowcharts, bullet points, checklists, and cue cards. Crisis management is a philosophy and, as will be mentioned, is susceptible to the frailties and failure of men and women. This book argues that it takes a crisis to make a crisis team. It takes a crisis to test a crisis plan. And, it takes a crisis to test the organization. Certainly, many organizations never consider emergency or crisis planning unless

Figure 15.1   As in this view of high water in North Dakota, flooding may cripple communication, transportation, and evacuation routes, and planning for such events should take this into account. (Courtesy of FEMA, https://www.fema.gov /media-library/assets/images/59697, June 26, 2011.)

or until something major has taken place or a near-miss has occurred. Decision making or lack thereof is equally important to a successful crisis management plan. That is, making the wrong decision can be just as damaging as not making a decision at all.

Crisis management teams are alike in so many ways and often detour into many directions. One immediate concern of crisis management teams is the fact of where they work, where they sit—hundreds or thousands of miles from the scene of the incident(s) taking place. Separation creates some immediate issues with respect to time. Time zones make it such that, while the crisis management team is operating on a 9–5 schedule, on Tuesday morning, the project team is simultaneously in the office on Wednesday midday. Communications as previously discussed might be an issue with respect to phone or Internet. Satellite phones may or may not provide adequate contacts.

Crisis management teams might suffer further from being set apart from organizational concerns by time and geography by the makeup and functions of the group. Just as a member of senior management might attempt to influence the team one way or the other (by either underestimating or overestimating the threat), so might the teams themselves succumb to feelings that, because of their crisis planning or crisis management abilities, the situation is well under control; in fact, however, it is nowhere near to being managed. If one particular member of the team is strong willed and able to convince others, this one person might sway the team to take action or choose not to do so. Through their statements, actions, tenure, or respect within the organization, overly dominant team members may be looked upon, especially by new team members or employees new to the team, as those whom "you don't mess with." Thus, whatever they say is considered to be the right way, the only way, to proceed and there are no challenges. If someone were brave enough to speak out, others might come to the defense of the much respected power figure and mildly, or not so mildly, put the dissenter in his or her place. Because the group is often made up of high ranking or the highest ranking members of the particular areas of emphasis (Human Resources, Legal, Safety/Security, Operations, and others), the team might have an air of infallibility about it. If there have been successes in dealing with crises in the past—no matter how small—this sense will be bolstered.

On the other hand, if the team has had its share of defeats, it might become paralyzed to move or take any actions that someone in hindsight or acting as a "Monday morning quarterback" might see as rash. Second guessing or seeking verification where there might be none will add to stagnation. Crisis team members are open to criticisms due to their separation from the project or expats in measured quantities such as time and distance; also, in many cases, the crisis team has no idea what the expat project or office team is dealing with in their work country. The old standby criticism—"How would you know; have you even been there?"—comes up again and again. For this reason, it is warranted and actually beneficial for someone from the crisis team (more than one member, actually) to visit the project or office. In this way, the team will benefit from direct observations by team members, and the team members may use their time making valuable government and private sector contacts that might be of assistance down the road. Then, when the question—"How would you know; have you been there?"—comes across the speakerphone in the emergency operations center, someone can pipe up and say, "Why, yes, yes I (we) have!" (Figure 15.2).

As mentioned before, it is often prudent to get a reality or *gut* check on what the team is recommending, what they are asking to be done, or what the team is not choosing to do during the buildup to or while the crisis is underway. It will cost lives and property to wait until the after-action report, when nerves and conditions have calmed and the dust has settled. By checking with what competitors or other corporations in the area or region are doing one might gather some insight into something that had

Figure 15.2 Emergency operations centers (EOCs) can adequately muster the correct personnel for crises. The trick is to operate as a team—independently, if necessary, of senior management interference. (Courtesy of FEMA, https://www.fema.gov/media-library/assets/images/51344, May 19, 2007.)

not been previously considered. That is, have other companies supplied their expats with open-ended one-way tickets, allowing them to arrive at the airport and get out of the country to hopefully safer locales? Have these same companies contracted with local shipping or charter boat companies in order to ferry expats to safety if the international airports are closed? Have they located privately chartered aircraft for the same reasons? In the same way, crisis and security management consultants may provide useful insight and suggestions to perk up a stale crisis management plan or free a floundering system from organizational rigidity. Do these consultants have a sanitized crisis management plan you might view? The more eyes looking at a program, especially outside experts, the greater is the chance for spotting a flaw or inadequacy within their own organization.

Consider an illustration of the intricacies involved in crisis management: A large manufacturing company has a field office in a country experiencing political turmoil. Weeks of nonviolent demonstrations have morphed into bloody confrontations between military and police forces against protestors. The protestors have been losing, badly. World opinion is for the protestors and against the government. The manufacturing company's home government has insisted that the military and police stand down and allow the protests to continue peacefully. The government vows to treat all subsequent protests as threats to its sovereignty.

Members of the Corporate Crisis Management Team (CCMT), specifically safety and security professionals, contact those in senior management to suggest the team be stood up in order to discuss the situation they feel to be percolating to a crisis condition. The request remains unanswered while, over the weekend, another bloody clash takes place between the government and protestors. The CEO, whose friend is the in-country project manager, contacts this manager and asks how things are going. The project manager says that everything is great, just great, and adds that the military and police will quickly quell this unrest and, by the way, will never side with protestors. The news shows vivid scenes the next day: Some of the protestors fight back, and people on both sides are hurt; 20 people die in the melee. Safety and Security managers approach senior management, which is resistant to calling the CCMT to meet. Efforts take place behind the scenes to attempt to convince the country manager to make such a request of senior management. But the country manager refuses, stating the situation is being blown out of proportion by the news media. Behind the scenes, Safety and Security begins to make inquiries of their home government and other sources to try to piece together the plans of governments or organizations that have expats in country. Some companies are beginning to remove their expats from the country, utilizing any commercial means possible.

As stated, the country manager is supported by senior management all the way up to the CEO. For these reasons, the Crisis Management Team is still not called up. Another round of protests ensues and, this time, over 200 protestors and government forces are killed. Governments of many other expats operating in the country advise them to evacuate as soon as possible. Slowly, word is received that companies are beginning to pull expats from the country, using commercial airliners as means to ferry employees to safe havens as soon as possible. Now, senior management and the CEO are interested in pulling personnel out of the country immediately, if not sooner. The company has previously contracted with an emergency medical and security evacuation outfit. This company is contacted and arrangements are made to have the company's expats proceed to a muster point and await airline tickets and a ride to the airport. While the expats are waiting, word is received that the government is halting the expat exodus by closing the airport to any further takeoffs or landings. Then, as if on cue, the government shuts down cellular phones and the Internet. The company has a dilemma. Its emergency evacuation plan is now curtailed, possibly out the window completely; the company spends the next 12 hours reestablishing communications and arranging for ground transportation and chartered aircraft to fly its employees to safety.

The next issue is that the only safe way to get the expats to the nearest airport where the charter craft may land and take off is through an area where many unofficial checkpoints have recently been popping up. It is obvious that a security detail is required to assist with the convoy of vehicles and attempting to get them safely from point A to take off point B. This is hurriedly arranged by members of the crisis management team but, now, the expats are unsure of how safe it is to drive the land route to the chartered aircraft—a very valid concern, to be sure. As discussions continue, there are reports of other cities where the expat conclaves have been ravaged, looted, and burned. The expats had previously abandoned these areas. The present location of the expats is not experiencing violence or looting, and the military is still present at checkpoints along the escape route to the chartered air location. The decision is made to make the vehicle convoy trip sooner rather than later. The checkpoints are cleared, with help from the former military indigenous security personnel contracted for this assignment. Along the route, the military is advising the convoy to hurry, to make good time to the airport, as the city they just left has been overcome with looting and rioting. As the convoy nears the airport, finally clearing the last government checkpoint, the landing strip is now less than a minute away. As the expats taxi down the runway, the pilot advises the passengers that reports are now being received that the military is in full support of the protestors and giving them assistance, including at checkpoints. The country manager, who knew so much about the comings and goings in the region where he had worked so long, had been incorrect. The delaying actions of this country manager had uselessly and carelessly stalled efforts to the point where every member of the project team had been endangered.

Dithering and wasting time don't work in crisis management. Allowing in-country managers to impede, slow, or otherwise impinge on crisis management planning or decision making places lives at risk. Anyone who spends too much time in country or on a particular project should not be the only deciding factor when it comes to planning and preparing for crisis management. In-country personnel may be reluctant to talk of serious things that can happen on the project. This might lead to other personnel not wanting to work on the project or to management thinking twice about remaining in country. Pulling up stakes in a crisis might endanger the project's completion or contracts in place. The company might suffer serious financial or public relations damage. The project manager may lose his or her job. For all of these reasons, precious time has been lost in crisis management and response. Preset, clearly articulated and formulated crisis management plans, supported by senior management who vow not to interfere with crisis operations, are what is required. The company does not need the country or project manager making a phone call back home, complaining that the project is at a difficult stage, that negotiations are tense right now, that *pulling up stakes* in the country right now won't go very far to dissuade nervous foreign clients of the company's intent to stay or not to stay.

Crisis management is not for the faint of heart. Crisis managers must understand that foreign operations can be very sensitive matters. Hopefully, the crisis management team has members who have been part of overseas multimillion dollar or euro projects that had much infrastructure and time and effort, that have run for years, and that are set to run for a few more. Hopefully, as well, these managers might have had emergency or difficult situations and can remember what it felt like to be concerned solely with life safety and not the bottom line. Maybe they will be the ones, who in spite of what competitors are doing or not doing in the country at the present time, are considering pulling their expats and flying or transporting their personnel to safety. Or, are the other companies in the region staying put and waiting to see what other companies are doing? Don't be a fence sitter; don't stick a wetted finger in the wind to check what others are doing. Has the government not made any recommendations yet? Because, let's face it, when the you-know-what hits the fan, foreign governments will have military escorts and fueled transport planes or helicopters warming up at the ready. Are there any helicopter charters to contact? Is this even practical? While you are sitting having your third cup of coffee or enjoying the drinks someone just ran out for, what are the expats doing? What if you are unable to contact them? What do they think you are doing? Do they trust your judgment to be for their benefit, or for the benefit of the company? What are the families of these expats thinking right now? Are they watching 24-hour news and getting the breathless reporting of the crisis junkie newspeople? Is the press even able to safely operate where your personnel are located? Should this be a sign from above for you?

Families worry about expats. Families who are not living with their expat husbands, wives, girlfriends, boyfriends, sons, and daughters worry about expats. They watch TV, they listen to the radio, they search online, and they read the papers. Crisis management teams, whether they have *stood up* in their emergency operations center or not, need to make a phone line available, 24/7, so that dependents and significant others can call in to get updates or receive or pass along critical information during emergencies or crises. Dependents need to be assured that

- Your company and your team have a crisis plan in place
- The safety of the expats is the most important function of your crisis team
- Your team is staying abreast of all of the latest information and mass media are not always the best indicator of what is really going on in the country
- Your team will do its best to keep everyone advised, should the expats not be able to contact their loved ones
- The caller is welcome to contact a designated member of the team at any time

If the people back home are happy, the expats will be happy. If the folks back home are not pleased with how things are being handled or the information they are receiving, there might be a mass revolt or exodus. What crisis teams do not want is for the expats to take any matters into their own hands or feel that the situation warrants their doing so. Expats have been known to panic in crisis situations: to band together, gather their supplies, and *circle their wagons*. Then, they often do the worst thing they could possibly do, given the circumstances: leave their residences, job sites, and office buildings and make their way outward on their own. Many a security, safety, or crisis management practitioner has been regaled by so-called world travelers with tales of how they "donned a ghutra and thobe and set out into the desert, to blend in and slip away into the night." These tales are nonsense. The likelihood of a Caucasian passing himself or herself off as native in sub-Saharan Africa are about as remote as finding palm trees at the North Pole. All James Bond and Jason Bourne abilities aside, a foreign-born and -raised individual will not be able to pass himself or herself off as local for very long, no matter the circumstances. And, with official and nonofficial roadblocks popping up everywhere, the chances of going quietly into the night are further diminished. Going off on one's own—even with proper maps; current GPS; satellite phones; adequate fuel; spare tires; trustworthy, mechanically sound vehicles; enough cash on hand; proper papers and personal documents; food and water; and first aid kits—is a risky endeavor. Intrepid travelers have often only made it as far as the first such checkpoint before they were relieved of said items, at the very least, and their lives in the worst-case scenarios.

This is why *standing fast* or hunkering down is often the best chance of surviving emergencies, depending upon the nature of the emergency. But, often, when there exists a lack of proper preplanning or emergency and crisis management plans and training, or in the event of the breakdown of communications, such actions are taken. Those on the ground in foreign locales have to be steadfast in their following of crisis plans. What if, although there are safe houses or pickup points and land travel is safe and warranted, the expats decide to go elsewhere and the crisis team is unable to locate these expats? What if the plan is to get an extraction team to the expats, but when that team arrives, no one is home? What if the evacuation plan called for a helicopter coming in for removal and the expats took off on motorcycles? No, crisis management plans that are set forth, agreed upon, trained upon, and relied upon must be followed, without deviation, unless and until the safety of the expats necessitates any changes. Crisis plans must be followed by the expats because, in the absence of reliable communications or the need to bug out and bug out quickly, the plan will be initiated without knowledge or input from the headquarters crisis management team back home. Hunkering down is important, of course, for several reasons, unless the situation is such that remaining represents a threat to life safety for the expats.

Such serious situations could include a chemical leak/cloud approaching or an evacuation necessitated by impending weather, such as hurricane, typhoon, etc., or of the man-made variety, such as house-to-house searches by rebels/terrorists or others looking to harm or kidnap expats. In other words, evacuating should only be undertaken if remaining poses the bigger threat to expats' lives and safety. Evacuating has so many variables: Is the route safe from a security standpoint or safety of the roadway and conditions? Are the vehicles adequate to make the trip? Is there enough room for everyone? Will the terrain be too tough for the vehicles? Another consideration is the destination. Are the destination and the route safe? When you are mobile, will you have reliable communications? Will a SAT phone work, or have you been relying upon Internet for communications with the home office? Are there police or fire stations along the route? Do you have their telephone numbers and addresses? Are these staffed 24/7? What about hospital, medical, or doctors' offices? Do you have telephone numbers and addresses for them? Will you make it there in one day; if not, will you be able to switch drivers to keep making time toward your destination? Is the route clearly mapped out and if, for some reason, it is not passable, are there alternate routes to be found? If the group is stopped, where will they go?

Bombs and bomb threats represent some of the most serious situations facing organizational managers and safety, security, and crisis management managers. The decision to evacuate or not evacuate buildings—for example, when a bomb threat is received—is a situation that might make or break a manager, or cause criticism from employees (for not evacuating) or from management (for overreacting and evacuating). Just what is the right call? Concerning bomb threats—more specifically, the threat from a certain type of bomb—another significant and ongoing threat to personnel working in hostile regions around the globe is that of improvised explosive devices, or IEDs. IEDs take many forms and sizes, ranging from a device planted in a brown paper lunch bag to a vehicle filled with hundreds or thousands of pounds of high explosives. These types of IEDs are generally broken down into the category of VBIEDs (vehicle-borne improvised explosive devices) and those carried by persons or MPIEDs (man-portable improvised explosive devices). Due to the difference in the amount of explosives each means of conveyance may deliver, each has preferred targeting. VBIEDs are more often used to attempt to destroy buildings. They may be parked outside buildings to cause major structural damage or be placed in parking garages under structures in an effort to bring them down. Often, VBIEDs are driven into security gates or other structures surrounding buildings or crashed directly into buildings. The bombs have such high concentrations of explosives that, even if detected or stopped by security services at checkpoints or gates, a detonation will still cause massive damage to adjacent structures and everything in between. But don't focus solely upon cars, vans, and trucks. VBIEDs have been placed on motorcycles and even bicycles to deadly effect.

The use of man-portable IEDs most generally targets the interiors of buildings or crowded areas, such as markets or outdoor meetings, speeches, and sporting events. Unlike the sheer size and pressure of car/truck/vehicle bombs, these are limited by how many kilograms of explosives the often suicide bomber may carry on his or her person or in a backpack or parcel. Those who carry these smaller bombs often pack them with ball bearings, nails, BBs, marbles, and even rocks in order to maximize the lethal potential of shrapnel emanating from the blast.

Methods for countering MBIEDs include sufficient use of security personnel for checkpoints and proper patrolling of grounds and surrounding areas, including use of closed circuit television cameras.

In many hostile regions or regions where car or vehicle bombs (VBIEDs) have been utilized, an effective countermeasure is to make use of increasing the standoff distance between areas where VBIEDs or IEDs in general might be detonated and the target structure. There are engineering charts and design ratios available for determining at which distance a control perimeter, checkpoint, or barriers might be effective for controlling the blast pressures and damage. Obviously, the larger the device is, the further from the building the barrier would need to be located. In addition, blast walls, sometimes no more than Jersey-barrier type concrete, sandbagging, or Hessco units, may be placed in order to absorb or deflect blast pressure waves. Vehicle inspections at checkpoints that include the use of mirrors, dogs, and electronic *sniffers* are effective countermeasures.

Methods for countering VBIEDs include use of security patrols along routes to be used for transporting personnel or supplies. Varying patrols might upset planning or constructing of IED threats along roadways. While driving, it is important to keep an eye out for unusual objects or items along the roadway. Be aware that an IED may be contained in anything from a soda can to an animal carcass. IEDs are often remotely detonated, so not seeing anyone in close proximity to a suspicious device is still not safe. As with all security, awareness is key and appearing alert is critical. If organizations are patrolling routes and appear to be aware of the roadways and surroundings, perpetrators might pick another easier target.

When traveling by vehicle, groupings of three or more vehicles are considered optimum. Vehicles spaced adequately (recommended distance is about two to three vehicle lengths apart) might make detonating a device at the ideal moment less successful. Route selection would be dependent upon patrol information and recommendations, and choosing alternate routes in order to confuse those intent upon attacks is advisable. Varying the rates of speed and the time of day that convoys are moving will help to thwart attacks. If, along your route, you observe items in or near the roadway such as boxes, trash bags, rocks stacked up, piles of dirt, or animal carcasses, go with your instincts and stop, turn around, and proceed in the other direction. Any such suspicions and observations must be immediately reported to the proper authorities. In some areas, the roadsides and shoulders and the countryside in general might be littered with unexploded ordinance (UXO), which consists of unexploded artillery shells or explosive rounds, bombs dropped, cluster munitions scattered, missiles fired, and land mines. Some countries have no idea and only rough estimates of how many of such devices are scattered across their countrysides. Somewhere between 15,000 and 20,000 people who come into contact with these ordinances die each year (United Nations, 2008). If you are going to be working in regions where UXOs are present, your crisis management plan must include first clearing them and figuring out how to deal with those you do not discover.

Ensure that vehicle convoys and personnel have proper personal protective equipment, including protective vests, helmets, and vehicle armoring. First-aid kits and properly trained medical personnel are critical, along with reliable communications if medical extraction or assistance is required. Communications are critical to convoys in preparing for and dealing with the possibility of IEDs/VBIEDs. If there is a detonation and injuries, or simply damage to vehicles that makes them inoperable, it will be necessary to phone for assistance. If satellite phones are the only viable option, they need to be in good working and reception order. If vehicles are using transponders and route tracking/emergency alert GPS devices (advised in areas supported by military/government forces), these as well need to be properly maintained and effective. Communications might be required to request mechanical assistance, response, protection or rescue from attack or criminality, and, in extreme circumstances, medical evacuation. Knowing grid coordinates and exact location will be vital to requesting emergency medical evacuation or security assistance if required. The methods of preparing for and requesting these services should be codified and drilled. Properly equipped first-aid kits, including trauma kits, should be made available to vehicle convoys, and medically trained personnel able to care for trauma should be part of the groups.

When dealing with VBIEDs or the potential for IEDs, at what point is the situation too risky for convoys to travel? At what stage does it become too dangerous to remain in a location, region, or country where IEDs/ VBIEDs are a way of life? Of course, the main question the crisis management team should ask themselves, and ask their corporate management, is whether the benefits of working in such regions are worth the risks that expats are taking by working there. These are more difficult management decisions to make.

One issue that often confronts employees working around the world is that of driving or being driven in rough terrain or under hazardous conditions. Road safety in foreign countries or in remote or harsh weather regions of the United States is critical to mitigating emergencies or disasters. A first step in determining the potential hazards for driving might be to check with the US State Department's country information pages for road safety information and suggestions. From this information, one might glean information such as the proliferation of land mines along roadways in former war-torn areas, or bandits and highwaymen plying their trade in regions, or merely the severely improperly maintained roadways where a pothole might become more of a sand trap. It is estimated that about one million people per year are killed in road accidents around the globe (World Health Organization, n.d.).

The number one killer of Americans abroad is such an accident (Boon, 2016). It should be a rule of thumb that the best drivers in other countries are qualified, trained, and safe drivers who are native to the country and, hopefully, the region. They will know not only how to drive, but also where and when to do so. The local drivers or anyone else operating vehicles should, of course, always use seat belts. They should be aware of any potential hazards or areas that are known to have dangerous roads. Defensive and evasive driving courses should be provided to drivers in areas where such training is warranted. Defensive driving is particularly useful in any driving situation. Evasive driving is of great use where criminal or terrorist activity has been perpetrated. Along with defensive driving, recognizing surveillance is of importance to those who are allowed to drive themselves. How to respond to car hijackings (give up the vehicle) or avoid carjackings (keep windows up and doors locked), for example, is a useful training topic.

One of the biggest complaints of expats working in foreign locations is that they feel the need or the right to drive themselves. Next to not wanting to provide travel itineraries to safety and security departments, this might be the biggest complaint. If you are going to advise an engineer or scientist, scholar, or construction worker that he or she is not going to be able to drive in a foreign location, be ready for an argument. "I have driven everywhere, in more countries than you!" they will scream. But, it stands to reason that expats driving in a foreign location, unless they have been raised since childbirth in that country and have driven since their teenage years in these locations, will simply not realize the nuances and *do*'s and *don't*'s of foreign driving. They will not have experienced the bumper-car rush hours or holiday and weekend traffic. They will be at the mercy of whoever would like to strike their vehicle and, in most cases, will be legally unable to make their case if such an incident takes place. They might be taken into custody by law enforcement, solicited for bribes in accidents, or, in extreme cases, beaten or killed by mobs of people. It is simply not worth it for expats to drive themselves in difficult or foreign locations—especially where language differences cause difficulty. If your expats want to drive themselves, tell them to stick to England, Ireland, or several other European locations. Driving along the beach in San Diego is a lot different from hitting a four-foot deep pothole at 45 miles an hour along a stretch of roadway in South America or North Africa. One is picturesque and enjoyable; the other will rattle your teeth, and, if you are lucky, you might be able to walk away from it with only a totaled vehicle and some injuries.

Various countries and regions have their own concerns and safety considerations. There may be issues with severe weather ranging from sudden snow or ice storms in the US Rocky Mountains, Pennsylvania, or Massachusetts, or sandstorms in Jordan or torrential rain in Indonesia. Weather conditions, ranging from wind velocity to amounts of rain and more recognizable seasonal affectations might be unknown to the beginning regional driver. Driving at night is bad enough in unknown areas, but add to this the likelihood of the probability of livestock or wildlife in the road and the chances for a mishap are increased dramatically. Difficult terrain is made more risky with the scarcity of lighting, highway or road lane or shoulder striping, road signs, stoplights, and traffic signals. Roadways may be narrow and poorly maintained. Travelers should be aware of the roads and routes to avoid because of these conditions.

Expats may be unaware of the local driving culture and nuances, the speed limits (even the Autobahn has limits in some areas), the practices of honking or flashing lights when passing, or merely the preponderance of honking in general. Pedestrian concerns are of major importance, with the proliferation of pedestrians, the lack of marked crosswalks, and the narrowness of roads just a few concerns. Aggressive driving is nothing new, but in some countries and regions, it is taken to a new level. In most countries, many drivers are inexperienced and, frankly, should not be driving in the first place. Having neither a license to drive nor insurance is nothing new. Add to the mix of lousy drivers the proliferation of cellular phones, being intoxicated in one form or another while driving, and vehicles that are not safe to be on roads in the first place, and roadways can be very hazardous to one's health.

In some countries, corrupt police officials look for out-of-town or out-of-country drivers in order to stop drivers for some reason and extract bribes for imaginary traffic violations or vehicle inspections. What small town hasn't at least been accused of or benefited from speed traps and other revenue-generating activities?

Drivers in foreign locales must be aware of all the aforementioned advice and ensure their vehicles are well equipped in hazardous driving areas and conditions. Carry spare tires and adequate tire-changing tools. Have extra fuel safely on board. Know the availability of and call-up procedures for roadside assistance. Make use of vehicle-mounted global positioning system (GPS) and global system for mobile communications (GSM) to know where corporate vehicles (or mobile units for rental vehicles) are located and if there are issues. These Internet-monitored systems will allow safety and security personnel to track your vehicle movements, and they will allow you to send an alert if you are in trouble, as well as what the nature of the trouble is.

Safe and defensive driving courses are recommended for personnel who absolutely must drive themselves in foreign locales. One method is to have security and safety personnel based in the home country take expats around and show them the different driving extremes and make recommendations on how to avoid traffic mishaps, what to do in case of emergency driving, and what to do in case of an accident. If these personnel are unable to convince the expat that he or she has no business driving, then you may be forced to attempt to pull some rank to back up your recommendation. Or you can let the expat drive and back him or her up with plenty of insurance and medical benefits because these will be needed at some point. Have the expat demonstrate car care techniques and aptitude. If the expat is unwilling or unable to change a flat tire on a US highway, will he or she be willing or able to do so in the Middle East? What if help is five hours away?

REFERENCES

Boon, Jane E. How Americans die abroad, *Time Magazine*, March 8, 2016. http://time.com/4250811/travel-safety.

United Nations. Demining. 2008. http://www.un.org/ed/globalissues/demining.

World Health Organization. Road traffic deaths. Global Health Observatory Data. n.d. http://www.who.int/gho/road_safety/mortality/traffic_deaths_number/en/.

16

9/11 and Y2K: Crisis Planning and Management Paradigms

Two incidents that have occurred in US history over the past 17 years probably best exemplify the successes and pitfalls of crisis management and contingency planning. These two events—the Y2K or the Year 2000 Computing Crisis, and the 9/11 attack on the World Trade Center—are examples of what succeeds and why we still fail in preparing for the worst.

Bob Bemer was a well-known mathematician and computer scientist. He was a computer programming pioneer and guru in the middle of the twentieth century. He was one of the first to have adequately heralded the issue of the Year 2000 Bug (Y2K) and publish a paper on this issue as early as 1971 calling it the *Millennium Bug*. In the 1950s and 1960s, of course, many people were getting into computing, and most programming utilized a two-digit reference for the date, such as "68" for "1968," and so on. When a special request came in from "a group of Mormons in the late '50s who wanted to enlist the newfangled machines in their genealogy project—clearly the kind of work that calls for thinking outside the twentieth century box. Bemer obliged by inventing the picture clause, which allowed for a four-digit year. From this point on, more than 40 years ahead of schedule, the technology was available for every computer in the world to become Y2K compliant" (Taylor, 1999). Programmers ignored Bemer's fix for decades to follow.

The buildup to the Y2K Millennium Bug mitigation, or the Y2K Crisis, or the Year 2000 Computing Crisis—whatever one chose to call this dilemma—was gigantic. Depending on whom one chooses to

183

believe—those within or those outside of the computer world—either a total disaster, such as the one predicted in the US banking and financial industry, was avoided, or computer programmers and experts used the hype surrounding the impending millennium to line their pockets and make a fast buck.

The August 1998 Government Accounting Office (GAO) report entitled "Year 2000 Computing Crisis: Business Continuity and Contingency Planning" pulls no punches from its opening paragraph salvo. It begins,

> The Year 2000 problem, while technical in nature, is primarily a business problem, with many organizations facing the risk of Year 2000-induced interruptions or failures of their core business processes. Time is running out and many federal organizations may not be able to renovate or replace all of their mission critical systems in time. Organizations must reduce the risk and potential impact of Year 2000-induced information system failures on their core business processes by implementing rigorous business continuity planning processes.

That's a pretty unambiguous statement from an independent, nonpartisan agency. It successfully captured what was the majority opinion among most of the world's computer experts and professionals—that something had to be done to avert impending doom. The theory of the Y2K crisis began, of course, years before 2000, but as exhibited by the 1998 GAO report, began to build in earnest two or three years before the millennium. Gun sales shot up, particularly in the United States. Sales of freeze dried food and survival gear spiked. Popular televangelist of the time, Reverend Jerry Falwell, stated, "I believe that Y2K may be God's instrument to shake this nation, humble this nation, awaken this nation and from this nation start revival that spreads the face of the earth before the Rapture of the Church" (Winerip, 2013).

No one knows how many people stocked up on provisions, including food, ammunition, and water and packed their families off to isolated locations to wait out the impending crash. But many know of such persons who did so. Camouflaged as a "family getaway or vacation," many people took off work and quietly yet covertly, so as not to attract ridicule, stashed their families in safe locations. The Clinton administration appointed a *Y2K Czar.*

> John Koskinen, chairman of the President's Council on Year 2000 Conversion, told a joint House committee hearing that even those federal agencies, such as the Defense Department and the Federal Aviation Administration, that have reportedly lagged in fixing their computers

for the Year 2000 computer problem will be ready by the end of 1999. Koskinen appeared before a joint hearing of the House Government Management, Information and Technology Subcommittee and the House Technology Subcommittee.

Orlando De Bruce (1999)
Federal Y2K Czar defends upbeat outlook

Many federal workers in the United States were given off the Friday before the millennium crept up, ostensibly so that the Feds could complete their pre-Y2K reprogramming efforts, but also perhaps because no one really knew what to expect.

The failure to identify, or simple overlooking of the issue which would present itself on the change in dates from 1999 to the year 2000—with computers capable of only registering dates beginning with the numerals 19, led corporations and government agencies in the United States to spend an estimated $100 billion dollars in programming costs (The United States Senate Special Committee on the Year 2000 Technology Problem, 2000). Estimates of precautionary spending around the world bordered on trillions of dollars. Predictions by US government agencies and computer experts ranged from US taxpayers not being able to receive tax refunds or file returns, to planes falling from the skies due to catastrophic on board or air traffic control system failures. Up to 40% of the US power grid was deemed at risk to fail, and hospitals were concerned that incubators containing premature babies would shut down at midnight on December 31, 1999. Many security, safety, and crisis management personnel around the world found themselves hanging out with their colleagues, eating pizza or snacking, watching TV or playing cards as the millennium approached. Many corporations and organizations had redeployed their information technology (IT) professionals months earlier to tackle the issue of determining which key company computer systems would be affected by the Y2K bug, and to make corrections to see this did not take place. Still, not knowing how the rest of the world did or did not prepare, many such Y2K watch groups were formed, especially in organizations that had worldwide technology concerns. After all, who could trust the Russians or Chinese to properly prepare for Y2K? How would the Internet as a whole fare when the clock struck midnight?

Naysayers point out that in comparison to the approximately $100 billion on computer system upgrades spent in the United States, Russia reportedly spent only approximately $200 million dollars (Doward, 2000). Some estimated a lot of the money was wasted and was spent unnecessarily. To fight the dreaded Millennium Bug, Aeroflot—the Russian national air carrier—spent $1 million dollars, while British Airways had $280 million to devote to the issue. "But, we had no money to fix the problem," said Professor Andrey Nikolaevich Terekhov, who oversaw the Russian Y2K planning center. "The World Bank gave us $14 million but this just went on consulting fees and paying the hotel bills of their representatives" (Doward, 2000). In addition, with much of the Russian computer system relying on software that had been illegally obtained from IBM and other software manufacturers, the Russian system was playing—pun intended—Russian roulette.

So, what was the Y2K in its essence? Was it in fact a bona fide issue? Was the United States, as the GAO (1998) reported, going to be responsible for being "...fully aware of the potentially devastating financial, organizational, and political consequences of the failure of one or more mission-critical information systems"?

Faced with daunting statements and prognostications, including from the religious, military, political, and social hierarchy, business and governments had no choice but to comply. The GAO identified and spelled out the processes which US private and public sector organizations needed to carry forward. It first recommended the establishment of project work groups dedicated to the business continuity of each organization. Next, each newly formed group would develop a strategy to seeing to this continuity. The key functions and business processes of each group must then be identified and prioritized. Assignments and the roles of the team participants should quickly follow. The group should set about establishing target dates and milestones, and a risk management and reporting protocol should be developed. All existing emergency, contingency, and business continuity plans should be assessed. And, finally, the resulting system should be audited.

Sounds like a perfect model for developing an organizational crisis management plan. Y2K blended the techies and nontechies. The bankers and the geeks. The pocket protectors and the pressed suits, the skateboarders, and the, well, you get the picture. Prompted by the US government appointment of a *czar*, Congress holding hearings, and IT experts writing voluminous accounts, industry and organizations kicked into high gear. Consultants were in high demand. Vendors were hounded by software customers. Entire customer service departments and staffs were hired just to handle an onrush of incoming phone calls and inquiries. Many organizations deferred and even canceled vacations for key personnel in order to work on the preplanning and corrections, and to be present while the world witnessed the rollover into the new century. No one single crisis,

CASE STUDY   DON'T DENY ME, DUDE

A multinational company had begun to expand into more and more foreign markets, which is a very good thing if this is your business model. The company thus began to send more personnel around the world in order to meet with clients and customers, for fact-finding trips, and for conferences. The Security Department for the company looked to expand itself with regard to the types of security, country, and travel intelligence, and US government contacts around the world. In order to accomplish this, the security department joined the State Department group OSAC, or the Overseas Security Advisory Council. OSAC was formed by the US State Department in 1985 as a means of providing an avenue to US private sector corporations to share with colleagues and the State Department best practices for securing people and assets around the world. In 2015, there were approximately 4600 US corporations that were members of OSAC.

But no one in senior management of this multinational company had heard of OSAC. The division leader had not heard of OSAC. And, even with a more than ample travel budget, the security personnel who visited the OSAC annual meetings, which were held at the State Department in Washington, D.C., continued to be asked about the cost-effectiveness of spending four days in Washington, with its $400 per night hotel rooms and costly round trip tickets, let alone the time spent away from the office. Maybe the security department was trying to rack up frequent flyer miles?

But, the security department stayed the course. The department built relationships with other constituent members of OSAC, and the many analysts, or country experts in security, whom they met at these gatherings. The security department attended the annual conferences, hearing the subject matter experts discuss the background and threat perspectives of the security concerns for regions around the world. If there was a rebel movement threatening US interests with attacks, or US citizens in another country or area were becoming at risk of kidnappings for profit, or the pickpockets in another location had begun to seriously become a menace for US tourists, this was the forum for such discussions. In addition, by meeting and getting to know colleagues from one of the thousands of other members who might share similar operations or geographical locations,

187

or similar threats or security issues, solutions or common methods of mitigation might be discussed.

Constituent members at these meetings shared their experiences around the world dealing with security and crisis emergencies. Best practices were discussed and shared. What worked and what did not, which security or crisis vendors could assist, and which ones didn't operate in certain countries. Trends and developments in these areas were discussed. Concerns for expats were brought up to the State Department subject matter experts for the particular countries and regions. As far as networking goes, this was time and money well-spent. But, to the bean counters back home, where was the payoff? It all sounded like a boondoggle to them.

Then, one Wednesday morning, bright and early, the security director whose trips to OSAC and expenses had been placed under such a microscope received a telephone call. The caller was a member of this OSAC group. The caller stated that one of the security director's company's senior management officers had attended a conference held by a group that was not particularly favored by activists. Some of the more extreme activists had stolen a list of the persons attending the conference which contained their company names and even their e-mail addresses. The extremists had asked for their supporters to begin denial of service attacks against the corporate websites of everyone attending. That morning, some attendees' websites had already been under attack, and the security director's company couldn't be far behind. Thanking the caller, the security director quickly contacted the information services (IS) director, who upon checking, noticed the beginnings of some strange activity. Over the next three days, the DOS attack strengthened in its intensity, but the early warning from the OSAC member had provided enough of a cushion for IS to deploy countermeasures that were effective enough to prevent the downing of the entire network, and the potential loss of millions of dollars.

Question: Do you believe the bean counters were ever again allowed to hassle the security director concerning any activity relating to OSAC?

or predicted crisis, as this instance could more properly be described, had existed prior to this. It is as if planet earth were to have discovered a comet that was hurtling its way, and the world had two years to prepare to destroy it in space. At first, many skeptics were saying the comet was too far from earth to worry about, then they claimed the course of the comet could not be properly quantified. Finally, some said the size of the comet by the time it reached earth might turn out to be the size of a grapefruit. Eventually, everyone decided to spend the money on a defense plan of rockets and laser beams.

Getting organizations to spend money on a crisis of which there were not quite so many naysayers, as there were with Y2K, but there were some, is a feat in and of itself. What about a threat, as exemplified in the case study "Don't Deny Me, Dude," of a denial of service? Is your organization susceptible, a target, or prepared? To have organizations spend the amount of funds they did on something that had never happened before (can you imagine explaining the concept of Y2K to a person living in Tombstone, Arizona in 1881? The biggest occurrence that year was the shootout at the O.K. Corral.). So, here is an event, predicted well in advance, which could conceivably cost untold billions or more in financial and other damages, medical devices could stall in hospitals, power stations might shut down and refuse to restart, and satellites might plunge from the heavens. And, add to this, not everyone was sure the efforts to mitigate the disaster would solve the issue. We couldn't count on developing countries, or our enemies, to do the right thing. On the contrary, might they not use this opportunity to attack us?

For crisis management professionals, the lesson, or template, under which the Y2K planning took place could be considered one of envy. Concerning the issue of the "19s" versus the "two zeroes" (20), many organizational resources were devoted, vacations were canceled or postponed. Massive overtime was paid out, countless consultants made their year in a few weeks by hiring themselves out to the highest bidders. Company IT plans were shelved and all hands were adapted into a fight to squash the Millennium Bug. As a crisis management event it was superb. Companies focused on one common foe. Resources and monies were made available, all eyes were glued to the progress reports. Most consumers had no idea of the late nights, the long weekends, the skipped birthdays and missed holiday parties. They might have assumed the lights burning all night at the corporate headquarters were for a new product launch or an acquisition, merger, etc.

In other words, the world took the warnings of crisis seriously. Not at first, of course. But, as more and more computer experts and consultants began reaching the mass media with their warnings, it took off like a forest fire. Magazine covers and TV programs were dedicated to the warnings. US commerce and worldwide businesses and governments had no choice but to comply with efforts to stave off disaster. Some did so more than others. And what were the results? What really happened after midnight on Deccember 31, 1999?

According to the February 29, 2000 GAO report, "While hundreds of computer problems have been reported since January 1, 2000, most have been quickly corrected and none have caused serious disruptions. Because there is no incentive for corporations or countries to openly report problems, the full extent of Y2K's impact may never be known" (The United States Senate Special Committee on the Year 2000 Technology Problem, 2000, p. 9).

Was Y2K good or bad for disaster or crisis planning? As pointed out, if one looks at it solely from the standpoint of a monumental focus on one impending (whether you believed in its inevitability or not) crisis of computers crashing around the world, the subsequent efforts of crisis planning, of the steps that were taken to fix the problems before these occurred, and yet to be ready for any crisis that might still develop, could be looked on as a lesson for all crisis planners.

"Y2K was the first instance during which emergency managers in all 50 states and the US territories were simultaneously operational and in direct communication with FEMA in anticipation of a single-source disaster or hazard" (The United States Senate Special Committee on the Year 2000 Technology Problem, 2000, p. 8).

When 8:46 AM took place in New York City on September 11, 2001, most Americans and many people around the world can tell you exactly where they were and what they were doing. It's as if that instant were permanently seared into our memories much like the searing heat of 10,000 gallons of aviation fuel contained within the first plane as it struck the North Tower. Within the next 77 minutes, 2981 persons would be killed at the Twin Towers, the Pentagon, and on the four airplanes used in the attacks. Crisis management reached heroic levels on this day, with many brave firefighters, police, paramedics, and coworkers diving into the chaos. Many gave the ultimate sacrifice and lost their lives in the effort.

After the dust had long since settled and the wreckage had been cleared, much has been investigated and written about concerning the crisis management planning before and the crisis response during the tragedies. But, what was known about the World Trade Center, or the Twin Towers, as more people called them, was that the location had long been a hugely desired target for terrorists around the world. But, to first understand what went on during and after the tragedy on 9/11, it is important to consider the first attack on the World Trade Center, which took place February 26, 1993.

February 26 was a chilly day in New York City. The cold temperature seemed colder than the mid-20s as the wind whipped between buildings and down streets and alleyways. Then, the normal hustle and bustle of the New York City lunch hour was rocked at 12:18 PM by a loud explosion emanating from the World Trade Center complex. New York City Fire Department Engine Co. 10 as well as Ladder Company 10 were located directly across the street and the explosion rattled their walls and windows. As they and other engine companies they notified arrived at the scene, heavy acrid black smoke was seen billowing through World Trade Center garage doors indicating the explosion or fire began below grade. Many assumed it to be a large transformer blowing up and catching fire. As more units of first responders began to arrive, the location of the fire seemed to be directly below the Vista Hotel, in the parking garage. The lobby of Tower 1 was now filling up with smoke. It was 12:27 PM. Soon reports of more smoke in Tower 1 and now of people being trapped were flooding in. Many more calls went out from the fire department for help. Being expert in Incident Command, the fire department quickly had set up a command post for coordinating the immediate concerns—those of life safety for those who were inside Tower 1 and the parking garage.

However, the first responders were immediately beset by communication issues.

> A major detriment to our ability to strengthen control of the incident was fire department on-scene communications. Communications were a serious problem from the outset. With 156 units and 31 chiefs operating at the height of this incident, try to imagine how difficult it was to gain control of the portable-radio operations frequency. Two command channels and one tactical channel were used. In many cases, runners were sent by a sector commander to communicate with the incident commander. (p. 7)

> Anthony L. Fusco (1993)
> *The World Trade Center Bombing: Report and Analysis*

There were simply too many fire companies and first responders using their radios. There were not enough channels to use and messages were being lost due to distance or frequency bleed or diffusion, or the inability to transmit through concrete and cement walls or steel structures. Fire couldn't speak with police, police couldn't speak with paramedics, and so on. To add to the mix, the blast, fire, smoke, and water took out the fire alarm and public address system, the Port Authority's fire command station was not serviceable, standpipes and automatic sprinklers were either totally inoperable or severely damaged, and emergency generators ran for only 20 minutes before overheating and shutting down, and then even the backup power to the building was gone (Fusco, 1993, p. 7).

When it was all over, six people had died and 1042 had been injured. The Ryder box truck the two bombers placed on the B2 level of the parking garage contained an approximately 1310-pound sophisticated bomb which was detonated after the pair lit a long fuse, estimated to give them 12 minutes to depart the parking garage. The parking garage was severely damaged by the blast or flooding on the lowest level, and both of the Towers had to be evacuated. The tremendous evacuation effort, with stairwells filled with smoke and the extreme lack of communications between first responders would be a test run for efforts that would take place eight years later when the second attack on the World Trade Center succeeded in bringing both towers down.

Remarkably, tragically, when New York City firefighters wanted to communicate with its crews inside the Towers, the radio system failed again, just like it had in 1993. Firefighters inside the North Tower didn't know the South Tower had just fallen. They continued to attempt to save everyone they could until their building collapsed. Police and fire crews were unable to communicate with each other. In a rush to get to the Towers as quickly and any way they could, firefighters and police officers left posts and grabbed rides in private vehicles in order to get to the scene, furthering the confusion of who was on scene and where they were located. In 1996, three years after the first attack on the World Trade Center, the city created the Office of Emergency Management. But, at the time of the 2001 attack, no joint disaster exercise involving the key agencies—New York police and fire department, and the New York Port Authority—had taken place (Dwyer et al., 2002).

Many don't realize that the City of New York's Mayor's Office of Emergency Management (OEM) was located on the 23rd floor of 7 World Trade Center, immediately adjacent to the North Tower. Many argued against placing the command center so near the target of the 1993 attack and location which many believed to be an ongoing target for terrorists. In addition, there were no plans for a backup OEM should this site fail (The 9/11 Commission Report, 2004, p. 284). The 7 World Trade Center building would in fact be destroyed when it collapsed hours after the Twin Towers had fallen due to a fire that raged in the building all day.

The Port Authority of New York in the aftermath of the 1993 World Trade Center bombing began to conduct fire drills at least biannually with prior notification of tenants in both Towers. The standard for the drills was for floor or fire warden fellow employees to lead their colleagues to the center of their floors where they would activate the emergency intercom system which would then be used by first responders during an actual emergency to advise employees what to do. For the most part, during these drills those participating were not advised to proceed to the emergency stairwells, or told about crossover or transfer hallways or fire doors which could lead them safely to alternate stairwells. Participants had no idea that they might in some circumstances have to walk up stairwells first in order to then catch another stairwell and walk down from there. Some tenants did cover such complexities during the fire drill and did utilize more robust drilling, but the plans and exercises varied across the board. Some participating in drills had no idea that doors leading to the roof were kept locked and there had been no plans for building occupants to be picked up from rooftops. In fact, no emergency response planning had gone into the possibility of persons trapped in the immensely tall high rises at the World Trade Center given the likelihood of some occupants not being able to walk down stairwells due to flames, smoke, or damage and who would subsequently require rooftop rescue. Many building occupants initially climbed up stairwells rather than descending downward. In any case, many occupants had not been trained or were not aware that as they reached lower floors they would be faced with crossover hallways and might come on smoke doors as they were attempting to evacuate. Smoke doors, for example, within the stairwells of the World Trade Center would have been closed once alarms were activated, but these doors were not locked (Ferreira et al., 2008, p. 3).

As will be pointed out more than once in this book, those responsible for crisis management and emergency response planning for private sector organizations need to be aware that the first few actions, the first few minutes of response are the most important.

> The "first" first responders on 9/11, as in most catastrophes, were private-sector civilians. Because 85 percent of our nation's critical infrastructure is controlled not by government but by private sector, private-sector civilians are likely to be the first responders in any future catastrophes. (p. 317)
>
> The 9/11 Commission Report (2004)
> *Final Report of the National Commission on Terrorist Attacks*
> *upon the United States (9/11 Report)*

In crisis situations, as has been pointed out, one cannot rely on first responders and response agencies. Persons must be responsible for their own safety and respond to crisis situations appropriately as groups or on their own individually. The more people who are able to evacuate themselves or others in the correct and safest manner, such as in a high-rise, office building, or other structures, the less time first responders will have to spend on doing so and they are able to focus on other areas.

In order to operate successfully as groups or individuals within a high-rise office or other facility emergency, clearly illustrated and trained/ exercised plans must be in place. Such plans should become almost second nature for building or facility occupants to the point that if a fire alarm were to be sounded, if there are no instructions given to groups assembled at a predetermined muster point where further instructions would be given by building managers or first responders, these persons could then get themselves to correct evacuation means such as emergency stairwells. They would not first go up stairwells rather than downward, and would know where crossover hallways or smoke doors might lie in their path toward safety. As in the Twin Towers in 1993 and again in 2001, radio communications were extremely difficult due to the nature of the structure itself, and other conditions.

> First, the radio's effectiveness was drastically reduced in the high-rise environment. Second, tactical channel 1 was simply overwhelmed by the number of units attempting to communicate on it at 10:00. Third, some firefighters were on the wrong channel or simply lacked radios altogether. (p. 322)
>
> The 9/11 Commission Report (2004)
> *Final Report of the National Commission on Terrorist Attacks*
> *upon the United States (9/11 Report)*

9/11 illustrates a common theme among disaster managers and emergency planning. Since 1993, New York City had 8 years, one might argue, to come up with suitable plans and to use the first attack as a template on which to build an ongoing crisis management plan. In the case of lessons from 1993 involving communications issues, primarily radios and their ineffective use within the towers, and the inability of agencies such as police and fire to communicate with each other, or communicate among themselves, the lesson was not acted on. The location of the New York City Emergency Operations Center within a building immediately adjacent to the Twin Towers was also a poor choice, given prior knowledge from 1993. Lives were lost in the Twin Towers due to the inability of first responders on the outside to notify those inside the towers that they needed to evacuate themselves immediately as first one then the other tower crumbled down. Think about for one moment how your organization is going to communicate to a group of your expat employees located in a dozen time zones across the world where radio and cellular phone, even satellite phone or e-mails, are sketchy at best. Add to this the unknowns of the infrastructure within the countries or regions where they work. For example, if a crisis strikes Panama, how much phone traffic will landline phone networks handle before crashing, how much will the cell towers be able to bear? If the Internet and phone service fails or is shut down by government or nongovernment actions in some far flung locales, how will headquarters keep in contact? Will your expat or employees in another city end up "waiting at the must point" such as those in the Twin Towers, for further instructions? Or will they be well trained and equipped enough to handle the crisis as is best suited when you are unable to give them the correct or any advice? In either case, training is key—the more training the better. Employees need to act as if it is rote memory, a muscle reflex, when responding to disaster or crisis. Crisis managers must operate in the same manner, as if they are on autopilot and each fiber in their being knows exactly what to do.

The case of the attack on the World Trade Center and discussions of the planning leading up to the year "2000, Y2K" concerns illustrate the good and not so successful with regard to crisis management. In fact, the upcoming millennium was a focus not only of computer programmers, the government and private sector with respect to what could potentially fail, such as computers combined with financial and defense institutions, but also a concern of counterterrorism officials around the world.

> On December 14, 1999, Ahmed Ressam—a 34-year-old Algerian—was arrested at Port Angeles, Washington attempting to enter the US with components used to manufacture improvised explosive devices. He subsequently admitted that he planned to bomb Los Angeles International Airport on the eve of the Millennium 2000 celebrations.
>
> Forensic scientists from both the Royal Canadian Mounted Police (RCMP) and the FBI examined the evidence in this case. An FBI Laboratory Explosives Unit examiner compared evidence found in Ressam's motel room with items seized in Port Angeles.
>
> Federal Bureau of Investigation (1999)
> *Millennium plot/Ahmed Ressam*

There had been much concern in the intelligence and military community leading up to the turn of the century that Al Qaeda would attempt

195

to make a bold statement and attack in the United States as celebrations for the incoming year 2000 were underway. The plot was thwarted, the arrest was made, and a crisis was averted. Most in the intelligence and government agencies felt the United States rested and relaxed after Y2K came and went without a widespread computer network failure and with this arrest being made with no subsequent attacks.

The lessons from Y2K and 9/11 are complex when combined and looked on as a whole. Y2K was a success for crisis management in that the threat of the computer failures was enough to convince private and public sectors to develop large sums of money in order to mitigate computers failing to realize the rollover from 1999 to 2000. But, would it lead to a backlash when the crisis didn't appear to be so monumental after all? Would this spell the end of crisis preparation involving the information systems of private and public sectors? Since the billions spent on the lead up to Y2K, nothing has captivated the information sector like the millennium bug. Information experts now focus on preventing hackers and denial of service attacks, which can cost private and public sectors millions of dollars in down time. And, as the news services are full of, stories of personal information including credit card or personal data are almost a daily treat. Y2K might seem silly to a young person in college or high school right now. It was something that appeared so simple and caused such dread and worldwide panic. People actually hid themselves away *off the grid* in order to wait out the collapse of society as it was known. It didn't happen, either because of the hard work of thousands of computer programmers or the built-in tenacity of the machines themselves.

After that 1993 attack on the World Trade Centers, one would have thought the towers would have done everything possible to plan for another attack on what had to be seen as the shining target in the sky of terrorists. Instead, planning was shortsighted and even though first responders called for improvements such as radio systems that allowed for interoperability and communications across multi-channels and agencies, this did not take place. The emergency operations center for the city of New York was located at the very sight that had been attacked 8 years earlier. One cannot blame the first responder agencies for failing to locate the emergency operations center in another location, or failing to provide enough radios, or radios and systems that could communicate across agencies. This was the work of politicians and bureaucrats who for whatever reason failed to accomplish this task. It is remarkable the first responders, the men and women of the New York City fire and police departments, the Port Authority, and others were able to save as many lives as they did. It is due to their shear courage and putting others above themselves that they did succeed. Many civilians were saved due to the actions and courage of their managers and their safety and security personnel, those who encouraged and mandated drills and exercises. Not tabletops or discussions of moldy plans on a shelf, but actual realistic changing and active planning and exercises. Some people panic in crisis; others see clearly what must be done and how to achieve it. This book is dedicated to those who plan and seek to help others, and most especially, to the brave men and women who place their lives on the line every day.

A FOOTNOTE: CRISIS MANAGEMENT IN THE TIME OF TERRORISM

In the 1970s, terrorism was a household world. Many forms of terrorism ranging from airline hijackings to bombs in parcels, letters, and trashcans were leading the evening news, radio, TV, and newspapers. Around 1970, there were upwards of 500 terrorist attacks around the world. By 1976 that number had dropped to almost 100. The next 30 years would see a steady decline in terrorist acts around the world. The trend has shifted to Iraq and South Asia being the most affected terror locales and regions and religious extremism replacing former territorial or political conflicts (Fisher, 2012). The numbers of dead in the 9/11 attack in New York City and at the Pentagon has been far surpassed by bombing, beheadings, and mass killings around the world. The new trend had added the term *lone wolf* to the lexicon of terrorism and crisis management concerns. The term lone wolf refers to those who are spurned on by ideology or actions for others within organized groups, but who are basically part of a *leaderless resistance* (Anti Defamation League, 2011). In recent years around the world, religious extremists within Islam have fostered the lone wolf attackers by publishing on the Internet detailed instructions and directions for home grown individual or small group types of attacks and attackers. Lone wolfs such as these are harder to detect because although some may have sought or have received direct training from terrorist groups around the world, many have not and plan their attacks in their homes or small nonconnected groups or cells.

Planning for and by crisis managers has remained equal in necessity but more complex in nature. While the United States experienced a devastating attack in New York City and at the Pentagon, the large-scale attacks of 9/11 have moved from the United States to other countries and regions. What the United States has been on the lookout for has been the lone wolf attacks within and outside of this country. And, the threat remains for larger car bombs, continued kidnappings, IEDs or other attacks to take place. As a result, US and other corporations need to plan for these as well. The success the United States and other countries have had in fighting terrorism and disrupting terrorist networks has broken up groups of those bent on destruction and fear and boosted the importance of the small cells or individual brokers. For this reason, organizations must ramp up their crisis and emergency management efforts to ensure programs, policies, and procedures are not only written, but updated, kept off the shelf, and second nature for all employees from the executive suite to the summer interns. It is going to be critical in the mid-2000s and after to maintain crisis management plans in the era of smaller domestic and international terror attacks designed to gather headlines. Sometimes, as with suicide bombings, the body count can be tremendous.

Terrorist attacks in the 1970s required upfront planning, operational techniques and coordination:

- *1970*: Palestinian gunmen force three planes (from the United Kingdom, United States, and Switzerland) with a total of 400 people onboard to fly to the Jordanian desert, where the hijackers blow up the aircraft after releasing most of the hostages. After 24 days of talks, the final hostages are freed in exchange for seven Palestinian prisoners.
- *1976*: The week-long hijack of an Air France airliner in 1976 is brought to an abrupt end at Entebbe Airport, Uganda, by Israeli commandos; they kill all the Palestinian hijackers and free 105 mostly Israeli hostages, but three passengers and one commando die in the raid.
- *1977*: German commandos storm a Lufthansa airliner in Mogadishu, Somalia, after a five-day stand-off during which Palestinian guerrillas killed the plane's pilot; three hijackers die in the raid, while 86 hostages are freed (BBC News, 2001).

Terrorist attacks in the twenty-first century have become smaller, low tech efforts:

In Tunisia, a man with a Kalashnikov hidden in a parasol shot dead 37 tourists at a beach resort.... In Kuwait, an Islamic State suicide bomber killed 27 people praying in a mosque. In Somalia, al-Shabaab militants slew a number of peacekeeping soldiers. And in France, a suspect decapitated his boss at a US-owned industrial gas plant which he allegedly tried to blow up.... What this says is that soft targets will always be able to be hit, said a senior defense official. We're still pretty good at looking at networks (terror networks—author), but it's much harder to go after the lone wolf.

Anton Troianovski and Dion Nissenbaum (2015)
Attacks in France, Tunisia and Kuwait revive concerns on security

Today's return to terrorism as a significant risk, a blast from the past of the 1970s and later, requires three things for international crisis management planning:

1. *Intelligence.* This is gained by relationships with private and public sector sources, in country and outside. It might include safety and security personnel from rival or competitor companies, or even government officials (trusted and vetted) from host nations or regions. Intelligence from private security and risk organizations is important, provided this information is timely and correct. Intelligence is required for forming rational decisions related to risk and mitigating such risks.
2. *Logistics.* This pertains to the materials and means by which things may take place such as moving people from one location to another, security or medical evacuation vendor providers, emergency or noncritical medical contract providers, relocating or locating assets and funding as required, supplying the things that people need in time of crisis, and the organization needs for recovery.
3. *Boots on the ground.* This does not pertain to military personnel, but in some cases, ex-military or law enforcement or security types who are able to be on site for your personnel as quickly as possible before or during a crisis and assess situations and make recommendations with respect to safety and security of people and assets.

One of the most important aspects of crisis management in most cases is to have someone from your headquarters get to the disaster area as soon as possible. This should be a qualified disaster team, not your CEO beating his or her chest and saying "I am here!" This is foolhardy. While it might build up the morale of the expat employees or employees on the ground, it's taking up a seat on the plane of someone from human resources, or safety or operations, or safety or security who are going to be required to soon work their butts off to get things done. If you want to improve morale, make sure you have an international telephone hotline or internal website or Skype set up so that families, loved ones, friends, etc. can communicate with employees. Keep in mind, communications may be limited or nonexistent. If your CEO wants to be useful, have him or her talk to the media about how you're taking care of your employees and their loved ones, and that your business will continue, and you will rebuild. Have the rest of the organization not involved in assisting in the crisis double down on working, keeping them busy supporting everything, which, after all, is why people are working there in the first place. This book is not going to speak about crisis communications, as almost as much has been written about concerning how to communicate to employees and the general public or consumers during a crisis as there has been in how to respond or mitigate such occurrences. While crisis communications is an important piece, having a comprehensive plan that contains this component is far more necessary and can save lives. Crisis management plans must be hard, fast, and steady, and be followed as closely as possible. If, however, the first priority, such as using commercial airlines for evacuation fails, and Plan B calls for charter aircraft to be hired, then Plan C should be the use of ocean liner, train, camel (or for that matter, even a hot air balloon), if feasible.

The point is crisis planning must be flexible to a certain degree.

A final word about crisis management exercises. Specifically, concerning tabletop exercises, the author of this book is not a fan. The author considers the words *training* and *exercise* to be similar in nature, and yet, sometimes, mutually exclusive. For example, when one is *in training*, say, for a boxing match, are you in essence *exercising* those muscles, the reflexes and the blocking, the punching? Isn't the boxer creating *muscle memory* during the *training* and, in fact *exercising* the body so that it becomes more familiar and accustomed to the art of boxing or the boxing match, which in this case would be the *crisis plan*? The author believes people don't learn a lot during tabletop exercises, given the way most tabletop situations are managed. For example, isn't it obvious during some tabletops that when faced with your manufactured, contrived, and often way over the top *crisis scenario* the first thing most participants do is refer to their crisis management plan? Are they going to have this plan with them when the real thing happens? Seriously? No, they're going to be in a plane or riding in the subway, or in an airport or at a wedding or a ballgame or at a dance recital, or in the lunchroom of a client or customer, etc. Do the right people know, by heart, by muscle memory, as if they have struck that imaginary crisis management punching bag hundreds of times the first three or four things they need to do during the crisis?

If they don't know the first things they should do given the crisis scenario, any of the crisis scenarios, the author believes they shouldn't be part of the crisis team. Do some participants keep their crisis management plan on the shelf in their office or in the trunk of their car and there it remains? It becomes the crutch, the checklist, the ball and chain they have to lug around with them. Are people really reading the plans, the updates you send out electronically? Do they know their part? There really can't be that much gained by an annual, biannual, or even a quarterly table-top, can there? And, seriously, how many organizations have the time or resources to conduct an exercise biannually or quarterly? No, tabletops keep the honest people honest. Tabletops are a means to shame those who haven't read their parts in the crisis management plan into doing so at some point, either while they are sitting at their collectively grouped table or in silence while the moderator is giving the tabletop instructions. When you conduct the vaunted tabletop exercise, do you realize you have the right people or the wrong participants on the crisis team? Did everyone show up, first of all? Did the backups come today or just the principals? Were several people on vacation? During the first moments of the tabletop, do you realize that Fred is a little more energetic and capable than Martha, or is Barbara not quite in touch with the latest with regard to logistics than Carol, who wasn't chosen to be part of the team? But Barbara always volunteers for these things and Carol seems too dedicated to working rather than volunteering. Michael seems a bit quiet and Frank is not much of a leader. Christine and Sharon seem to be doing nothing but arguing deciding what the first steps should be. Joey was great last year but she retired. Cindy took her job and she has spent more time out of the room and on the phone putting out brushfires in her department. How many moderators and observers did you ask to help today? We only have time for one scenario today, and you think you, as the moderator, chose the proper and most likely scenario. But what about the 10 other possible scenarios? Oh, we can get to those in the five-year plan. Next year we will do tsunami, this year it's hurricane (Figure 16.1).

Chances are the scenario you are choosing is not the one that will happen next. The scenario that happened last year is not something that will ever happen again. Tabletops are a crap shoot, a shot from the three-point line, or a *Hail Mary* pass. Tabletops perhaps fill some necessity function for training, if this is all the training your weakest team member or the team is receiving, but if this is all the training your team receives, that they take in, or that you are delivering, you will be hoping for the best and will not be prepared for the worst, when this happens.

201

Figure 16.1 If a region has experienced a tsunami, earthquakes, or volcanoes, why not prioritize the types of plans to be put into place? (Courtesy of USAID, https://blog.usaid.gov/2014/12/lessons-learned-a-decade-after-the-indian-ocean -tsunami.)

So, what to do? Well, several things, actually. First, your team should be supplied with experts in their fields. Your public information officer should be an expert in his or her field, and if possible, one who has dealt with true crisis scenarios. So should your IT professional, your human resources team member, and so on. Your company should have someone in safety, risk management, or security who has dealt with crisis as part of their job description. They should be tasked with considering your crisis management plan from the aspect of one who is an expert in crisis and risk management. This team should meet monthly, especially in a company that has experienced crisis in their operations around the world or is in risky operations of any nature. Monthly meetings will serve to ensure that plans are maintained and kept current. Each focus group—human resources, travel, risk management and insurance, etc.—should be tasked with developing crisis plans that serve the functions of their particular groups. For example, human resources would be tasked with developing a crisis plan involving aspects of crises ranging from how does the company pay employees when the servers, computer systems, and recordkeeping/ timekeeping are inoperable? How does the travel department route employees to safer locations when all airlines are grounded? How does finance pay a vendor in Africa in that country's currency when they are asking for money in advance? In order to develop working relationships within organizations, human resources should take its crisis plan to particular business units and projects and work with them to develop how they would assist these divisions and areas given their particular needs and requirements. For example, human resources might work with a project in a remote location in providing medical resources or recommendations, or in identifying mental health professionals who could be contacted to provide counseling to employees in the wake of a crisis.

If a corporation or organization is sincere and invested in crisis management, none of the aforementioned suggestions will be of consequence. The recommendations will be agreed on and any obstacles of time or money or project priorities will stand in the way of the team. It's by putting their money where their mouth is that organizations show their true concern for employees and for mitigating a crisis situation in the correct manner.

So, first of all, let me assert my firm belief that the only thing we have to fear is fear itself—nameless, unreasoning, unjustified terror which paralyzes needed efforts to convert retreat into advance."

Franklin Delano Roosevelt
Franklin D. Roosevelt Library, First Carbon Files, 1933–1945,
National Archives Identifier: 197333, inaugural address 1933

REFERENCES

The 9/11 Commission Report. "Final Report of the National Commission on Terrorist Attacks upon the United States (9/11 Report)." Executive Agency Publications, July 22, 2004. http://www.9-11commission.gov/report/.

Anti Defamation League. Explaining lone wolf terrorism, May 24, 2011. http://archive.adl.org/main_terrorism/lone_wolf_terrorism.html#V4_cf9J96Ul.

BBC News. History of airliner hijackings, October 3, 2001. http://news.bbc.co.uk/2/hi/south_asia/1578183.stm.

De Bruce, Orlando. Federal Y2K Czar defends upbeat outlook, February 22, 1999. http://edition.cnn.com/TECH/computing/9902/22/upbeat.y2k.idg/.

Doward, Jamie. Russia Y2K bill "shows West overreacted." *The Guardian*, January 8, 2000. https://www.theguardian.com/business/2000/jan/09/y2k.observer business.

Dwyer, Jim, Flynn, Kevin, and Fessenden, Ford. Fatal confusion: A troubled emergency response; 9/11 exposed deadly flaws in rescue plan. *The New York*

Times, July 7, 2002. http://www.nytimes.com/2002/07/07/nyregion/fatal
-confusion-troubled-emergency-response-9-11-exposed-deadly-flaws
-rescue.html?pagewanted=all.

Federal Bureau of Investigation. Millennium plot/Ahmed Ressam. FBI Press
Release, December 14, 1999. https://www.fbi.gov/history/famous-cases
/millennium-plot-ahmed-ressam.

Ferreira, Michael J., Strege, Steven M., Peacock, Richaerd D., and Averill, Jason.
Smoke Control and Occupant Evacuation at the World Trade Center. National
Institute of Standards and Technology, June 21, 2008.

Fisher, Max. Terrorism's global decline, explained in charts. *Washington Post*,
October 22, 2012. https://www.washingtonpost.com/news/worldviews
/wp/2012/10/22/terrorisms-global-decline-explained-in-charts/.

Fusco, Anthony L. *The World Trade Center Bombing: Report and Analysis*. New York:
US Department of Homeland Security, February 1993.

The United States Senate Special Committee on the Year 2000 Technology Problem.
"Y2K Aftermath—Crisis Averted: Final Committee Report: Summary of
Committee Findings," February 29, 2000. http://permanent.access.gpo.gov
/lps90964/y2kfinalreport.pdf.

Government Accounting Office (GAO). "Year 2000 Computing Crisis: Business
Continuity and Contingency Planning," August 1998. http://www.gao.gov
/special.pubs/bcpguide.pdf.

Taylor, Chris. The history and the hype. *Time Magazine*, January 18, 1999. http://
content.time.com/time/world/article/0,8599,2053906,00.html.

Troianovski, Anton and Nissenbaum, Dion. Attacks in France, Tunisia and Kuwait
revive concerns on security. *Wall Street Journal*, June 26, 2015. http://www
.wsj.com/articles/attacks-on-three-continents-revive-concerns-on-global
-security-coordination-1435330519.

Winerip, Michael. Revisiting Y2K: Much ado about nothing? *New York Times*,
May 27, 2013. http://www.nytimes.com/2013/05/27/booming/revisiting-y2k
-much-ado-about-nothing.html?_r=1.

APPENDIX

EMERGENCY FUNDS CONTACT LIST

As referenced in Chapter 2, one thing that can easily be overlooked in crisis planning is the fact that during an emergency or crisis the need for ready access to funds can be critical. Whether the need is to order five generators with light plants or to arrange for a charter aircraft to carry 15 employees out of a hotspot, money talks and you know what walks. Employees on the ground need to know who to contact and how in order to obtain their credit card or credit assurances or international wire transfers in order to make things happen. If you haven't attempted an international wire transfer of funds, then you don't know how complicated these things can be. Make sure you have the right people at the ready, 24/7 if and when you need them.

The Global Offices must establish a means for rapid receipt of emergency funds with the company. There should be persons designated to request, approve, and disburse emergency funds. All appropriate contact information should be provided to projects.

There should be three people who can physically receive these funds:

1.
2.
3.

(Include appropriate contact information)
Spell out the specific procedures to follow. One of the five management representatives, listed above, will initiate procedures with the company (Bank) representatives.

1.
2.

(Include bank contacts and whom within the company to initiate withdrawals)

INFORMATION COLLECTION PRIOR TO DEPLOYMENT

As referenced in Chapter 4, deploying employees and dependents to a foreign assignment requires many departments and divisions to operate in coordination. From taxation, visa/passport and other requirements to safety and security, up front planning can cut down on time and issues down the road during a crisis. If you are sending employees to extremely risky and dangerous locations (and hopefully this book has illustrated how you determine such things), then additional pretrip planning and documentation should take place. Such things as pretrip safety and security briefings, more close scrutiny to emergency stand fast or evacuation planning or obtaining additional security resources would be required.

International Travel Security Management

The Corporate Crisis Management Team must have the critical information prior to an employee departing for an area of civil unrest:

- Personal information should be included on the sheet such as
  - Name: first, middle, last, nickname
  - Physical description: height, weight, color of eyes, color of hair, identifying scars, marks, and tattoos
  - Permanent home address and telephone
  - Work site in country: address and telephone number in country
  - Marital status
- Detail all biographic data on spouse and children such as full name, physical description, school attended, school schedule; detailed medical information and emergency contact information.
- Include all medical information such as allergies, medicines, chronic conditions, shot records, name and contact instruction for family doctor and dentist.
- Have at the ready copies of official documents such as passport: date and place of issue, expiration date; visa: date and place of issue, and expiration date.
- Have expats collect and maintain their income tax forms.
- Notate all languages spoken by the expat.
- Any special skills they possess (medical, dental, finance, logistics, etc.).
- Indicate what are available for personal vehicles, the description, license number, vehicle identification number (on engine block).
- Have photographs of all personnel and dependents.

- What was their arrival date in the country.
- Ask expats to maintain copies of passports and visas.
- Produce extra copies of in-country itineraries.
- Produce copies of flight information or other travel arraignments.

The traveling employee should have with him or her:

- Open-ended airline tickets.
- An extra set of passport photos.
- A map and directions to the nearest friendly embassy.
- Map and directions to nearest appropriate country embassy or consulate.
- Map and directions to a predetermined safe haven.

The traveling employee should have on his or her person at all times:

- Passport and visa.
- Emergency contact numbers including those of all local management (with dialing instructions).
- List of the nearest appropriate country embassy or consulate telephone numbers (with dialing instructions).
- Corporate Crisis Management Team telephone number (with dialing instructions).
- Emergency 24-hour Incident Response Team telephone number (with dialing instructions).
- All transportation contact numbers.
- All pertinent hotel/lodging contact numbers.
- Local police telephone numbers.
- Local medical emergency telephone numbers.
- Adequate local currency.

SECURITY AND EVACUATION PLANNING

As referenced in Chapter 4, the following information is useful as a planning guide or checklist in dealing with items of severity which might crop up in hostile regions and locations. It is useful as an overarching security management and security/safety evacuation plan for normal to hostile situations. This plan describes levels of threat and recommended steps commensurate with such situations. No one plan may act as a catchall, one size does not fit all. But, thinking and planning along these lines can be beneficial in assessing the current capabilities of your project, your

TRAVEL SECURITY TIPS

Also important to keep in mind that you will need to explain, briefly, and provide general traveling security suggestions:

- Discuss travel plans on a need-to-know basis only.
- Telephone operators and secretaries should not advise callers and visitors when an executive is out of town on a trip.
- Remove company logos from luggage.
- Luggage identification tags should be of a type that allows the information on the tag to be covered. Use the business address on the tag.
- Do not leave valuables and/or sensitive documents in the hotel room.
- When sightseeing, observe basic security precautions and refrain from walking alone in known high-crime areas.
- Always have telephone change available and know how to use the phones. Learn key emergency phrases of the country to be able to ask for police, medical, etc.
- Joggers should carry identification.
- Men should carry wallets either in an inside jacket pocket or a front pants pocket, never in a hip pocket. The less money carried the better.
- Have available the telephone numbers of the appropriate country embassy or consulate, and company employee contact numbers should be carried with employees at all times.
- Always carry the appropriate documentation for the country being visited.
- When traveling, ask for a hotel room between the second and seventh floors. This is because more burglaries may be perpetrated with first floor access and many fire departments don't have ladders of sufficient height to reach above the seventh floor.
- American-type hotels usually offer a higher level of safety and security inasmuch as they offer smoke alarms, fire extinguishers, safety locks, hotel security, 24-hour operators, English-speaking personnel, safety deposit boxes, and normally will not divulge a guest's room number.

- Choose taxis carefully and at random. Be sure it is a licensed taxi. Do not use independent nonlicensed operators.
- Be as inconspicuous as possible in dress, social activities, and amount of money spent on food, souvenirs, gifts, etc.
- Stay in or use VIP rooms or security zones when waiting in commercial airports abroad.
- Minimize the amount of time spent in airports.
- When traveling internationally, keep all medicine in original containers and take a copy of the prescription.

staff, the situations you are presented with, and allows for input from all those concerned.

Emergency situations include, but are not limited to:

- Medical emergencies and evacuation
- Nonmedical evacuation
- Natural disasters
- Civil unrest
- Political instability
- Terrorist activities
- Bomb threats/improvised explosive devices (IED)
- Kidnapping

Sources of emergency information:

- Television (like CNN International, BBC World News, Sky News, Radio: Voice of America)
- Hospital emergency contacts

Example Plan

This has been created for Company XYZ project for the Jakarta High Rise Office Security and Evacuation Management.

Introduction

The Security and Evacuation Management Plan (the Plan) provides guidelines and direction for actions to be taken in response to various emergency situations, which might impact the safety and security of Company XYZ professionals around the world. The Plan provides direction to managers who are tasked with emergency planning responsibilities with the intent being to assist in developing sound processes by which to make decisions during emergency situations. The Plan further provides actions to be taken by employees during emergencies. It clarifies the appropriate responses to specific situations and explains the sequential responsibilities as each pertains to the different emergency options available. The Plan identifies situations that vary from those confined to specific facilities/sites in a local area to those that impact on the entire country. Additionally, this Plan defines the various interfaces applicable to external organizations.

Safe Haven

Safe Havens are predesignated locations selected as rally points for personnel to meet or where personnel can wait until a period of short-term unrest passes or they are directed to deploy elsewhere. Normally, Project Sites are considered Safe Haven locations. There may be periods when employees are directed to relocate to another site or seek refuge at a US government or, in some cases, host country government facilities.

A headcount will be prepared and maintained at the Safe Haven for force/locator reporting.

The Security Team Leader will determine/designate Safe Havens to be used in case of an emergency or evacuation. The Safe Haven selected should be accessible to all personnel, provide safety and security, and the capability to support personnel for a period of time (personnel may have to wait a period of time for the unrest to settle). Depending on the threat and situation, other groups may also be using the same rally point that could create crowding, confusion, and demand a team approach to problem-solving under pressure.

The company Security Team Leader must be prepared to arrange charter, standby, and/or reservations promptly if out-of-country evacuation is ordered and commences from the rally point/Safe Haven.

Transportation/Vehicles

Transportation to and from the support site, work site, office, as well as any other transport requirement for professionals may be handled by

COMMON CRIMINALITY

BACKGROUND

As some expatriates may be working overseas or in the host countries for the first time, it is essential for them to review some of the general differences between living in the United States and living outside of the United States relative to criminal activity exposure.

Criminal activities are often quite different from the problems one would experience in cities in other locations around the world. All project professionals are expected to be cautious and avoid those areas where they would most likely be vulnerable to be selected as a random target of violence. For example, in some countries, it is obviously unwise for project professionals to be walking around alone outside the confines of the project site and alone in the city or built-up areas.

PERSONAL/RESIDENCE SECURITY

The most important part of personal security is being cautious and following one's intuition. However, it is each expatriate's responsibility to be prudent in their actions to remain as safe as possible. To further promote a secure environment, all expatriates are encouraged to share any unfortunate experiences including cultural nuances with one another as a learning tool to avoid future confrontations.

TRAVEL SECURITY

Travel to and from locations in host countries must be carefully planned. All project professionals should communicate directly with project management or their designee their travel plans. In some countries, travel outside of secure locations might include escorts.

TERRORIST ACTIVITY/THREAT REPORTING

Any person discovering or otherwise acquiring knowledge of actual or potential terrorist activity will report such information immediately to the Project Manager and Corporate Security Manager. This includes terrorist threats as well as actions impacting professionals and assets.

The project/office management shall assess the actual or potential impact on professionals and assets and shall report their assessment to the Home Office and Corporate Security. The Security Team Leader has full authority, based on current events, to determine actions to be taken at project sites. The Security Team Leader shall take appropriate actions including but not limited to:

- Assigning additional guards to observe fixed assets or to escort professionals as needed.
- Implement adequate security measures to protect project professionals.
- Varying routes for movement of professionals and equipment to avoid routines.
- Reporting all suspicious activities to appropriate authorities.
- Evacuating or relocating professionals as required.
- Restricting professionals to designated locations (lockdown).

project drivers, thus normally eliminating a need for other professionals to drive and the need to obtain mandatory documents to drive.

NONMEDICAL EMERGENCY EVACUATION PLAN

Scope and Purpose

It may become necessary to evacuate nonessential and/or all project/office professionals from selected and/or all site locations depending on safety and security conditions. The Security Team Leader, in coordination with the Corporate Security Manager, will determine initiating the implementation of this Plan. When the decision to evacuate project/office professionals for nonmedical reasons is made, the Security Team Leader may direct implementation of parts or all of the Plan. The Plan provides guidance and responsibilities; options available for in-country and out-of-country relocation and evacuation; Company XYZ professional responsibilities; criteria concerning primary and alternate locations; actions to be taken at various levels of the operation; and mode of transport to final locations as appropriate.

Applicability and Responsibility

This Plan applies to all company expatriates, business travelers, and associated visitors. In some situations, the Team Leader may deem it appropriate to include foreign expatriate employees in evacuation plans. Appropriate actions in this Plan will be directed by the Security Team Leader based on his/her assessment and evaluation of the situation and local conditions, in consultation with the other members of the management team, client, embassy or consulate general, and the corporate office as necessary.

Travel Documentation

The Project Manager ensures all personnel possess the necessary official travel documents prior to any site evacuation. Business managers at each site maintain a photocopy of all professionals' visas and passports (picture page). Specifically, each individual must have the following documents in hand:

- Passport
- Official IDs
- International certificate of vaccination
- Emergency communication

In an emergency or in standby conditions, the project/office telephones will have a 24-hour watch. The telephone watch will be coordinated and established by the Crisis Team Leader. The fax line will be operational 24 hours. All project locations will initiate and maintain a 24-hour telephone watch until stand down is directed by the Team Leader.

If telephone communications are disabled, alternate emergency communication to the appropriate Project Managers, Security Manager, etc. may be established by telephone communication to the satellite, cellular, and e-mail systems.

XZY Company and Expatriate Professional
Asset (Personal Property) Protection

Under most conditions, it is safe to presume that the company project/office professionals and staff will not be in any significant position of risk and they will be able to stay on the site or relocate to a US government/private vendor/government or host country facility. If leaving the site, transport/convoy should be coordinated/arranged with the Corporate Security Manager. The Business Manager (business manager) and the staff under the business manager's supervision will maintain security of all company physical assets (funds) and company project documents. All professionals should maintain a current inventory of personal items at site/office/lodging for insurance or possible company reimbursement.

Out-of-Country Evacuation

If it is determined, due to the nature of the threat, that out-of-country evacuation is necessary, the Plan will be implemented to evacuate employees from project locations to designated locations to await required air/ground transport. The Security Team Leader may direct only nonessential professionals be evacuated out-of-country or he or she may determine all professionals be evacuated.

If out-of-country evacuation is not immediately feasible, professionals will seek refuge at a designated site location, US government/private vendor/or host country government facility, if feasible, or in a United Nations facility nearest to their location (if established).

The Security Team Leader will coordinate in-country relocation and out-of-country evacuation with the Corporate Security Manager to ensure the safest evacuation for company expatriates.

Based on the nature of the threat, out-of-country evacuation may preclude any stopover in any designated in-country location.

Evacuation out-of-country may involve ground transport to an in-country location where either US government, private vendor, or charter air assets will be utilized for further transport out-of-country. Depending on the threat, US government or private vendor air transport could be used to relocate professionals to another in-country location for further transport out-of-country or to relocate professionals out-of-country.

Evacuation Using Air from a Designated Location

If an out-of-country evacuation is planned and air is to be utilized, the primary and alternate in-country destinations will be the international airport; or any other designated US/host government facility with capability or a United Nations facility, if established.

If commercial, charter, or US government/private vendor air is utilized from the international airport, the designated manager, when directed by the Security Team Leader, will take those actions necessary to coordinate required evacuation of company professionals located in the immediate area.

Transportation to a primary and/or alternate in-country designated location for out-of-country evacuation will normally require ground transport. Often, there are limited transport assets to rapidly relocate professionals from their normal location at one time. The Corporate Security Manager in coordination with the Security Team Leader will ensure proper escort (which might include private armed/unarmed security) is available for all evacuating professionals to the designated location and air departure location. Depending on transportation availability, close coordination of transport assets and qualified security personnel will be essential.

Out-of-country egress may be established for groups or individuals as short-term or long-term evacuation, based on the nature of the threat and the needs of the project.

- Short-term country evacuation will be to Country A or Country B. Visas may be purchased upon arrival in both countries.
- Long-term out-of-country evacuation will be to the evacuee's home in the United States or country of origin.

Evacuation Using Ground Transportation Only

If out-of-country evacuation cannot be supported by air as a result of security conditions at designated locations or due to lack of air resources, evacuation may be conducted using ground transportation to another host country where air transport can be arranged. Professionals may be directed to rally at a designated location as required prior to convoy movement using these routes. US government/private vendor/host country support for these convoys should be considered and requested. All professionals should carry their Evacuation Kit.

Evacuation to Country A Border

The Regional Crisis Team Leader in coordination with the XYZ Company Security Manager and Site Security Managers will organize and direct ground convoys to proceed to Highway # X and on to Highway # Y (stay on the route marked Alpha and Bravo) and move north to the Country A Border and continue on to designated location where there is an international airport where air transport can be arranged to designated final destinations.

Previous reconnaissance and use of the route to the Country A Border by Company XYZ employees report that travel time from office/facility to the border is approximately 3.0 hours with approximately 30–45 minutes travel through the city of XXXXX.

Evacuation to Country B Border

The Senior Project Manager in coordination with the Company XYZ Security Manager and Site Security Managers will organize and direct ground convoys to proceed to Highway # T and on to Highway # U and move west to the Country B Border and on to XXXXX where air transport will be arranged to designated destinations.

Previous use of this route by Company XYZ persons traveling to Country B report that from office/facility to the Country B border is approximately 8 hours and approximately 3 hours from the border to XXXXX. Convoys may experience up to 3.0 hours delay processing through the border point.

The Director, Business/Administration should be fully prepared with funding arranged by the Company XYZ Senior Project Manager and will receive instructions to promptly purchase air travel tickets on the most suitable outbound flight to Country C or XXXXX within three hours of notice for either short-term or long-term evacuation.

If ground transport to XXXXX and/or a destination in Country A is utilized, the Director, Business/Administration should be fully prepared with funding arranged by the company Senior Project Manager and will receive instructions to promptly purchase air travel tickets from these locations on the most suitable outbound flight if appropriate.

Project Reporting during Evacuation Period

If work continues on the project, the business manager and the staff under the business manager's supervision will provide daily reports on activities and progress to the project office. In a situation where the project is to be permanently shut down, the business manager will make the arrangements for the recovery of company assets and documents.

Evacuation Procedures

Evacuation operations include personnel notification procedures, assembly of professionals to be evacuated, passing information up and down the organizational chain, and mobilizing personnel and resources.

Evacuation operations will be divided into three stages, which also serve to inform personnel of the status of the operation:

- *Warning/Level One.* Professionals are ready and transportation and related procedures are in place.
- *Assemble/Level Two.* All professionals to be evacuated move to designated marshaling areas ready to travel.
- *Proceed/Level Three.* Evacuate the area by the prescribed method to designated locations.

LEVEL ONE

Threat

General internal social, political, and/or US government/private vendor instability that may be manifested in the occurrence of incidents that may or may not be directed specifically against the company or other US interests in the region. Additionally, regional political tensions or heightened US government/private vendor activity may exist that potentially affects US regional interests. This is a period during which routine collection and assessment of information about local and international events are in progress.

Actions

All expatriate professionals will be briefed regarding personal security at their place of work, support location, and in-transit to and from work. Emphasis will be placed on maintaining a low profile, avoiding troubled areas, and avoiding provocative behavior.

- Security and/or guards and drivers will be briefed and placed on alert.
- Identify and be prepared to evacuate nonessential professionals.
- Implement additional security at the support location, office, and job-site (tighter access control, locked down, and additional security staged around the above areas).
- Establish communications with local contacts, to include the US government/private vendor and monitor the situation.
- Notify the Home Office.
- Maintain liaison with the appropriate government authority and the Corporate Security Manager.
- Keep professionals informed. It is important to develop a procedure to deal with rumors that have a tendency to emerge with the onset of any crisis situation. Left unattended, rumors can have a demoralizing effect.
- Documents (company or client sensitive) should be identified or set aside for possible future destruction. Thought should be given to begin copying of data to disks and destroying all hard drives and systems.
- Previously established routes to the designated primary and alternate safe locations and airport should be checked for traversability under emergency conditions.
- Ensure that fuel and gasoline storage levels are adequate or available.
- Review previously established staging areas for assembling employees.

LEVEL TWO

Threat

This phase should be initiated when, in the judgment of the Security Team Leader (or directed by Embassy/Consulate personnel) a situation has reached a level of tension or instability that could lead to partial or complete evacuation of expatriate professionals. The earlier an evacuation decision can be made, the more likely it can be affected in a calm, secure, and less politically sensitive atmosphere.

Activity primarily applies to site and local incidents, but may apply to regional and national incidents. Activities include intensification of regional conflicts, and escalated internal social and political instability.

Actions

In addition to all activities identified in Level One, the following actions will be implemented:

- Normal work routines should continue; however, certain definitive actions such as obtaining required clearances and conducting programmed document destruction of company- or client-sensitive documents to begin on the order of senior management should be undertaken as appropriate.
- Copying of data to disks and destroying all hard drives.
- Order *stand fast* for all personnel.
- Notify security/guards (if present) to strengthen security (reassign security/guards to office entrances/exits to offices, support site, and job site), as appropriate. Add security if none is present.
- Place primary and alternate Safe Havens on notice.
- If incident endangers professionals, nonessential staff and others may be transported to previously identified Safe Haven locations.
- Secure personal and company property.
- Notify Home Office. Provide accurate list of personnel (professionals, visitors, etc.) to include locations and telephone numbers.
- Validate Emergency Contact List data.
- The possibility of having to secure or abandon personal property should be addressed.

LEVEL THREE

Threat

This phase should be initiated when, in the judgment of the Security Team Leader; the situation has deteriorated to the point that the decision to evacuate is imminent or has already been made. Generally, when there is a breakdown in the ability of the local authority to control the frequency and severity of incidents against project work/support sites, the situation has deteriorated where there is imminent danger. It is probable that regional and national incidents have heightened and caused potential antisentiment or regional chaos. It is assumed that total withdrawal of professionals will not meet active resistance from the local authorities.

Actions

In addition to the actions described in Level Two, the following actions will be implemented:

- Coordinate with Home Office for evacuation assistance as required.
- If incident is national in nature and it is not safe to remain *stand fast* and an evacuation to designated Safe Haven location or from the country is required, establish the links for transportation. (Notify if at all possible in advance and of the destination.)
- Coordinate payment of foreign expatriates and local staff and agencies for services rendered.
- Coordinate the release of all local hire personnel.
- Coordinate the evacuation of all nonessential personnel.
- Be prepared to evacuate essential professionals.
- Ensure communications to Home Office, Corporate Security Manager, Embassy and/or Consulate and others as appropriate are completed and if possible authorization for an evacuation has been obtained.
- Advise client of evacuation.
- Initiate shutdown of project to include secure storage or destruction of sensitive documents and records as required.
- Order evacuation of personnel with armed escorts as required.
- Rally at designated Safe Haven location and/or at the airport as directed. Coordinate the release of airline tickets and emergency cash.
- Notify Home Office and/or Corporate Security on arrival to the Safe Haven location or airport.

MOVEMENT

Site Evacuation

Modes of site evacuation to primary or alternate in-country destinations are ranked by preference.

- By road to international airport and fixed wing aircraft to Country A, B, or country of origin.
- By rotary lift aircraft to international airport (this movement can commence at the project sites).
- By road to Country A border (continue to designated city for air transport).
- By road to Country B border to XXXXX (for air transport).
- Coalition facility and US government/private vendor or charter air to out-of-country destination.

If over-land evacuation is to be undertaken to international airport or to designated primary or alternate locations, the Team Leader will ensure all vehicles are fully serviced and fueled, and provisions for refueling are established. The Security Team Leader, through the company business manager, will ensure necessary provisions of food and water are established for all evacuees.

Each evacuee will be permitted one suitcase and one carry-on bag during implementation of this Plan.

Coordinating Instructions

Coordinating country egress or evacuation involves proactive planning; therefore, when evacuation becomes a reality the remaining steps are well in place. Through daily close review and daily scrutiny of events reflected in credible news sources and continuous close contact with the appropriate sources, the Senior Project Manager and Corporate Security can stay abreast of unrest, terrorist activities, and political uprising. As a result of this continuous scrutiny, the Senior Project Manager is always prepared to initiate appropriate action at a moment's notice to ensure the safest egress for professionals.

COMPANY XYZ SECURITY (NONMEDICAL) EVACUATION ALTERNATIVE

Although the procedures to support a rapid nonmedical evacuation are best arranged at the local level, should local assets fail to perform to the level expected by the Senior Project Manager, International SOS provides another alternative for the Project Manager to consider. SOS can support emergency nonmedical cases of civil uprising, insurrection, war, or demonstrations/attacks against project personnel and other civil disturbances and disasters.

Extraction Directed by the US Government/ Private Vendor/US Embassy/US Consulate

Under certain circumstances the situation may be of a nature that requires the US government to have command and control. This command and control includes the possibility of a US government/private vendor extraction. In all cases, the Senior Project Manager will follow and fully comply with the directions provided by the US government/private vendor and the US Embassy/Consulate General.

CASUALTY OR INJURY NOTIFICATION EXAMPLE PLAN

As referenced in Chapter 5, injuries or fatalities may happen on any project in any location or region around the world. Organizations should always have a plan in place for how to address such events as these occur.

Casualty Notification Plan (Continuing with the Example, Company XYZ)

In the event of an employee fatality:

1. A member of the company's upper-management team, including a Human Resources Representative, makes a *best effort* to inform the spouse/family in person of the accident. If it is not possible to make a face-to-face notification, a member of clergy or a police officer may be a possible candidate. The goal is to notify the

spouse/family quickly. A phone call is a last resort because of its impersonal nature.

2. The company representative remains at the professional's home until other family members arrive or for as long as he or she can.

3. The media may attempt to contact a family member. You cannot prevent them from talking to the media. It is their right to speak to the media if they wish.

4. Determine whether the professional's family is in need of money to cover small expenses. If so, it may be appropriate to provide assistance in this area with vice president of Human Resource's approval. The few dollars spent will come back in goodwill.

5. Maintain contact with a relative or close friend of the spouse or family to ensure that funeral arrangements and related items are being handled.

6. In case of local national employees, follow procedure as above and any local customs as appropriate.

Note: If the fatality involves a nonemployee, contact the individual's employer for notification procedures. Contact your insurance company and legal counsel as soon as possible.

Fatality Notification

In the event of a professional's fatality, you may be called on to notify the spouse or family member. This is a traumatic event for both the relative and you. Here are some guidelines to help with this process.

Do your homework. Obtain the full name, address, and social security number of the deceased. Next, get the full name of the next of kin, the relationship (wife, brother, mother, etc.) and determine if the family members are English speaking. Gather all information relative to the case so you can provide an explanation.

Determine where you will meet. Will the contact be at home, work, or school? If it is outside of the home, arrange with the relative's employer or school for a private place to meet. Verify that you are talking to the correct person, that is, "Are you Sandy Johnson's sister?"

Do not go alone. Take a fellow professional, friend of the deceased, member of the clergy, or police or fire official to support you.

Decide in advance what you will say. There is no easy way to say that someone has died, so do not even try. Speak simply and directly. Using terms like *mortally wounded* only confuses people. While it is not necessary to be blunt or cold, at some point it is necessary to say *dead* or *died*. Example: "Mrs. Jones, there was a very bad accident this morning at the project. Charlie was moving a ladder and fell over a guardrail. The paramedics did everything they could, but he died instantly."

Do not lie. If you tell a mother that her son died with her name on his lips but she later learns his death was immediate, there is a conflict. It may not be necessary to offer all of the details. Example: If the spouse asks, "Did he suffer much?" an appropriate answer might be, "I don't think so."

Be prepared for emotions. There will be shock, denial, grief, numbness, and anger. These emotional reactions will be directed at the deceased, at you, and at the medical staff. Let the relative vent these feelings. Use common sense and do what seems appropriate at this time. Some people will appreciate a touch of a hand; others will not.

Decide what not to say. By not preparing what to say, you may end up saying things that you will later regret. Example: In an effort to offer words of comfort, do not say, "He's with God now," or "You're young and will find someone else." Instead, say, "I'm so sorry this has happened to you," or "What can I do to help you right now?"

Always listen. The formula is 90% listening and 10% talking. If the relative needs to go to the hospital or funeral home, you may offer to drive or get a cab. If there are children involved, help arrange for a sitter or a friend to look after them. When appropriate, offer assistance in getting in touch with the life insurance company, social security, and so forth.

You have gone through an extremely stressful event. Take care of yourself now. Use your critical-incident stress counselor to review the difficult process you went through. No one ever gets comfortable with this part of the job.

HOSTAGE AND KIDNAPPING EXAMPLE PLAN

As referenced in Chapter 5, if a region is prone to kidnappings, hostage taking, or terrorist activity, it is prudent to take into consideration what to tell family, loved ones, and friends during such occurrences.

In the event of an employee kidnapping:

1. A member of the company's upper-management team, including a Human Resources Representative, makes a *best effort* to inform the spouse/family in person of the kidnapping. If it is not

possible to make a face-to-face notification, a member of clergy or a police officer may be a possible candidate. The goal is to notify the spouse/family quickly. A phone call is a last resort because of its impersonal nature.

2. The designated company representative remains at the employee's home until other family members arrive or for as long as he or she can.

3. The media may attempt to contact a family member. You cannot prevent them from talking to the media. It is their right to speak to the media if they wish.

4. Determine whether the employee's family is in need of money to cover small expenses. If so, it may be appropriate to provide assistance in this area with a senior member of Human Resource's approval. The few dollars spent will come back in goodwill.

5. Maintain contact with a relative or close friend of the spouse or family to ensure that related items are being handled.

6. In case of a local national employee, follow procedures as above and any local customs as appropriate.

Note: Implement the hostage reporting procedures outlined in this section.

Note: If the kidnapping involves a nonemployee, contact the individual's employer for notification procedures. Contact your insurance company and legal counsel as soon as possible.

Provide appropriate embassy or consulate contact information.

1. Name, phone number, and e-mail of person reporting incident
2. Date of incident
3. Time of incident
4. Location of incident (as specific as possible)
5. Brief description of what happened
6. Description of people involved
7. Description of vehicle involved
8. Hostage name/nationality
9. Employee name
10. Name, phone number, and e-mail address of person who will take follow-up questions from embassy, law enforcement representatives

Note: If your organization has a kidnap plan, make sure any governmental or law enforcement contacts are handled by the experts only.

TRAVEL SAFETY AND SECURITY INFORMATION

As referenced in Chapter 7, if your organization is fortunate enough to have travel tracking and intelligence vendor assistance, and assistance by quality travel booking and other organizations, the following information can be very useful.

Company XYZ Travel Safety and Security Pre-Planned Travel Intelligence and Tracking, Travel Evacuations Plan

A *Lifeline* is a conceptual and tactical program that consists of a Corporate Crisis Management Team, a Corporate Security Department, Safety Department, Travel Department, Human Resources Department, Legal Department, and others working together to ensure the safety and security for employees traveling the world. Procedures and technology are put into place to identify risks before employees book travel to high risk locations, the employees and their managers are *pushed* information concerning recommended vaccines and safety and security precautions (intelligence), and the travel is tracked in order to locate or evacuate employees in dire situations such as medical or security emergencies. When combined with an international medical intelligence and response program, such protections offer employees protection wherever their travel takes them.

Company XYZ and the Corporate Crisis Management Team has examined the current status of corporate international travel and determined the following: Prior knowledge of employee/senior management international travel and ability to know where all employees are traveling at a moment's notice is required (accomplished by a travel tracking software interactive program). Employees and security management should be provided with current and ongoing trip safety, security, and health information while on their trip. A mechanism should be in place that provides for an automated system to know where employees are located in the event of emergencies. A system needs to be in place to provide one single source provider of international emergency medical and security evacuation assistance should the need arise.

Company XYZ Comprehensive Travel Security Program

Travel security should be designed to do the following:

- Provide Company XYZ with advance notification that employees are intent on traveling to a specific location.
- Ensure the destination is one that is safe for employees to travel to for business.
- Provide employees with the necessary information in order to safely travel to desired location (safety and security).
- Provide employers with any necessary security briefings and measures in order to travel to desired location.
- Provide for emergency contact and notification capabilities in the event of a worldwide or country-specific emergency.

In order to function properly, the following mechanisms must be in place for a successful travel security program:

- *Executive Travel*
  - A policy should be enforced limiting the number of senior management/corporate officers who are allowed to ride together on the same aircraft.
  - Corporate security should conduct a risk analysis prior to any senior management/corporate officer foreign travel. Where appropriate, one-on-one briefings should occur.
  - Security and safety briefing packets should be provided for senior management/corporate officers who are traveling as groups to foreign locations.
- *Lifeline*: Implementation of a corporate *Lifeline* program, which mandates that each internationally traveling employee (outside of the United States), prior to departing for his or her trip, identify another employee (not a spouse, significant other, relative), but someone who works for Company XYZ and would have knowledge of where the employee is traveling to and for what purpose. That person, the Lifeline of the traveling employee, would provide the traveler with telephone numbers that the traveler could reach 24/7 in the event of an emergency. Likewise, the Lifeline would be provided by the traveling employee with emergency

contact telephone numbers (including cellular phones) for the traveler while they are in country.

The Lifeline should not be a person who travels extensively himself, but rather someone who would most likely be available for contact while the traveler is outbound/inbound and in country.

In the event of a natural or manufactured disaster, the Lifeline would be contacted by corporate security to determine if the traveling employee had contacted the Lifeline in order to pass along their status. If no such contact had been made by either the Lifeline or the traveling employee, corporate security would assist in such emergency contacts and verifications.

All travelers should be advised that no reservations will be made unless the traveler supplies the travel department with the name and contact information of their Lifeline. Any such information should be electronically collected and maintained, preferably by means of an electronic travel security platform.

- *Electronic Traveler Security*: A 24/7 software-based and control center monitored travel security program, such as Travel Tracking and Intelligence Vendor or competitors, should be initiated. Travel Tracking and Intelligence Vendor utilizes the electronic travel agency records, which activates the following travel security protocol:
  - Approximately 15 minutes after the PNR is initiated, each traveler, based on e-mail address, will receive a request to update their Travel Tracking and Intelligence Vendor travel security profile.
  - Following the activation of the profile, travelers will receive active *pushes* of e-mailed security and safety information relating to their destination country or region.
  - Travelers receive only the pertinent security information for the duration of their trip, for example, if traveling on May 10–May 15, all information ceases on midnight of the 15th.
  - In the event of an emergency, designated corporate security and Safety personnel may query the Travel Tracking and Intelligence Vendor database, which plots travelers by worldwide country maps, for flight and lodging information. If there are multiple travelers affected by country, simultaneous e-mails may be sent with Travel Tracking and Intelligence Vendor, which might state to contact corporate security immediately, remain in your lodging, etc.

- *Additional Requirements*
  - Immediate supervisor approval for employee travel outside the United States or Canada.
  - The travel service vendor travel group and corporate security agreement on areas to be considered high risk travel areas (Iraq, Afghanistan, Algeria, Colombia, etc.).
  - The travel service vendor group notification of corporate security of employee reserving of potential travel to high risk areas.
  - Corporate security consultation with employee (traveler) about necessity of travel to high risk areas, and verification of supervisor/manager approval for employee to travel to such areas.
  - Corporate security assessment of transportation security (including vehicle travel in country), lodging security, site or destination security, emergency evacuation plans, and examination of current country security risk status by review of US State Department secure website and contacts with regional security officers (RSOs), use of private intelligence databases, and benchmarking with corporate security colleagues operating in the area.
  - Corporate security provides security briefings to employee, and, if necessary, corporate security arranges to accompany employee or makes arrangements for in-country security protections.
- *Requirements for Successful Travel Security Program*
  - Timely reservations reporting by the travel service company.
  - Providing of travel reservations information to corporate security manager.
  - Senior management commitment to the Lifeline program.
  - Corporate policy or instruction of Travel Security program.
  - Educational awareness training of employees.
  - Contracting with travel intelligence/travel tracking vendor.
- *International Emergency Medical Evacuation/Routine Medical Referral and Emergency Security Situation Evacuation Program*: Employees based in foreign countries or traveling for business in foreign countries would benefit from emergency medical referral and possible evacuation while in country or to a country that can first stabilize the patient and then transport for follow-up treatment. Employees would also benefit from recommendations for non-critical medical care, such as for doctor, dental, or clinic visits.

A vendor such as International SOS provides these services and in addition will transport (in most circumstances) employees out of host countries in the event of natural or manufactured disasters (such as coups, terrorist actions, etc.).

EMERGENCY EQUIPMENT AND SUPPLIES

As referenced in Chapter 8, the following information contains a brief rundown on emergency equipment and supplies for remote or standalone locations and facilities.

The local crisis management team will verify that these basic supplies are available, as needed, and in proper working order and mark the locations of emergency equipment on the site map when a map is provided.

From the local crisis management team the Project/Facility/Office Manager will identify an Emergency Supply Manager. The emergency supply manager will maintain and control the emergency supplies.

Checklist

- 20 lb (or two 10 lb) fire extinguisher (A, B, and C classes)
- First aid/trauma kits
- Personal eye wash
- Blood-borne pathogen kit
- Emergency food (MREs)
- Water and fuel to sustain the site/camp for a minimum of 3 days (stored in a secure location)
- Flashlights, batteries, maps, compass, etc.
- Additional equipment as needed

IMPROVISED EXPLOSIVE DEVICE (IED) AND BOMB THREAT PLAN

As referenced in Chapter 3, if your projects/offices happen to be located in areas where there are bomb threats, bombings, or frequently found or received suspicious packages and parcels, then security/emergency/crisis planning with regard to such threats can be critical. What is often overlooked is that merely having a plan, without training and drills, in the

BASIC GUIDELINES

- Keep areas near exits and extinguishers clear.
- All trailers/offices must be equipped with smoke detectors and fire extinguisher readily available.
- Designate one vehicle as the emergency vehicle; place hospital directions and map inside; keep keys in ignition or readily accessible during field activities.
- Inventory and check site emergency equipment, supplies— refer to Emergency Equipment and Supplies section.
- Ensure every person in the camp worksite has a *bug out* bag packed with essential items, personal medical items required, personal identification documents, and water.
- Security Managers will establish a warning signal for the site and brief all personnel on the warning signal and actions to take on hearing the signal.
- Security Managers will, during periods of heightened threat, brief camp/site personnel on additional security requirements (e.g., have body armor with the individual at all times and wear the body armor and vest at all times, etc.) for the site/camp.
- Security Managers will maintain an up-to-date roster of personnel in the camp/site for use by crisis management team leader in accounting for personnel.
- Security Managers will establish standard operating procedures for response to different incidents (direct and indirect fire, incidents during travel, actions to take if personnel are away from the camp/site and return to find the camp/site evacuated, etc.) and will brief all newcomers to the site. Additionally, the Security Manager will, during periods of heightened threat, rebrief the camp/site personnel on responses to incidents, alarms, and warnings and additional security requirements.
- Security Managers will establish an Evacuation Plan for their site. Evacuation Plans are a *close hold* item and should not be discussed outside of the local crisis management team, until there is a requirement, based on heightened threat, to do so. Security Managers will liaise with adjacent US

government/private vendor units for evacuation assistance and MEDEVAC assistance, if available. Security Managers will be in charge of the evacuation of a site, assisted by other members of local crisis management teams.

case of such threats can be detrimental to planning for mitigation and ensuring successful outcomes.

Scope

The history of IEDs and bombing threats are familiar violence recorded in the many regions of the world. These activities have created a requirement that practical basic knowledge be made available by the appropriate security manager to expatriate employees, consultants, visitors, and local hires. Knowledge of explosive devices may help employees to better cope with the increase of violent activities by some individuals or groups resorting to the use of IED/bombs to further their own interests.

IED/Bomb Threats

Typically, there are two reasonable explanations for an IED/bomb threat to be transmitted to a specific installation or individual.

There is real or suspected knowledge that an explosive device will be placed or has been placed in a specific facility or along routes traveled by friendly/contractor personnel and he or she wants to minimize personal injury or property damage. The informer may be the person who placed the device or someone aware of such information.

The informer wants to create an atmosphere of anxiety and panic that could result in disruption of normal installation activities.

Objective

The objective of the IED/Bomb Threat Plan is to ensure reasonable actions are taken to protect employees and property if there is an IED/bomb threat incident.

Authority and Responsibility

Professionals working on a project/in an office must be instructed when anyone is informed of an IED/bomb threat to the project/office or project site personnel. That person immediately informs the Senior Project Manager and Corporate Security Manager, who in turn:

- Decides whether project personnel should continue work or be immediately evacuated from the project site or rally at a pre-arranged point outside of the office or facility. (Senior Project Managers identify rally points and locations are clearly marked.)
- Informs on-site Security personnel (if any).
- Informs COMPANY senior management as appropriate (when time allows).

Receipt of IED/Bomb Threat

Regardless of who receives the IED/bomb threat or the bomb threat call, the recipient attempts to remain calm and receives and prepares to record as much information as possible.

If possible, the informer or caller is informed that the structure is occupied/route is being used and detonation of a bomb could result in death or serious injury to innocent people. This may cause the informer or caller to reconsider actions that may lead to other conversations that may reveal the location of the IED/bomb.

When listening to the informer or caller, the recipient tries to detect voice characteristics to help identify the informer. The recipient pays particular attention to the exact words spoken by the informer or caller and documents immediately comments or statements made.

Although the informer or caller should not be interrupted, the recipient determines an appropriate time in the conversation to ask for the informer's name and/or group affiliation.

The recipient tries to determine if the informer is familiar with the facility, the work being conducted at the installation, someone working there, or involved with the project.

In the case of a telephone call, the call recipient must keep the line open (do not hang up) following the call. This may allow authorities to trace the call after the caller hangs up. At all times during the call, the call recipient does everything possible to remain calm and keep the conversation moving and gathers as much information as possible. As soon as the call recipient can do so, he or she records specific notes of the conversation to aid in postincident identification of the caller.

There may be differences with the capabilities of host governments and countries and law enforcement in the region. But, it is important that you work with them whenever possible. And, they will be in charge of many efforts.

Other Types of Threats

Mail handlers, drivers, couriers, and any office personnel who handle mail need to look for suspicious letters and packages. If a suspicious letter or package is noted, the recipient remains calm and notifies the Project/Office Manager, and Corporate Security Manager immediately. Everything pertaining to the letter or package is not to be handled and is to be saved to assist in the investigation that will follow.

Postincident Action

If suspicious items are determined to be safe by Site Security or local authorities, the company Team Leader makes a determination about whether to return professionals to their place of duty. If a suspicious item is found and/or deemed unsafe (further actions required) and the office/job site had not yet been evacuated, the Team Leader may order an evacuation based on his assessment of the location and size of the suspicious item. If office/job site professionals discover the suspicious item, they are not to touch, move, or jar the item in any way. All suspicious items will be evaluated by Site Security, US government/host country law enforcement/ private vendor/personnel as far as disposition of the items are concerned.

After suspicious items have been cleared, the Team Leader or Corporate Security Manager makes the decision concerning return to work.

Postdetonation Action

It is possible that a bomb could be placed in a facility or office space and not located or a bomb threat call to announce the threat of the bomb is not received. In an effort to consider all related possibilities surrounding this type of incident, it is valuable to list the basic responsibilities of the project/office management in case a bomb explodes unexpectedly at a project office or job site. Management's first responsibility, in case of a detonation, is to account for all expatriates, other professionals, and visitors as required. Once this has been done, the following is accomplished as soon as possible:

- Ensure those injured in the blast receive medical treatment as quickly as possible.
- Notify Site Security and appropriate authorities so that an investigation of the incident can begin quickly.
- Inform corporate senior management and client as soon as possible of the situation, extent of damages, injuries, and casualties.

As the worst-case situation may result in injury or death to the Team Leader, the project staff must have a clearly defined chain of command so that order can be restored quickly to ensure the welfare of the project expatriate personnel and other employees.

Once Site Security and appropriate authorities have finished their investigation and corporate senior management postdetonation requirements have been fulfilled, the Team Leader in coordination with Corporate Management must determine the next steps insofar as the project is concerned.

The Corporate Security Manager provides a complete postdetonation incident report to Senior Management as soon as possible after the incident.

INDEX

241